Finding God's Fingerprints in our Daily Lives

A Daily Devotional

By:

Jean Howell Kopp Heffern

authorHOUSE

1663 LIBERTY DRIVE, SUITE 200
BLOOMINGTON, INDIANA 47403
(800) 839-8640
www.authorhouse.com

First published by AuthorHouse 07/07/04

ISBN: 1-4184-5812-0 (e-book)
ISBN: 1-4184-3490-6 (Paperback)

This book is printed on acid-free paper.

Dedicated to the memory of my Grandfather, W. A. J. Kopp,
who encouraged and nurtured my love for creative writing.

and

To all who have participated in bringing this book
to completion,

Thank You!

FORWARD

The title of this daily devotional has an intimate meaning for me that I hope you will share:

FINDING: *"Ask and it will be given to you; seek and you will find; knock and the door will be opened to you."* *(Matthew 7:7)* Within these pages I have examined different events from my own life, looking for God's fingerprints in each. As I did I discovered each event in my life mirrors and reflect God's presence.

GOD'S: *"for it is God who works in you to will and to act according to His good purpose."* *(Philippians 2:13)* God is my soul's purpose and direction. I must look within myself, seeking God and become aware of where He is working in my life. Nothing is about me; everything is about God.

FINGERPRINTS: *"You hem me in – behind and before; You have laid Your hand upon me."* *(Psalm 139:5)* The presence of God's fingerprints is evidence of a lasting mark on my life. Within each event in my life I look for God's hand; then isolate that one integral piece of it that contains His fingerprints. I find His fingerprints are scattered liberally throughout my life, if I just look for them.

IN OUR: *"because the One who is in you is greater than the one who is in the world."* *(I John 4:4b)* God is with me always. It is He within me that transform ordinary daily events in my life into witnesses of His power and glory. If I remain open to Him He will touch me, leaving His fingerprints on everything that is within my life.

DAILY: *"Sing to the Lord, praise His name; proclaim His salvation day after day."* *(Psalm 96:2)* The more I seek God's presence in my life the more God reveals Himself to me. When I daily search for His fingerprints they become easier to find.

LIVES: *"Know that the Lord is God. It is He who made us, and we are His; we are His people, the sheep of His pasture."* *(Psalm 100:3)* God made me and gave me life: He didn't have to. Nothing I can ever do or will ever do shall make me deserving of the life God gave me. My life belongs to God and, as such, I need to seek to find Him in every event of my life, every day.

CONTENTS

Contents Page 2

Contents Page 3

Contents Page 4

Contents Page 5

Contents Page 6

NEW BIRTH INTO LIVING HOPE

I Peter 1:3

At the stroke of midnight New Year's eve my husband and I were kneeling at the altar rail sharing in the Lord's Supper. Shortly thereafter we lit candles and silently filed out of the church with about thirty-five others into the night.

The night was crisp and calm with stars hovering like pin lights in the sky. In unison we lifted our candles high and sang "Amazing Grace." Not another sound was uttered as we prayed for our country, for world peace and new beginnings. All around us were the bursts of lights and the occasional popping of fireworks.

There was something magical in the moment: A New Year was being born.

Suddenly the words Peter the Apostle wrote in I Peter 1:3 popped in my head:

"Praise be to God and Father of our Lord Jesus Christ! In His great mercy He has given us new birth into a living hope."

Can't you just see the bursts of lights and hear the popping of fireworks as the passion in Peter's words explodes across the centuries?

It seemed so natural for us to usher in the New Year surrounded by friends in God's own Home holding fast to His promise of new life. The light we took out from His altar into the world that night sealed for us the promise of the new birth of a new year into the living hope God offers us all in His great mercy.

Happy New Year!

GOD'S PURPOSE

Genesis 45:5

When Joseph's brothers sold him into slavery they never expected to see him again. But God had a purpose and worked through the brothers' cruel act to save lives.

In fact as Joseph revealed his true identity he said to his brothers:

"Do not be distressed and do not be angry with yourselves for selling me here, because it was to save lives that God sent me ahead of you." Genesis 45:5

What's this? His brothers sold Joseph into slavery. Yet, he is telling his brothers to never mind about that. It really was God who sent him?

That was because God used the brothers' act of personal animosity toward Joseph, not only to save their lives, but also to save the lives of many nations that came to Egypt to buy food in the face of the famine.

We can take Joseph's words to his brothers to heart. Let's not be distressed or angry with ourselves over things we've done in our past. Rather, let us take courage knowing God will use what ever those things was for our good.

God still has a purpose today and can work through even our most thoughtless acts. He still uses everything to His Glory.

Isn't this a wonderful way for us to begin a New Year?

Just think. God has freed us all from our past by using our past to pave the way to our future.

This is the year for us to realize that God has a purpose for our lives.

TEMPTATION'S STRATEGY

Genesis 3:4

One of my New Year resolutions was to read through the Bible in a year. Of course, one of the first stories I read was that of Adam and Eve and the fall of man.

While I was reading about the serpent tempting Eve to eat of the Tree of the Knowledge of Good and Evil, I noticed something. Eve let the serpent trick her. What the serpent in Genesis 3:4 did was to get Eve to focus on the forbidden tree by suggesting that God was keeping something good from them. That diverted Eve's full attention on that tree instead of the bounty God had provided.

"'You will not surely die,' the serpent said to the woman. 'For God knows that when you eat of it your eyes will be opened, and you will be like God, knowing good and evil.'"

Eve could have pointed out, "Yes, but that is only one tree, serpent. Why would we need another tree? Just look at this garden full of trees of whose fruit we can eat!"

But she didn't. Eve allowed the serpent to focus her desires on what she didn't have.

Isn't that exactly what I do today in my own life? I tend to focus on the things I do not have instead of all the blessings God has given me. Oh how many times has that serpent gotten me to focus on the forbidden instead of God's bounty!

Re-reading this old familiar story provided me with a fresh insight. My first line of defense against temptation is to keep my focus on God, His goodness and provisions.

Never on the restrictions. Never on the circumstances. Never on what I don't have. But always on God!

THE WORD

Genesis 1:1 & 3   John 1:1-2

Genesis 1:1 begins: *"In the beginning..."* John 1:1 completes that thought: *"In the beginning was the Word..."* Genesis 1:3 tells us whose Word by stating, *"God said..."* John 1:1 continues to piece together the concept of that Word: *"The Word was with God and the Word was God."*

Thus, we discover the Word is alive. God spoke and His Living Word created the earth and all that is within it. The book of Genesis makes that very clear. We even read that God saw what His Living Word created and called it good. So, who is God's Living Word? Well, the gospel of John tells us exactly who the Word is – Jesus Christ.

"He was with God in the beginning. Through Him all things were made; without Him nothing was made that has been made." John 1:2

Jesus is the Word who, before the beginning of time, brought the world into existence. God spoke the Word and the Word was with God and the Word was God. God spoke and Jesus created.

Does it surprise you to learn that Jesus was always there? He didn't just begin to exist the hour Mary gave birth to the Son of God. Jesus is the Word that created all life and then, out of His great love, came down to dwell among us. Jesus still remains the Word for us today.

Jesus is our Creator, our Redeemer, and our Lord of life. No one comes to the Father unless he comes first through His Son. And who is His Son?

His own Beloved Word, Jesus.

STANDING IN THE GAP

Exodus 1:15-18

You know, there are no "stand alone" or unrelated stories in the Bible. Just take the story about the midwives in Moses's time.

"The King of Egypt said to the Hebrew midwives, whose names were Siphrah and Puah, 'When you help the Hebrew women in childbirth and observe them on the delivery stool, if it is a boy, kill him, but if it is a girl, let her live.' The midwives, however, feared God and did not do what the King of Egypt said. They let the boys live. Then the King of Egypt summoned the midwives and asked, 'Why have you done this? Why have you let the boys live?'" Exodus 1:15-18

God used these midwives to "stand in the gap" between the Hebrew women and Pharaoh. Because of this many male children of the Hebrew race were saved. The midwives allowed the Hebrew sons to live so that the people increased and became more numerous.

Just as the midwives did back then for the Hebrew women we have Someone who "stands in the gap" for us today – Jesus Christ.

Although we may not always feel His presence Jesus is constantly with us through all our heartbreaks or trials.

It's Jesus who stands in that gap between the way things are and the way things should be, allowing us to live, to increase, and to become more numerous.

No wonder we call Him Savior!

EPIPHANY

Matthew 2:11

We have just taken down our Christmas tree. We can see signs all over the neighborhood, stores and streets that Christmas is over. Well, at least it's over for the secular world.

The Christian calendar, however, sets aside a special day to keep Christmas alive. The 6th of January is Epiphany. Epiphany is when we commemorate the coming of the wise men to Bethlehem to worship the Christ Child with gifts. They had been following the Star of Bethlehem along dusty back roads, traveling mainly at night for that was when they could see the Star. Matthew 2:11 says this:

"On coming to the house, they [the wise men] saw the Child with His mother, Mary, and they bowed down and worshipped Him. Then they opened their treasures and presented Him with gifts of gold and of incense and of myrrh."

Their arrival in Bethlehem was extremely important. But, somehow in the flurry of Christmas, Epiphany is overlooked and we miss the manifestation of Jesus Christ into the Gentile World. The wise men were not Jews. They were of the secular world.

Today in the Christian church, although it marks the end of Christmas and the beginning of a new church season, Epiphany provides us an occasion to reflect again on the real reason for the Christmas season. After all the Christmas trees have been taken down and the secular world has put away Christmas until next year, we continue to celebrate the Living Christ.

Epiphany. It's the holiday the retail industry has not discovered. It's the holiday that embraces Jesus alone.

JANUARY 6

GOD'S EYE

Luke 6:41

One Saturday as I cleaned house I listened to Barbra Striesand's CD "Higher Ground." One of the feature songs she sang in duet with Celine Dion was entitled, "Tell Him." One line in the chorus caught my attention. It went something like this:

> "Tell Him, tell Him that the sun and moon rise in His eye. Reach out to Him...."

As I listened I thought, "Yes, the sun & moon does rise in God's eye. Everything's in His eye. He sees everything. Then God allowed the realization of that thought to flood my senses.

What if the whole world exists in His eye?

If the whole world exists in God's eye we have a choice. We can choose to either to be part of His seeing or to be part of the proverbial "mote" in His eye.

I just have this feeling that God is counting on us to be part of His seeing. How else can He accomplish His work here on earth?

Jesus must have been aware of that in the Sermon on the Mount when He asked,

"Why do you look at the speck of sawdust in your bother's eye and pay no attention to the [mote] in your own eye?" Luke 6:41

Jesus knows we can only be part of God's seeing when we see as God sees.

NOT BY WORKS

Ephesians 2:8-9

A while back I met a woman who told me about all the good deeds a friend of hers always did. She volunteered for all kinds of charities and had virtually become the salvation for hundreds of people. Never was there a person whose heart was so big, kind and generous.

This woman felt that her friend was a true saint because she was doing the type of good works described in the Bible.

It didn't matter – she went on to say – that her friend wasn't a Christian. She surely would go to heaven. After all, just look at all the good she was doing and the lives she was saving.

Wouldn't God reward her for that?

I was instantly reminded of the passage in Ephesians 2:8-9.

"For it is by Grace you have been saved, through faith – (and this not from yourselves, it is the gift of God) – not by works, so that no one can boast."

We tend to lose sight of the fact that Salvation is a gift. No matter how hard we work and how many good deeds we pile up in our favor, Salvation can't be earned.

Yet, Satan will send us all kinds of "Do-gooders" filled with good works and acts of false righteousness so we will be tempted to testify to their goodness, turn from God and follow them instead.

Any work not done in the name of Jesus serves the wrong master.

LOOK ALIKE

Ephesians 4:12

Not so long ago a coworker of mine who has twin teenage daughters was relating to me the astonishment of her twins with people's difficulty in being able to tell them apart. One even cut her hair short while the other left hers long. Still, people confused the two.

I suddenly recalled a friend of mine in high school who insisted on calling me Nancy-Jean. When I asked her why she told me she never could tell my sister and me apart. So she put our names together. That way no matter which of us she was interacting with, she would always be half right!

Now, that was the time I was astonished.

I had brown hair, hazel eyes, was tall with long legs (earning the nickname of "Daddy Long Legs" from some). My sister was over two years younger than I was, 5'2", tiny and petite with blond hair and brown eyes. I was painfully shy and withdrawn while she was outgoing and vivacious. We were nothing at all alike, except in family facial structure.

Then it occurred to me that maybe that is one reason why the name, "Christian" was coined. Like my friend having trouble distinguishing between my petite sister and myself, perhaps the non-believer in Jesus' time found it hard to tell the believers apart. As Christians we are all sizes and shapes. Sometimes we're nothing alike, except in our family faith structure. But the Bible tells us that we are

"...all members of one body." Ephesians 4:12

That makes us all, although different, the one and the same in Christ.

SUNBEAM

Revelations 1:7

Remember that song?

> "A sunbeam, a sunbeam. Jesus wants me for a sunbeam. A sunbeam, a sunbeam, I'll be a sunbeam for Him."

When I was eleven or twelve years old I remember looking up at the sky and seeing glorious sunbeams shooting out from the billowing clouds. It was so beautiful! Then the Sunbeam Song resounded in my head over and over again.

I was just a child, but even then I think I knew Jesus was calling me. Even today I can still feel that same peace and warmth and experience that same awe I had then of being in the presence of Someone Great!

Since then I have experienced many types of sunbeams flung gloriously across the sky and across my life. Every time I do the Sunbeam Song welds up within me. For instance: A few years ago a pastor at my church was fond of telling me I was the "cheerleader" for my chosen ministry. Somehow her words to me were like sunbeams and I immediately thought of the Sunbeam Song.

I get this feeling that Jesus is tapping me on the shoulder. He's saying, "Remember? You are still My sunbeam." I can feel the presence of Jesus "beaming" at me, as He did back then, waiting.

Revelations 1:7 tells us

"Look, He is coming with the clouds, and every eye shall see Him!"

So yes, Jesus,

"A sunbeam, a sunbeam. I'll be a sunbeam for You."

ACTS, CHAPTER NINE

Acts 9:1-2

Chapter nine of Acts talks about the conversion of Saul from persecutor to Christian. In it we read:

"Saul went to the High Priest and asked him for letters to the synagogues in Damascus, so that if he found any there who belonged to the Way, he might take them as prisoners..." Acts 9:1-2

You know Saul must have known almost everything there was to know about Christians and the Way or Christianity. Knowing the passion of Saul, he would have made a thorough study, for a true adversary always knows his opponents well.

It's interesting to note that Saul, probably knowing more about Jesus Christ than we do today, had to be struck blind before he could see!

Friends, I gotta tell you. We are no different today. Most of us have an idea of what Jesus Christ and Christianity is all about but, like Saul, we most likely retain that knowledge in our heads. There it stays until something happens that moves that knowledge from our heads to our hearts.

Only then, like Saul, will the scales fall from our eyes. Only then can we turn from what we are doing and follow Jesus Christ without hesitation.

This blinding experience of Saul's turned Saul into Paul, the most effective Christian missionary the world has ever known.

TRUST

Psalm 20:7

It's funny. Usually none of us find it difficult to trust God with the eternal. After all, we consider that His department. His job is to take care of the eternal and the universal, while sitting on His throne overseeing the world.

Right?

What we do find difficult though, is to trust Him for the small things such as our daily bread, this month's car payment, day-to-day relationships, or those unexpected things we all experience. Those things we consider our department. We are not so quick to take those things to Him.

Yet, when our daily living becomes entangled we turn around and blame God. We completely ignore the fact that we get ourselves into the messes that we're in because we left God out. It never occurs to us that God will only work in our lives when we ask Him in and give Him room to work.

No, we lock God out, then demand to know why He wasn't there!

God is so patient with us. We're talking about the Almighty God who keeps the sun in the sky and the seasons on track in perfect sequence. Why is it that we so often think that we can't trust Him to keep our lives on track just as perfectly? It's sad but we seem to rely more on man and self than we do on God. As Christians we are called to trust in God for everything. Psalm 20:7 says,

"Some trust in chariots and horses, but we trust in the name of the Lord our God."

It doesn't go on to say "as a last resort" or "when everything else fails." It simply states, "We trust in the name of the Lord our God."

TURNING POINT

Psalm 91:14-16

There's always a turning point that occurs in just about every crisis we face. And with turning points come choices.

It's true: Most of our turning points hinge on our choices. While we are likely to try most anything in a crisis, it's our choices that determine the directions we take. Our choices can either save us or drag us down.

In other words: When we are sinking in a storm-tossed sea we can either grab a life buoy or an anchor!

Jesus came to be a life buoy for us. When we choose to grab Jesus, we experience the turning points that lead us to Salvation. In fact God Himself describes what happens when we choose to grab Him as our life buoy:

"Because he loves me" says the Lord, "I will rescue him; I will protect him, for he acknowledges My name. He will call upon Me, and I will answer him; I will be with him in trouble, I will deliver him and honor him. With long life will I satisfy him and show him My Salvation." Psalm 91:14-16

It is wonderful that we have a God who loves us so much that He will personally deliver us and shower us with His Salvation if we but ask Him.

The next time you experience a crisis, call on God and claim His promises for your own.

Choose to grab Jesus and allow Him to lift you from your crisis. Let Him be the turning point that will change your life forever.

God said, *"Because you love Me I will rescue you."*

FAITH

Hebrews 11:1

How many times do we do things on faith?

How many more times do we resist doing things because we doubt?

One morning as my husband got out of bed he heard birds singing. Now he always heard that birds sing as the sun begins to dawn, but these birds were singing their hearts out in the dark! There was no hint of light at all. He couldn't understand why they were singing.

Later in the day during his devotions he came across Hebrews 11:1.

"Now faith is being sure of what we hope for and certain of what we do not see."

All of a sudden he knew! He shared this "tid-bit" with those he encourages through the Internet with this insight:

"Faith is the bird that feels the light when the dawn is still dark!"

As he shared that with me, I was reminded of all the times that I quit singing because I couldn't see the dawn. I guess we all have times like that even though we know the dawn will come.

There's an old saying that goes,

"It is always the darkest just before the dawn."

I often find myself quoting that in the midst of trouble. But just as often, the darkness of that trouble overwhelms me and I give up when the dawn is almost within my grasp.

I asked my husband, "Is that because I don't have as much faith as a little bird?"

THE ONE AND ONLY TRUE GOD

Exodus 3:19-20

God said to Moses, *"...I know that the king of Egypt will not let you go unless a mighty hand compels him. So I will stretch out My hand and strike the Egyptians with the wonders I will perform among them. After that, he will let you go."* Exodus 3:19-20

It always bothered me why God allowed plagues to occur before Pharaoh would let God's chosen people go. Then through my Disciple Bible Study I finally was able to understand what God was doing and why He had to do it this way.

You see each plague was directed against an Egyptian god or sign. God used the plagues to permanently discredit all gods but Himself.

For instance: The plague of frogs was to prove frogs (the Egyptian symbol of regeneration) had no regeneration powers. The plague of gnats and flies was to contradict that gnats and flies (believed to be the eyes and ears of the Egyptian gods) had no such powers. The plague visited upon the cattle was to negate two Egyptian gods who were worshipped in cow forms – Hathor, the god of love, beauty and happiness and Apis, goddess of fertility – reducing their powers back to mere livestock. The plague of boils neutralized the powers of Imhotep, the Egyptian patron of medicine. The next two plagues, hail and locusts, were directed against the powers of Nut (the sky goddess), Isis (the goddess of life) and Seb (the protector of life). Then God used darkness against Ra, the Egyptian sun god. The final plague was the most important – the death of all first born. It rendered Osis, the Egyptian giver of life and Pharaoh's own personal god, completely and utterly powerless.

One by one God annihilated every Egyptian god until only He, the One and Only True God, was left.

LIFE STORIES

II Timothy 2:15

There's an old saying:

"Every life has a story."

That might be putting it a bit simplistically, but never the less it's true. Yet, how often do we remember that?

I know there's been many times in the past that I was so wrapped up in my own life that I remained oblivious to the life stories unfolding around me.

Just think of all the opportunities I've missed by allowing that to happen. Each life story that touches mine leaves a bit of itself in my life while taking a piece of mine with it. So that makes it my responsibility to make sure the pieces of my life others take with them is God filled.

As Paul told Timothy in II Timothy 2:15, we need to

"Do our best to present ourselves to God as ones approved, workmen who do not need to be ashamed..."

I am now trying to stay more conscious of the life stories unfolding around me. And, when someone's life story touches mine, I try to make sure the piece of my life they take with them is uplifting and encouraging. I know from experience that when I do, I find the bit of their life story they leave behind in mine is twice as great.

So, when someone's life story touches mine I try to pour all the love and blessing I can into it.

What I walk away with is usually more priceless than I ever imagined.

YOUR PEOPLE

Exodus 32:7 & 11

We have adopted a little gray cat that came to us a few years ago. She appeared as a stray at our back door. My husband said he didn't want a cat so though I fed her, we would not let her come in the house. Then one night it rained so hard that he, concerned over the little kitten, went out, found her and brought her out of the storm into the house.

You guessed it. She stayed.

So now we have this rule. Whenever it rains she is his cat and he has to take care of her. Sometimes when he's teasing me, he'll say, "She's your cat." Then I firmly remind him with "I don't have a cat. Remember? She's your cat!"

Recently I caught the end of Derek Prince on the radio. His message that day was centered on when God spoke to Moses on Mount Sinai. When Moses was so long in coming down, the people made for themselves an idol to worship. So the Lord said to Moses,

"Go down, because your people, whom you brought up out of Egypt have become corrupt." Exodus 32:7

"But Moses sought favor of the Lord, his God. "O Lord," he said,

"Why should Your anger burn against Your people, whom You brought out of Egypt with great power and a mighty hand?" Exodus 32:11

You see neither God nor Moses wanted to claim the Israelites! Because of their great sin, God said to Moses, "They are your people." Moses firmly reminded Him, "No, God. They're Your people!"

DID HE KNOW?

I Peter 1:18-20

Did He know?

He who brought the world into being and made everything in it? He who separated the earth from the waters and made seasons for all things to flourish and grow?

When He scattered the seeds for the grass and vines to grow and planted the flowers and the trees, did He know?

I wonder. Did He know that among those trees He planted, one would someday be fashioned into His Cross? Did He tend that tree as tenderly as He did the rest? Or, did He make it stronger by watering it with His tears?

I Peter 1:18-20 reminds us, *"For you know that it was not with perishable things such as silver or gold that you were redeemed from the empty way of life handed down to you from your forefathers, but with the precious blood of Christ, a lamb, without blemish or defect. He was chosen before the creation of the world, but was revealed in these last times for your sake."*

We know Jesus didn't go to the Cross as a last resort or because He couldn't think of anything else to do. No. Remember, He was chosen before the creation of the world.

The Cross was always the only way, planned before the creation of time for our sakes. It was always meant to be.

Did He know? He planted the tree and watched it grow. And I think that whenever He sent the breeze to stir its leaves He thought about you and me.

Yes, I think He knew.

SIN-TRASH

John 1:29

I was just relaxing, enjoying a rare quiet moment, when an unwanted thought popped into my head. It wasn't anything I had been thinking of and I had no idea where it came from. It simply was there. So I promptly dismissed it.

But the damage had been done.

My quiet moment was over.

The message of the pastor at the baptism of our granddaughter, Emily, focused on trash collecting. He pointed out that because we know which day trash pickup is scheduled in our neighborhoods we go around gathering up our trash the night before so that the trash collectors at the appointed time can take it away.

His question to us was "Why don't we do the same thing in our daily lives?"

He said we should schedule prayer appointments with God. Then, through soul-searching, gather up our sin-trash before our prayer time so that our Master Trash Collector at the appointed prayer time can take it away.

Our Master Trash Collector is Jesus.

John the Baptist identified Him as such for us:

"The next day John saw Jesus coming toward him and said, "Look, the Lamb of God who takes away the sins of the world!" John 1:29

So, look at your schedule and set up your prayer appointments with Jesus. Then gather your sin-trash so that at the appointed prayer time you can give it to Jesus to take away.

OUTSIDE YOUR EXPIRATION DATE

Hebrews 2: 3-4

One of my grandfathers use to be part owner of a major distribution center that serviced all the food stores and grocers in Pensacola, Florida. Food products would arrive to his warehouse by rail, then be distributed out to the stores by trucks. Occasionally food products would arrive near or after their printed expiration date and could not be distributed. Since my Grandfather could never stand to see good food go to waste he would bring a number of those products home to us. You see he knew that the printed expiration date was to alert the stores of when to pull the products from the shelves. It was not some magical date of instant spoilage.

So, you might say I was raised on expired food!

The other day Chuck Swindoll's message was about that time line between a product's printed expiration date and the date it actually becomes unfit. He was comparing the printed expiration date to the times we fall short of our potential, due to sin and human nature. He emphasized that we also have a period of time after we have fallen short before we reach the point of eternal condemnation. He called this span of time God's "grace period." Then he asked a thought-provoking question:

"Are you living outside your expiration date? For if you are, you need to repent and seek to live within God's Salvation."

The writer of Hebrews encourages us to always be aware of where we are living because

"How shall we escape if we ignore such a great Salvation? This Salvation, which was first announced by the Lord, was confirmed to us by those who heard Him. God also testified to it by signs, wonders and various miracles, and gifts of the Holy Spirit distributed according to His will." Hebrews 2:3-4

GOD'S WORD

Matthew 24:35

When my husband and I set our wedding date for January 21, 1966, I asked a very dear friend to be my maid of honor. Because she was of a different religious faith, she told me she had to ask her church if she could. I remember how hurt I was when she told me her church would not allow her to attend our wedding. She said her church did give her permission to attend our reception, if she wanted, as long as it was not held on our church property.

Time has since healed my heart, but I still remember those words.

I was reminded of that when Chuck Swindoll on the radio the other day cited a similar circumstance that happened in his life. In speaking of it he said that words, once spoken, remain forever no matter what we do. The spoken word can never be erased or cease to exist. We can soften it or make necessary amends and even choose to forgive, but we can not make it not exist.

Now, John takes this one step further, reminding us about the Word that endures forever. He begins by telling us that before time was the Word existed and will continue to exist beyond the end of time. We learn that the Word was not only with God but that the Word was God. The Word was Jesus becoming flesh and dwelling among us.

We know that is true because Jesus Himself confirms it for us in Matthew 24:35. He said:

"Heaven and earth will pass away, but My Word will never pass away."

A word, once spoken into being, can not cease to exist. Sometimes that word can hurt. But when that Word is Jesus it will always fill our hearts and souls with peace, love and joy.

OVERSTATEMENT

Genesis 3:1

It all began in the garden.

Adam and Eve were doing their thing. You know, being fruitful, increasing in number, filling the earth and subduing it, just as God told them to do in Genesis 1:28.

Suddenly up slithered the serpent. He approached Eve with a theological question about God.

(Definitely a smart move; Eve loved to talk about God!)

Slyly the serpent made a deliberate overstatement:

"Did God really say, 'You must not eat from any tree in the garden?'" Genesis 3:1

(The serpent knew Eve would correct him.)

"No, God didn't say that…"

(He was right! Eve corrected him!)

Then, as if to drive home her point, Eve made her own overstatement…

Hey, it was a natural response. Eve was just trying to match the serpent's passion with her own. Only, by doing so, she played right into the serpent's court. She was now focused on that one tree God withheld from Adam and her.

That's how come God found them hiding, with apple juice still dripping off their chins!

Mark Twain once said (and I paraphrase)

"Given Man's nature, maybe God should have made His own overstatement. He should have told Adam and Eve not to eat the snake!"

GOD CARES

Psalm 8:4

When a friend of our e-mailed us searching for a 3-legged stool to use in her Emmaus talk, I was struck with how much God cares for each and every one of us. No detail is too small for Him.

You see, our friend remembered seeing a 3-legged stool and thought every Emmaus fourth day group must have one. So when her fourth day group didn't, she thought of us. Perhaps we would know where she could find one.

We had just moved. So I had just recently mailed all our family and close friends a change of address, which also included our e-mail addresses. Therefore, when our friend thought of us, our e-mail addresses were right there at her fingertips.

As soon as I received her e-mail I immediately replied. Amazingly enough, I had just unpacked the box containing our 3-legged stool! I knew exactly where it was.

Had our friend tried to contact us earlier, she would not have had our e-mail addresses. She would have had to track us down through other means, using valuable time she didn't have. Or, if she had contacted us before I had unpacked that box, I would not have had any idea which box contained our 3-legged stool.

As it was, the timing was perfect.

That humbled me. I whispered Psalm 8:4 to God:

"What is man that You care for him, the son of man that You care for him?"

There are millions of things in this world needing God's attention, and God is concerned with this minor detail. My friends, He will do the same for you.

BIRTH

I John 3:9

Recently I began thinking about the stable in which Jesus was born, and it occurred to me that it not only represented the birth of our Savior into the world, but also the birth of our Savior into our hearts.

Jesus, the Holy, Infinite and Perfect Son of the One and Only God, drew His first breath in a dirty unkempt animal stable. I imagine that the first thing Jesus would have seen – besides the face of His mother, Mary, and Joseph – was some old dust-laden spider webs rippling in the night air.

Or maybe field mice scampering about looking for food. Or the face of a cow or two, a donkey and some sheep!

Not exactly what we would have thought to give our newborns.

Yet, through His birth in the world, salvation came to all.

When we accept Jesus as our personal Savior and invite Him into our hearts, Jesus eagerly comes in. As He draws His first breath in our dirty, unkempt human hearts, I imagine the first things He would see – besides the love we just professed for Him – are the years of dust-laden webs of sin within us.

Or maybe a few bad habits we just can't seem to give up. Or some hidden desire or two seeking to devour us.

Not exactly what we would have thought to give our God. Yet, through His birth in our hearts, we are wiped as clean as newborns.

How do we know this? I John 3:9 explains:

"No one who is born of God will continue to sin because God's seed remains in him; he cannot go on sinning because he has been born of God"

WIN-WIN SOLUTIONS

Romans 15:1-3

I ran across an article on prayer recently, in which the author stated:

"When you pray to win, you are actually praying for someone to lose."

I was floored!

You mean, all those times I prayed to come out on top; to be the one picked for that desirable job; to excel at some competitive based activity; I had done so at someone else's expense?

To be a winner implies that there must be a loser, yet I had never looked at it that way before. I mean, how caring is it to pray for someone to lose?

So then, how in the world could you ever pray for what you want?

That question just about stumped me until it occurred to me that maybe my whole approach of "praying to win" was wrong. Then, while I was searching the Scriptures for an answer, I came across Romans 15:1-3.

"We who are strong ought to bear with the failings of the weak and not to please ourselves. Each of us should please his neighbor for his good, to build him up."

That was it!

Instead of praying for my own success where there is competition for the outcome, I should be praying for my competitor to find greater success than I should. I need to pray for the Lord to open another door for the individual I'm in competition with instead of for me to win at his/her expense.

I am now learning to pray for win-win solutions.

GOD'S HEART

Genesis 1:1

In the beginning God decided it was time to create man in His own image…

Actually, God has no beginning. He always was and always will be. Also the creation of man was not a rash or sudden decision. God always knew He would create man. He looked forward to the fellowship and oneness He and man would share. Yet, before He could form this perfect creation called man, He needed to create just the perfect place for man to live. So

"In the beginning God created the heavens and the earth." Genesis 1:1

Now the earth needed to be a suitable place – one that would sustain life and be perfect in all aspects for man to flourish.

And God knew just how He was going to do it. All God did was to look into His own heart. That is the place God designed for man to live. There is no greater perfection than that.

So God took His own heart, shaped it and set it in the most perfect spot of His created heavens, the universe. He gave it His Spirit and gently blew order to the waters and stimulated the beginning of life – first in the seas and then on land. Then, just when the atmosphere and the growth process was ideal, God created man.

Sounds a little on the tall tale side? Let me assure you that it's not.

God simply took the "**H**" from the beginning of His **H**-E-A-R-T and moved it to the end:

‑E‑A‑R‑T‑H

WHERE ARE YOU?

I Kings 19:11-12

God whispered, "Child, I love you." I yawned, changed my position and fell back to sleep.

God shouted, "Here I am. I will protect you." I got up and shut the window to close out the sound of the thunder.

I dreamed God called "Come to Me" from within a burning bush. I ran for some water to douse it.

I was exhausted. I had not slept well. The day was wet and dreary and I felt like I had been running around in circles, spinning my wheels, and putting out fires all night!

I cried out, "God, where are you?"

I have discovered that the reason I can't find God is that I don't look for Him in my daily life.

Oswald Chambers in his classic daily devotional; "My Utmost for His Highest" helped open my eyes to this. Oswald maintains that God is with us all the time but sometimes we never realize it. Elijah also experienced this as he was fleeing from Jezebel and was hiding in a cave on Horeb, the mountain of God.

"The Lord said, 'Go out and stand on the mountain in the presence of the Lord, for the Lord is about to pass.' Then a great and powerful wind tore the mountains apart and shattered the rocks before the Lord, but the Lord was not in the wind. After the wind there was an earthquake, but the Lord was not in the earthquake. After the earthquake came a fire, but the Lord was not in the fire. And after the fire came a gentle whisper." I Kings 19:11-12

Elijah expected to find God in the wind, earthquake and fire. He may also have cried "God, where are you?" But God was there all along. God was in the gentle whisper.

HEALED

I Peter 2:24

A few years ago I attended the Women of Faith Conference, "Outrageous Joy." I was blessed to be able to hear and meet such spiritual giants as Patsy Clairmont, Barbara Johnson, Thelma Wells, Shelia Walsh and Marilyn Meburg.

Each speaker shared her heart and soul with us and had us laughing, crying and rejoicing as never before. As each speaker told her story, hearts were touched and hurting souls were healed that day.

God put me there that day to further that healing in three lives.

At different intervals through out the conference, three women sought me out. They each had the need to verbalize their histories again. As they did, I sensed in each of them the beginning of a new healing.

I am a Stephen Minister, but I don't think that that is why they sought me out. None of these women would have known that about me. Also, it wasn't because I listened nor that the hurts they suffered were so similar to the ones the speakers were sharing. Although that was also true.

It was because for the first time each of these women realized that, through Jesus, they were already healed!

Peter, the rock upon whom Jesus built His church, put it this way:

"He [Jesus], Himself bore our sins in His body on the tree, so that we might die to sins and live for righteousness; by His wounds you have been healed." I Peter 2:24

Sometimes it's only when we realize that we are healed that we can be healed.

THE OLD HAS GONE

II Corinthians 5:17

A commentary I recently read on the book of II Timothy centered on chapters 4 – 8: The solemn farewell charge of Paul to Timothy.

Paul knew the day of his execution was near and was not sure if he would have another opportunity to write Timothy again. The battle-scarred warrior of the Cross was looking back over the long and bitter fight in which he had engaged his life on behalf of Jesus. Sure enough, shortly after Paul wrote this letter he was executed.

The commentary stated, "Our guess is that when [Paul] got to heaven, his very first act, after rendezvous with the Lord, was to hunt up Stephen to beg his forgiveness."

That statement bothered me. I mean, I get this picture of Stephen sitting in heaven nursing anger toward Paul and then Paul, upon his arrival in heaven, running scared of Stephen's retaliation! Not quite the picture of heaven I always imagined. After all, didn't Paul himself say in II Corinthians 5:17

"Therefore, if anyone is in Christ, he is a new creation; the old has gone, the new has come!"

So I really don't think it would have even crossed Paul's mind to seek out Stephen in hope of receiving forgiveness.

God had already forgiven Paul for his persecution of the Christians and his part in Stephen's death. That meant the past simply did not exist anymore. It had been completely erased by God's mercy – I believe – for both Paul and Stephen.

After all, Heaven is a place of joy, worship, peace, and new beginnings.

The old has gone.

TOYS

Psalm 122:1

When our grandchildren came over to spend the night I told their mother to have them pick out a favorite toy to bring with them. When she dropped them off she told me that they had not wanted to bring their toys; they wanted to play with our toys. We keep a small box of assorted toys for our grandchildren in a corner of the closet in the guestroom.

Several days later I shared this with a friend of mine. She was amazed that our grandchildren would leave their favorite toys home in order to come to our house and play with ours.

Usually when we go to church on Sunday, most of the time we come bringing our own favorite issues, notions, beliefs, and all that stuff – you know, our own toys. However what we should do is exactly what our grandchildren did: We need to leave our favorite toys home when we come to God's house and play with His.

When we bring our own toys to God's house we end up so busy playing with them we miss out on receiving the wonderful and glorious things God has in store for us.

We should leave our toys home and remember the words of Psalm 122:1 written by David, the shepherd boy who became king:

"I rejoice with those who said to me 'Let us go to the house of the Lord.'"

and play with God's toys, because our greatest blessings are in the toys we find in God's house.

RE-SOULING OUR SOULS

Ezekiel 36:26

The other night as I began to clean the kitchen from supper, I happened to step into the hall and noticed my husband's cowboy boots sitting by the door.

They hadn't been there before, so I asked him, "What are your boots doing by the door?"

He answered, "I set them there to remind me to take them to the shoe shop in the morning to have them resoled."

As I turned back to the kitchen, the thought crossed my mind, "How ironic it is that we tend to pay more attention to our shoes' soles than we do our own souls."

Just as we take our shoes to the shoe shop for repair, we should take our souls to the Lord for renewal.

The resoling done to our shoes extends its wearable life. The renewal done to our souls extends us eternal life.

We may not be able to put our souls by the door as we can our shoes to remind us to take them to the Lord for renewal. But we can put our souls before the Lord in prayer, confident that He will remember for us.

After all, He promises,

"I will give you a new heart and put a new Spirit in you." Ezekiel 36:26

God will resoul our souls when we recognize our need to bring them to our wonderful God, the Almighty "Soul Doctor" for repair.

THE CENTER IN OUR LIVES

I Corinthians 2:9

When our youngest daughter was in pre-school she had to take allergy shots weekly, so every Saturday morning she and I would make the trip to the doctor's office.

One morning as we were returning from the doctor's office she suddenly asked me, "When I get big can I marry anyone I want?"

I answered, "Sure, Honey. As long as he loves you and you love him."

Then she announced, "I guess I'll marry Daddy."

Realizing how serious she was, in spite of my wanting to laugh, I very gently and thoughtfully explained that although she couldn't marry her Daddy, she would one day find someone just as wonderful her age to marry. Her young mind pondered that a moment then she told me with a deep sigh, "I don't know anybody else. If I can't marry Daddy I don't know who I'll marry. I guess I'll just be an old maid!"

You see, because of her young age our daughter couldn't imagine any other man in her life but her daddy, the one she trusted and adored. The thought that someone could ever replace him as the center in her life was inconceivable to her.

Actually this is a perfect example of how God wants us to love Him. He wants us to never be able to imagine that anyone or anything could replace Him as the center in our lives. God in I Corinthians 2:9 tells us,

"...No eye has seen, no ear has heard, no mind has conceived what God has prepared for those who love Him."

As long as we keep God as the center in our lives, He will reward us with blessings too wonderful for us to even imagine!

THE MOST PRECIOUS GIFT

Mark 14:22-24

Recently I participated in a very moving ceremony called Clown Communion, or "The Gift." The Gift, of course is what Jesus did for us on the Cross.

It's a Gift we have trouble understanding fully, but gently Jesus leads us back to the Cross over and over again until we begin to get the idea.

It's kinda like peeling an onion. Our understanding comes in layers. Jesus willingly became our sacrificial Lamb and by doing so He not only gave us a very priceless Gift – His life – He reminded us we have the most precious Gift of all in God. In Mark 14:22-24 we find that

"While they were eating, Jesus took bread, gave thanks and broke it and gave it to His disciples saying, 'This is My body.' Then He took the cup, gave thanks and offered it to them, and they all drank from it. 'This is My blood of the covenant, which is poured out for many,' He said to them."

Then through the Cross He poured out His greatest Gift on us.

Jesus, by example, showed us that even everything we have and everything we are already belongs to Him. We need to give back to Him daily out of our stores of gifts. We need to give according to the measure He continues to give us, which will be different for each of us. My all may not be your all. My gifts may not be your gifts. Jesus understood that.

And He knew we could only begin to understand this in layers.

Over and over Jesus continues to lead us through our gifts to our Giver! I pray that Jesus continue to lead you through the gifts He has given you to the most precious Gift of all – Our Giver!

WHO MOVED?

Hebrews 13:8

In the years I worked with alcoholics I became aware of a pattern. Some alcoholics were able to stay in recovery but some could not, even though almost everyone who moved into recovery did so for the same reason, regardless of their personal histories. Most had experienced some sort of crisis that caused their alcoholic way of living to stop working for them.

Sometimes, while in a crisis, it's easy to turn to God when nothing else seems to work. So, why are some able to stay in recovery but others keep relapsing?

It could be as time passes, some might find that the sameness of daily routine becomes mundane. When that happens they could find themselves relying more on self and less on God. Soon they discover that they are alone, unable to cope, and right back where they started.

Most of them will tell you that they have no idea how or when God left.

…Or did He?

A pastor friend of mine once said: "If you feel far away from God, ask yourself, who moved?" Hebrews 13:8 gives us a clue:

"Jesus Christ is the same yesterday and today and forever."

However, today when I experience the humdrum routine of life, it sometimes catches me off guard and I slip into relying more on self and less on God. When that happens I have to stop and take note of where God is in my life.

If you, like me, sometimes feel far away from God, ask yourself: "Who moved?" I bet it wasn't God.

SHIELDED

Deuteronomy 33:12

My husband and I were in line at a traffic light a short while ago that seemed to stay red forever. You know the type. As the light turned green and we waited for the car ahead of us to move, I observed a very common incident occurring in the lane next to us. A vehicle in that lane had not responded to the movement of the car in front of it fast enough to suit the driver in the vehicle behind it. That driver began to blow his horn. As I turned to look at him I noticed him also yelling at the car ahead of him while rudely motioning for it to start moving.

This was incredible because although I observed this, I could not hear a thing! The glass in our car windows shielded me from all outside sound.

Then I thought, how like Jesus to speak to me once again through circumstances.

Jesus is like that glass for us in life. Moses in Deuteronomy 33:12 said,

"...Let the beloved of the Lord rest secure in Him for He shields him all day long."

Jesus shields us from harmful and evil forces in our lives just as my car window shielded me from those angry outside sounds. I could have chosen to roll my window down, removing the glass and thereby exposing myself to those angry sounds, just as we can choose to step away from Jesus, removing His protection and exposing ourselves to all sorts of harmful and evil forces.

However, if we choose to stand behind Jesus nothing can pierce His protection of us. We can rest secure in Him for He will shield us all day long.

THEN THEIR EYES WERE OPENED

Luke 24:31

Our youngest daughter and her husband have a cat named Cookie who loves to play ball. When a ball is tossed, Cookie runs after it, picks it up and drops it back at the feet of the person who threw it.

Then she waits expectantly for the ball to be thrown again.

One day, as our daughter was quilting, she noticed her pincushion missing and remembered Cookie had just been in the room. Thinking that Cookie might have thought it was a ball, she began looking for it.

She found the pincushion downstairs and around the corner. Except it now contained no pins. Since she knew exactly how many straight pins she had placed in the pincushion, she began searching the area for them. When her husband came home that night she was still searching, so he took a flashlight and began helping her, without results. Not wanting to take the chance that Cookie may have swallowed the pins, they took her to the Vet to be x-rayed. Sure enough, Cookie had swallowed a pin that the Vet had to remove surgically.

Then, when they got back home that night and started upstairs to bed, there on the staircase landing in plain sight were all the other pins in a neat tidy pile!

As our daughter shared this with me, I knew beyond a shadow of a doubt that this was divine intervention. Had she and her husband found those pins earlier they might have dismissed the missing one and failed to take Cookie to the Vet. Luke 24:31 says, *"...Then their eyes were opened...."*

Only after Cookie was out of danger were their eyes opened to see the other pins.

THE CHAIR

I Corinthians 3:11

Frank E. Peretti, author of "This Present Darkness," was a guest speaker on Dr. Dobson's Focus on the Family one morning. He was talking about Jesus being the foundation on which we need to build.

To illustrate this, he used an analogy about a chair. He told us to imagine ourselves in a big room that is completely round and black. We can't see a thing. We are trying to figure out just where we are. However, the sameness confuses us and we feel hopelessly lost! We lack a fixed point of reference to set as a foundation on which to build.

Then, suddenly we bump into "The Chair." It's different. We can feel it and sit in it. We realize that now we have a fixed point of reference – a foundation on which to build. We know exactly where we are. We are in "The Chair!"

Using "The Chair" as our fixed point it becomes easy for us to begin to explore and reference our relationship to the rest of the room. With "The Chair" as our homing device, we can now venture out without becoming lost.

Jesus is our fixed point of reference in life. We can count on Him. He's different. He is the foundation on which we can build.

"For" (Paul says*) "no one can lay any foundation other than the one already laid which is Jesus Christ."* I Corinthians 3:11.

Once we accept Christ as our fixed point of reference our relationship to the rest of our life will be revealed in His light.

By using Jesus as our homing device, we are no longer lost.

FEEDING WOOD – AND SOULS!

Isaiah 55:2-3

One of my mother's hobbies was fixing and refinishing old or antique furniture in our basement. She always had a project of some sort in progress and she became quite good at restoring broken down, tired and misused pieces. I learned quite a lot from her and take pride in the pieces I inherited from her, as well as other pieces I have added to my home over the years.

Recently my husband was polishing our living room pieces and noticed that one table was beginning to look shabby. The wood had started to dry and crack. As he called my attention to it, I knew it had been caused by my neglect.

I remember my mother telling me over and over: "Wood cracks if you don't feed it."

As I shared this with my husband he looked at me and said, "You know that can also happen to our souls. Our souls can crack if we don't feed them."

Wow! What a marvelous insight!

Just as wood cracks if you don't feed it, so does your soul.

I am so blessed to have a husband who continually feeds his soul and nourishes mine at the same time.

Little did he know that he was polishing more than our furniture that day. He led me to the invitation God extends to us in Isaiah:

"...Listen, listen to Me and eat what is good, and your soul will delight in the richest of fare. Give ear and come to Me; hear Me that your soul may live." Isaiah 55:2-3

DISPELLING DARKNESS

John 8:12

I must admit that when I walk into a dark room and flip on the light switch I don't consider it a miracle.

I just take it for granted that when I turn on the light the darkness will be dispelled.

I must also admit that I can be that way with God. I sometimes just take it for granted that when I turn to my prayer time my soul's darkness will be dispelled.

When we turn on a light in a dark room the room floods with light giving us security and warmth. But if there happened to be a break somewhere between the switch and the bulb, no light would appear. If that happens we must first find the cause of the break and repair it before we can again have light.

Likewise, we must practice that same principle in our prayer life. If there happened to be a break in our prayer connection to God we would lose His Light. We must first find the cause of the break and repair it before we can again have the security and warmth of His perfect Light.

John 8:12 tells us,

"When Jesus spoke again to the people He said, 'I am the Light of the world. Whoever follows Me will never walk in darkness but will have the Light of life.'"

God has given us a Light in Jesus much stronger than any man-made light. Jesus is the Light that will dispel all darkness forever.

It gives you something to think about the next time you flip on a light switch. That light will only dispel our darkness temporarily but Jesus is the Light that will dispel our darkness forever.

THE PURSE

Matthew 11:28

Several months ago my best friend and I were asked to perform Clown Communion for the deaf community's weekly chapel time.

Clown Communion is a mute reenactment connecting the sacraments used in the Lord's Supper to what Jesus did for us on the Cross. It really brings home the significance of the Cross with the blood and broken body, as represented in the Eucharist. Because it is done in complete silence it is a perfect testimony for the hearing impaired community.

Especially for one young woman.

She was the first to come up for Communion after our reenactment. Then she remained standing beside us as we served the others. It was obvious that, maybe for the first time, she had made the connection of the Eucharist to the Cross.

Later, one of the staff told us the miracle that had taken place.

That young woman had recently come to them with only one item in her possession – her purse. It was the symbol of her identity. She took her purse everywhere with her. She refused to go anywhere or do anything (even shower) without it.

However, during Clown Communion, she rose and came forward, <u>leaving her purse in the pew</u>! Then she stayed by our sides without bolting back to get it! It was the major break-through for which the entire staff had been praying.

Maybe Jesus Himself had whispered in her permanent silence, as her eyes heard what we were saying:

"Come to Me all you who are weary and burdened, and I will give you rest." Matthew 11:28

ARE YOU THE ONE?

Matthew 11:2 & 3

John the Baptist was the first to identify Jesus as the Son of the Living God. Yet he could only have known this through the divine revelation of God Himself. There is no other way he could have known.

Up until this point, John the Baptist probably knew Jesus as simply his younger cousin who lived in Nazareth. He may have even heard a few stories and rumors about Jesus. Yet when John was called to prepare the way for the One God would send, he never questioned why it was his cousin, Jesus, who came forward.

While John was in prison he had time to reflect on these things and in spite of that hardship, he remained steadfast and true to the One God sent. I imagine it was not due to disbelief that John sent his disciples to ask Jesus,

"Are You the One who was to come, or should we expect someone else?" Matthew 11:2-3

I think John was sending his disciples to Jesus so that they could hear first hand that Jesus really was the One.

Or perhaps the question was John's way to get his disciples to leave him and go follow the true Master.

It's interesting that we sometimes still ask that question today. "Jesus, are You the One?"

Jesus is very intentional in His ways of answering us, for He always answers us. But so often we don't stop to listen. We hurry off to the next things on our agenda before we hear His answer.

Then someone, like John the Baptist did with his disciples, has to come and send us back to Jesus so we can hear first hand that He is the One.

CONFIDENT IN OUR DIRECTION

Hebrews 10:25

I got picked. For jury duty, that is. I had to report to the heart of down town San Antonio. Since I was unfamiliar with that area, I asked my husband to draw me a map.

I always rely on his maps when I'm uncertain of my way. But this time he really outdid himself.

The night before I needed to be there he drove me with the map along the route I was to take. We made note of lane changes, one-way streets and located surrounding parking areas. We pinpointed the exact location in which I needed to report.

The next morning I drove straight there like I had been doing it all my life.

My husband had me study the map and then he showed me the route so that when I had to continue alone I would not get lost. I was able to press on my way – confident in my direction.

It's the same thing we do in Bible study. Hebrews 10:25 is our summons to Bible study:

"Let us not give up meeting together as some are in the habit of doing, but let us encourage one another – and all the more as you see the Day approach."

We gather together to study God's Word. We take His Word and make note of life changes and the right paths. We locate how to give and receive forgiveness and mercy, and we strive to pinpoint our Lord and Master, Jesus Christ.

We continue to study together so that when we are absent from one another we will not get lost. We will be able to continue on the way that leads to eternal life, confident in our direction.

LIGHTHOUSES

II Corinthians 4:6

Those who know my husband know he collects lighthouses. For him they are a symbol of hope – a beacon guiding the lost to the light of Salvation.

For me they represent what Jesus is doing in his life. I watch my husband ministering to a discarded and forgotten people by bringing them the Word and Communion each month. As I see God's light growing stronger and stronger in him, I praise God that He chose to use my husband as one of His beacons to guide others to Christ.

Slowly lighthouses and representations of lighthouses are taking over our home, just as Jesus and His Holy Spirit are taking over our souls. You see there are very few things that can represent the strong light of salvation radiating from Jesus better than lighthouses.

A lighthouse stands firm and unmoving, throwing it's light out into the piercing darkness. It can be seen in the distance forever. Nothing else can guide a lost ship to port like the beacon of the lighthouse.

Likewise, there is nothing else that can guide a lost soul to salvation like the One and True Light – Jesus.

Paul said it best in II Corinthians 4:6:

"For God, who said, 'Let light shine out of darkness', made His Light shine in our hearts to give us the light of the knowledge of the Glory of God in the face of Christ."

The image of a lighthouse shining in the darkness, giving light to ships for safe passage, reminds us of God giving His light to shine in our hearts. God, as our Lighthouse, gives us His Light in the form of His Son so that we might become the beacons to shine that light for others, guiding them to Christ.

AS RUTH LOVED

Ruth 1:16

One well-known verse often used at weddings comes from the book of Ruth:

"Where you go, I will go, and where you stay I will stay. Your people will be my people and your God my God." Ruth 1:16

This classic expression of selfless loyalty captures the very essence of love. It's no wonder that (except for 1 Corinthians 13) this passage is an all time favorite for couples in love.

Would it surprise you, then, to learn that these words were not spoken by Ruth to her beloved'? No, this expression of such beautiful and true devotion poured from Ruth's heart to her mother-in-law!

However, that is exactly what makes Ruth 1:16 so wonderful. It is a perfect example of love that knows no bounds. It's a love that transcends the ordinary.

This had to have been the type of love Jesus wanted for us. Maybe the love of His ancestor, Ruth, came to His mind as He instructed us to love one another, as He loved us.

He could have added, 'and as Ruth loved Naomi.'

After all, like Ruth did to Naomi, Jesus promises to be with us always.

That means: Jesus will go where we go, stay where we stay. Our people will be His people and He will be our God forever.

VALENTINE'S DAY

LOVE

I Corinthians 13:4-7

Several years ago in my Disciple I class we studied 1 Corinthians, Chapter 13, which is the "Love" chapter. This is a beautiful description of love and one of the most commonly known and loved chapters in the Bible.

As an exercise we were asked to take I Corinthians 13:4-7 and insert the word "I" for the word "love".

"I" am patient, "I" am kind. "I" do not boast, "I" am not proud. "I" am not rude, "I" am not self-seeking, "I" am not easily angered, "I" keep no record of wrong doing: "I" do not delight in evil but rejoice with the truth. "I" always protect, always trust, always hope, always persevere."

Wow! That really opened our eyes!

Not to what love is but to what love is suppose to make of us. Until we "put on" love it will just be a word and will have little or no personal meaning for us.

This little exercise taught us that we had to live love in order to know love.

This Valentine's Day as we give and receive symbols of love, let us remember that it is not how much love we give or get, it's what love makes of us.

Put yourself in I Corinthians 13:4-7 and God will put I Corinthians 13:4-7 in you.

LOVE IS NOT A GIFT

Galatians 5:22-23

The book, "Porcupine People" by Lee Ezell, talked about the fact that love is not a gift as some may believe.

A gift implies it's given to us – to some more than others – and we simply just receive the amount allotted us.

In answer to this Lee said, "If you can find someone who can lay hands on you and impart the gift of love, please call me!"

The thought that someone could "zap" you with the gift of love is ridiculous. Yet, in spite of Lee's humor, her answer makes the point well.

Love is not a gift. No where in the Bible do we find love listed as a gift. I know. I looked. However, Galatians 5:22-23 list love as being the first characteristic found under fruits:

"But the fruit of the Spirit is <u>love</u>, joy, peace, patience, kindness, goodness, faithfulness, gentleness and self-control."

Its funny, but when I considered love a gift, I thought that somehow we just magically received it.

However, seeing love as a fruit changes that.

A fruit has to grow and ripen to be good. Fruit requires effort, nurturing, weeding and wise tending in order to grow.

Also, like a fruit we must cultivate love if it is to take root and blossom inside us.

You see love is not our actions but the product of our actions.

FEBRUARY 15

TRAINS AND STATIONS

Ecclesiastes 3:6

I couldn't believe it. All of a sudden I was dwelling on a worry that I had let go and given to God some time ago. Now after all this time, here it was back again.

I was puzzled so I silently asked God, "Why?"

That's when the thought occurred to me that the passing of time might have made no difference. Maybe I still had a welcome mat out for them.

Perhaps my fears and anxieties were so comfortable with me (and I with them) that they kept coming back every chance they got!

Even though I thought I had let go, maybe they hadn't.

Then I recalled something I had heard at a contemplative prayer workshop I had attended some years ago.

"Our thoughts are like trains and our minds are like stations."

Even though we have little control of which thoughts flood into our minds at times, we do have control of which thoughts we actually keep. We can choose which thoughts will pass on through our minds and disappear or which thoughts will stay.

Solomon, in his beautiful revelation on time in Ecclesiastes, touched on this. He said,

"[There's]...A time to keep and a time to throw away." Ecclesiastes 3:6

I can't stop thoughts from coming. I can only keep them or throw them away.

In other words, it's my choice whether my thought trains stop and stay in my mind station or simply leave and pass on through.

PULL YOURSELF TOGETHER

Acts 17:27-28

You remember that old joke:

A man walking along the railroad tracks came upon a leg. "That looks like Henry's leg," he said and walked on. Then he came upon the other leg. "That looks like Henry's other leg," he said and walked on. Then he came upon an arm. "That looks like Henry's arm," he said and walked on. Then he came upon the other arm. "That looks like Henry's other arm," he said and walked on. Then he came upon a torso. "That looks like Henry's torso," he said and walked on. Finally he came upon a head. He looked at it and said, "Henry, I thought that was you. Pull yourself together, man!"

We groan, not only because it's a horrible joke, but also because we know that scenario is impossible.

Yet, Henry's inability to pull himself together is not totally unlike our inability to pull ourselves together in other aspects of our lives.

The point is we can't pull ourselves together by ourselves. God tends to bring us back to that same point over and over again in our daily lives until we get it.

In fact, Paul tells us in Acts 17:27-28:

"God did this so that man would seek Him and perhaps reach out for Him and find Him though He is not far from each one of us. For in Him we live and move and have our being."

Never is it recorded that God ever looked down on us, without compassion, and said, "Henry...Jeanne...Mary...George (or, whatever your name is), pull yourself together!"

So when we become fragmented and unable to pull ourselves together, look to God for help. For its only God who can pull all aspects of our fragmented lives together and make the pieces work.

FEBRUARY 17

OUR CHURCH HOME

Psalm 122:2-3

It's hard to change church homes. Whether it's due to a move to another town or a search for Truth, it isn't easy to make a choice out of all the church homes available to us.

So what's a person to do?

I have been told that there are three things a person should look for when choosing a church home:

1. First, it must be a church that edifies the Word of God, breathing it in through proclamation, prayer and praise. It must be "God-Breathed".
2. Second, it must be a church whose focus is outside itself, extending to others compassion, community and comfort. It must be "God-Focused".
3. Finally, it must be a church that encourages its members to use their individual gifts, equipping its saints to boldly build up the body of Christ. It must be "God-Equipped".

We need to find a church that is God-Breathed, God-Focused and God-Equipped.

Look for a church that is built like a home in which its family is closely knitted, standing together and reaching out. Once we are certain the church home we have chosen is God-Breathed, God-Focused and God-Equipped, we will know we have found a good church home.

Then we can proclaim with David:

"I rejoice with those who said to me, 'Let us go to the House of the Lord.' Our feet are standing in your gates!" Psalm 122:2-3

GOD'S PLAN

Hebrews 11:40

For years I had been the volunteer coordinator for the San Antonio Stephen Series Leader Training Course (LTC). So I really felt sad when St. Louis notified me that a change in the registration procedure had eliminated the need for volunteers.

There was no need for us to be there to help with registration.

But my husband and I couldn't stay away! On registration day we went down to the training site anyway.

We wanted to say hello to our friends on the LTC Adjunct Staff and to visit the resource center. We needed to purchase a few special Stephen Ministry items for our new class that we were commissioning the following Sunday. We had planned a wonderful day for Commissioning Sunday, which included a luncheon in honor of our newly commissioned Stephen Ministers after church.

When Sunday came, imagine our delight to discover that our friends on the LTC Adjunct Staff had chosen the same restaurant for lunch that we had! Not only did we get to see them again but also our newly commissioned class of Stephen Ministers was able to meet them.

Yet, even more delightful to us was the realization that we could not have planned this perfect ending to our commissioning day.

Only God could.

Doesn't that remind you of Hebrews 11:40?

"God had planned something better for us so that only together with us would they be made perfect."

THE RIB

Genesis 2:18 & 21-24

At a wedding I recently attended the "Wedding Song" was sung.

It gave me the opportunity to really listen to the words. The "Wedding Song" is such a beautiful piece. I love the completeness of it. However, this time, as I listened, one phrase really stood out for me.

"Woman draws her life from man and gives it back again. And there is love … there is love."

It's true! From Adam's rib God formed Eve. That's how woman drew life from man. But woman? Though she drew life from man, she turned around and gave it back to him.

What hit me was, this was something only woman could do. Woman is the only one of the two that can bear and produce life. So, not only does woman become one with man in marriage, she takes their union and multiplies it!

Woman drew life from man. He then considered his job done. But woman didn't stop there. She took that life and proceeded to fill the earth with it!

"The Lord God said, 'It is not good for man to be alone. I will make a helper suitable for him.'"

"So the Lord God caused the man to fall into a deep sleep; and while he was sleeping, He took one of the man's ribs and closed up the place with flesh. Then the Lord God made a woman from the rib He had taken out of the man and He brought her to the man. The man said, 'This is now bone of my bones and flesh of my flesh; she shall be called "woman" for she was taken out of man.' For this reason a man will leave his father and mother and be united to his wife and they will become one flesh." Genesis 2:18 & 21-24

ANGEL CHECKS

Job 1:21

Some years ago my husband was "down-sized" from his chosen profession. Although it was the beginning of some marvelous blessings in our lives, living through that unemployment period had its moments!

We were forced to put our home up for sale and negotiate with our creditors. Yet, we both had agreed on one obligation that would remain non-negotiable - our tithe commitment to our church.

Under the circumstances we both knew how easy it would be to call the church and reduce or discontinue our tithe obligation. In fact, that's what a few individuals advised us to do. But that would be ignoring that everything we had already belonged to God.

I like to think the way we looked at our dilemma, on a small scale, was not unlike the way Job looked at his. He said,

"Naked I came from my mother's womb and naked I will depart. The Lord gave and the Lord has taken away; may the Name of the Lord be praised!" Job 1:21

Like Job we remained steadfast, sometimes financially hanging on with mere fingernails and prayers. As a result, whenever our money was gone before our obligations were satisfied "angel checks" would arrive in the mail.

Usually it was money we had coming that we had forgotten about, but it would always arrive just in time and in the amount we needed. Job said, "The Lord gave and the Lord has taken away."

Even though our situation couldn't begin to compare to Job's, we join in his praise, adding, "And He gives again!"

SEE JESUS

Luke 24:27

Sometimes I'm exactly like Cleopas and his friend walking from Jerusalem to Emmaus. Cleopas and his friend were walking with Jesus but they didn't know it!

They didn't expect to see Jesus.

Oh, they knew someone had come up along side of them and joined them in their travels. Only they did not recognize him to be the Christ. After all, hadn't they had watched Him die?

So Jesus walked quite a ways with them, trying to comfort them by explaining why their Savior had to suffer crucifixion and enter His glory.

"And beginning with Moses and all the prophets, He explained to them what was said in all the Scriptures concerning Himself." Luke 24:27

How many times do I do the same thing? I look at something – or someone – and do not see because I do not expect to see.

When God is busy at work in my life and miracles are occurring all around me but I take them for granted, I don't see them. When I chalk them up to simply good luck or coincidence, I don't recognize Jesus in them.

We are all on a journey like Cleopas and his friend – confused and searching. Often we forget that Jesus is walking that journey with us.

We must always expect to see Jesus everywhere and in every situation.

Or, like Cleopas and his friend, we won't see Jesus working in our lives simply because we don't expect to.

THE SWEET SPOT

John 3:16

Do you play tennis?

I haven't in a long time, but I did take a semester of Tennis as one of my Physical Education requirements in college. I learned such tennis terms as "love" and "sweet spot" among others.

A short time ago my husband and I attended a special candlelight service in which the attending pastor compared the game of tennis with our Christian life.

He said that in tennis the term "love" means zero, zilch, nothing. Love means you lose. But in Christianity love means everything. Love means we have won. Then he made a special note of the "sweet spot" found in the center of a tennis racket. The "sweet spot" is the spot you want the tennis ball to hit on the racket so the ball can be controlled at all times. He emphasized that you must keep your eye on the ball (which is the goal and objective of the game). Then you must hit the ball, making sure it makes contact on the racket within the "sweet spot".

Jesus is the tennis ball whom God served to us, using love as His racket:

"For God so loved the world that He gave His one and only Son that whoever believes in Him shall not perish but have eternal life." John 3:16

We must keep our eye on Jesus (who is the goal and objective of our faith). Then we must proclaim Jesus to others, making sure Jesus makes contact within their hearts, which is the true "sweet spot".

CHOOSE JESUS

Joshua 24:15

In an election year, campaign speeches and promises abound. Each candidate promises just a little bit more than the one before. Each tries to make us want to choose him/her on Election Day.

We listen to the issues and we listen to vague promises and solutions. We get caught up in personality struggles and underhanded accusations that have little or nothing at all to with the issues or the election itself. We are hounded, lied to, fed conflicting data; then we are asked to choose.

Sometimes I feel like I'm only voting for the lesser of the evils represented on the ballot!

Aren't we glad we don't have to choose our God that way? Jesus never pressures us, never hounds us, and never lies to us to make us choose Him. He just sticks to the Truth. He never allows Himself to get caught up in a debate of underhanded accusations with Satan.

To do so would draw Jesus' entire attention off of us and on to His arch competitor. Jesus would never allow that to happen.

We already know who the winner will be. So our only choice is to choose whether or not we want to be on the winning side.

I think Joshua stated it best:

"But if serving seems undesirable to you, then choose your yourselves whom you will serve, whether the gods your forefathers served beyond the River, or the gods of the Amorites, in whose land you are living, but for me and my household, we will serve the Lord." Joshua 24:15

Be on the winning side. Choose Jesus!

WITNESS

Proverbs 12:17

For some years now my husband and I have been bringing a worship service on the first Sunday of each month to the residents of a local assisted living home.

Just about a year ago a new resident began to join us in our worship service. She listened with great interest to the witness but always refused Communion for she was of a different faith. However we would, when we served Communion and came to her, give her a blessing instead. This seemed to mean so much to her.

Through the months she was very faithful in her attendance and never missed a first Sunday. Several times she would tell us how much the worship service meant to her and how much she was learning from our witness. Occasionally she would ask a few questions.

Then one first Sunday, a few months ago, she told us she would like to know more about this man called Jesus. We were able to put her into contact with someone who could better answer her questions by using her own faith background.

My husband and I praised God for allowing us to be His instrument. He used us to open her heart, which started her on her journey toward Jesus.

My husband's message and our faithful presence every first Sunday helped create the foundation and witnessed to her.

It's like Proverbs 12:17 claims:

"A truthful witness gives honest testimony, but a false witness tells lies."

If our witness had been less than true, or our presence less than faithful, her heart would not have sought Jesus.

MULTI-TALENTED

I Corinthians 3:9

Our youngest daughter is such a multi-talented individual. Now I know that I'm her mother but I assure you, it is true! There's nothing she can't do if she puts her mind to it. For instance:

I showed her the keys on the piano, named the octaves, and explained the basics of reading music. She, on her own, not only learned to play the piano but how to personally record the notes of the songs she liked best.

I showed her how a sewing machine worked, how to thread a needle, and how to place and cut patterns on material. She, on her own, not only learned how to sew but how to mix patterns to create styles of her own.

I encouraged her to dance, took her to dance lessons, and watched her fall in love with it. She, on her own, not only learned to become an accomplished dancer but also chose it for her life's work.

That has to be the way God thinks about each of us, don't you think? After all, He created us. He knows our every potential.

He knows we are all multi-talented in our own ways – within our own gifts.

Even Paul confirms that for us in I Corinthians 3:9

"For we are God's fellow workers; you are God's field, God's building."

In other words, Paul is saying,

"There's nothing any of us can't do once God puts our minds to it!"

FOLLOWING OUR FATHER

John 5:19

Late last summer I stopped by one of our daughter's homes to drop off a few things I had collected for them. Her husband, my son-in-law, and their son, my grandson, were mowing the yard.

Actually, my son-in-law was mowing while my grandson was following – running after him, pushing his toy mower.

I stopped to watch them a minute, wishing I had a camera with me.

I noticed that every move my son-in-law made was being duplicated by his son – down to the exact angle he held his head while pushing the mower to the way he wiped his brow as he paused to maneuver the mower around in order to tackle another row. I was touched to see my grandson following and imitating his father in every detail, wanting to be just like him.

There is another Son who adores his Father in much the same way as my grandson adores his father. His name is Jesus. And like my grandson, He follows His Father, running after Him, duplicating every move.

In fact, when He was asked about His special relationship with His Father

"Jesus gave them this answer; 'I tell you the truth, the Son can do nothing by Himself; He can do only what He sees His Father doing because whatever the Father does the Son also does.'" John 5:19

ONE BAPTISM

Acts 19:3-6

Our pastor, during his sermon one Sunday spoke of Baptisms. He quoted Mark 1:4 – 11 which states that John the Baptist came preaching a baptism of repentance for the forgiveness of sins.

John's message said,

"After me will come One more powerful than I...I baptize you with water but He will baptize you with the Holy Spirit."

Interestingly enough, Paul again pointed out this difference when he reached the town of Ephesus in his travels. There he had found some disciples and had asked them if they had received the Holy Spirit. When he found that they had not even heard of the Holy Spirit

"Paul asked, 'Then what baptism did you receive?' 'John's baptism,' they replied. Paul said, 'John's baptism was a baptism of repentance. He told the people to believe in the One coming after him, that is, in Jesus." On hearing this they were baptized in the Name of the Lord Jesus. When Paul placed his hands on them the Holy Spirit came upon him."* Acts 19:3-6

The Baptism true Christians receive today is the Baptism of the Holy Spirit through the Name of Jesus.

I was baptized as a baby so I don't remember my Baptism but that never lessened the Holy Spirit I received into my life that day. I have always been a special child of God's, filled with the Holy Spirit from the day of my Baptism.

Only those who since the beginning of Jesus' ministry only had received John's baptism of repentance needed to be baptized again in order to receive the Holy Spirit.

Today, whether we are baptized as babies or adults, one Baptism, as long as it is in the Name of Jesus, is all we need.

TEMPTATION

I Corinthians 10:12-13

We all come face to face sometime in our lives with temptation. I'm no exception, of course. It seems I fight it almost daily. Most of the time I succeed in defeating temptation but there are those times temptation win.

We've all been there and know that as we grow older it doesn't get any easier. It reminds me of that saying:

"Man's weakness is Satan's strength."

Man's weakness is exploited by the temptations we fall into and when temptations prevail Satan gains strength.

It's hard to recognize temptations when they present themselves because 90 % of the time Satan has disguised those temptations as acceptable types of choices, much like the ones we already make everyday.

So often I know I fall in temptation because I have lulled myself into believing that what I am doing or thinking or planning is the right thing.

More often than not I fall in temptation when I begin to rely on self instead of God.

Temptation is not a new thing. It began in the Garden of Eden and still thrives today. So the Bible offers us lots of encouragement and tools we can use to resist literally any temptation.

It helps to remember the wisdom contained in I Corinthians 10:12-13

"So, if you think you are standing firm, be careful that you don't fall! No temptation has seized you except what is common to man. And God is faithful; He will also provide a way out so you can stand up under it.

WILL YOU DIE FOR ME?

Romans 5:8

Ash Wednesday is the beginning of the 40-day (excluding Sundays) period of penitence before Easter, called Lent.

To enter into this period, designed to prepare our lives and hearts for Easter, we should keep in mind why Jesus went to the Cross:

"But God demonstrates His own love for us in this: While we were still sinners, Christ died for us." Romans 5:8

Jesus went to the Cross to save us from sin and to give us everlasting life. The 40-day period of Lent calls for us not only to repent from our sinning ways but also to focus on Jesus and how we can live for Him.

Just perhaps Jesus would ask us:

WILL YOU DIE FOR ME?

Will you die for Me like I died for you?
Will you pick up your cross if I asked you to?

When I knock on your door will you let Me in?
Will you cleanse your heart and confess your sin?

Will you die for Me?

Will you care for Me like I care for you?
Will you serve the people I send to you?

When I knock at your door will you let Me in?
Will you cleanse your heart and confess your sin?

Will you die for Me?

Jh 1996

MARCH 1

THE CHICKEN OR THE EGG?
Genesis 2:19

At one of our Lenten services the speaker for the evening asked us the age-old question:

What came first, the chicken or the egg?

Now, we know an egg is called an egg regardless of it origin. It could be a hummingbird egg, an ostrich egg, an alligator egg, a fish egg, a reptile egg or an insect egg, just to name a few. There's so many! Each egg's difference is not just in size and color.

Then we read,

"Now the Lord God had formed out of the ground all the beasts of the field and all the birds of the air. He brought them all to the man to see what he would name them; and whatever the man called each living creature, that was its name." Genesis 2:19

The question now is: If God had brought the man just the eggs to name, how would he have known which living creature was inside which egg or what type of creature it would be once it hatched? Would the man even be aware that eggs hatch? After all, the rest of the living creatures God brought to the man didn't. Also, an egg must have warmth to hatch. How was that warmth supplied if no egg had ever hatched yet and each hatchling type creature was still in its shell?

The last time I checked the jury was still out on the answer to this age-old question.

Perhaps the man held each egg and named whatever would emerge, sight unseen. Then God cradled each egg in the palms of His hands to hatch them.

If we follow the egg naming theory, man might have mistakenly named a chicken "spider!" Oops! (If that were the case would we be eating "fried spider" today?)

So, what came first, the chicken or the egg? I think that as long as we put God first it really doesn't matter!

STAY WITH US

Luke 24:28-29

"As they approached the village to which they were going, Jesus acted as if He was going farther. But they urged Him strongly, 'Stay with us…'" Luke 24:28-29

Sometimes in our walk with Jesus we get to where we thought we were heading and then are surprised when Jesus keeps going! As Cleopas and his traveling companion did, we usually urge Jesus to stop and stay with us.

However, more often than not, we stop because we have completed our own agenda and never noticed that Jesus kept going!

When that happens to me I am really surprised. I look around and exclaim, "Why isn't this working? Why do I feel all alone? I know I was following God's will – He was just here….

Hey! .. Where did Jesus go?"

We need to slow down and meet Jesus where He is so we can discover for ourselves more about His agenda. When we do, we become attuned to Jesus and our agenda change, aligning more accurately to His.

The way we do this is through prayer, Bible study, and fellowship with other believers. We must prepare ourselves. We must be ready to run when Jesus runs, walk when Jesus walks and stop only when He stops.

We need to open our eyes and see where our Lord is working; then join Him there.

If we stay with Jesus He will stay with us.

THE SINGER NOT THE SONG

Luke 21:33

I remember one Friday night just after I had graduated from high school a group of us got together to go to the drive-in movies.

It was the 'thing to do' back then. All drive-in movies were double-headers in that the current popular feature was always linked with another "B-rated" movie.

I've long since forgotten which movie we actually went to see, but I have never forgotten that "B-rated" movie. The name of it was "The Singer Not the Song."

In a nutshell: The movie was about a young priest who was sent to a small South American village, deep in the heart of Mexico, to start a church. Soon that young priest had the whole village attending the church services and under his direction Christianity began to flourish. Even people from outside the village began to flock into that small village to be saved. In fact, this young priest did such an outstanding job that the church soon reassigned him to start new churches in other areas where God was not yet known! But as soon as the young priest was reassigned and left the village, the church died! The villagers had only come to church because of their love for the "Singer" (the young priest) not their love for the "Song" (God). So as soon as their beloved "Singer" left, the people left. The young priest had not taught them the "Song"!

This movie really impressed me. It showed me that what counts is not who brings us the message (who the "Singer" is). The thing that really counts is the "Song" (God). We go to church to learn from the "Singer" about the "Song". Our "Song" is Jesus who makes us strong and keeps us together. In Luke 21:33 Jesus said,

"Heaven and earth shall pass away but My Words will never pass away."

"Singers" will come and go but the "Song" is over 2,000 years old and is still growing stronger every day!

THE LIGHT

John 12:36

We all have moments when we feel on top of the world!

That's when we usually claim that nothing could be better, and we earnestly wish that things would just stay that way forever!

Yet they won't. And we know it.

Those "on top of the world" moments we all have never last. No matter how hard we try, we can never recapture that exact feeling again.

Yet we keep trying. That's because when we lose our "on top of the world" feeling we start to feel cheated. Then we spend our time trying to chase the elusive shadows of those feelings.

In John 12:36 John reminds us

"While you have the Light, believe in the Light."

Ummm... So, does that mean we should chase after those wonderful moments we remember? Or could it be that John is trying to tell us to stick with Jesus and let Him be our Light through the lows in our lives as well as the highs?

Now there's food for thought!

Jesus is the Light and He shines within us: During our darkest moments as well as in our brightest. Putting on Jesus (or turning on His Light within us) doesn't always feel good. No, Jesus never promised us it would.

But He did promise to shine within us. Especially, I think, when we feel it the least for that is when we need Him the most.

Remember that His Light can break even your darkest fear.

NEVER WILL I LEAVE YOU

Hebrews 13:5

"A two-fold existence; I am where thou art.

Hark! Hear in the distance the beat of my heart."

Today my husband left on a business trip that will take him out of town for an extended length of time. As we said goodbye we were both aware that although time may go slow for us in time we would be back together.

We may be apart for a while in miles but we will always be together in heart. It reminded me of Hebrews 13:5 because no matter what, God is always there for us.

God assures us

"Never will I leave you, never will I forsake you."

Sometimes we may not feel His Presence and we may even think God has left us. But our Heavenly Father is always there for us in every situation. He keeps watch on both my husband and me where we are.

He keeps us together in the triangle of His love.

God joined us together in marriage in 1966 and made us extensions of each other. We are truly one. In fact my husband often states that when he begins a thought I finish it and vise-versa!

While we are apart in miles we talk on the phone every night. Quite a bit like we talk every night to God, using prayer instead of the phone.

The only difference is that I can audibly hear by husband's voice as I share with him. God responds back to me using other means.

Yet, no matter how He responds, He is always assuring us,

"Never will I leave you, never will I forsake you."

COTTON CANDY JESUS

John 10:17-18

This weekend I had occasion to attend a special worship service where the pastor referred to Jesus as being "cotton candy!" That didn't sound quite right, so it really got my attention.

The pastor was recounting the resurrection of Jesus by pointing out the sequence of events after the crucifixion. In the garden after the stone had been rolled away, Mary assumed Jesus was the gardener. She said to Him, *"Sir, if you have carried* [Jesus] *away, tell where you have put Him."* Jesus simply said, *"Mary."* She recognized Him. Then He was gone.

Later that same day, on the road to Emmaus, Cleopas and his friend assumed Jesus was a fellow traveler and asked Him to stay and eat with them. When Jesus blessed the bread and broke it, their eyes were opened and they recognized Him. Then He was gone.

Each time Jesus appeared, He vanished. Jesus, full of compassion and love, comes to us and just as we taste His sweetness, He melts away – just like cotton candy!

Jesus even tells us why.

"The reason My Father loves Me is that I lay down My life – only to take it up again. No one takes it from Me but I lay it down of My own accord. I have authority to lay it down and authority to take it up again." John 10:17-18

If every time Jesus came to us we caught Him, He would not be free to work His miracles all over the world. Jesus must remain free to come and go.

He knows just what we need. We taste His sweetness and know His love. It melts in our mouth and leaves us with the lingering hunger for more. We come again and again to Jesus, never tiring of His cotton candy sweetness!

WHOM WILL YOU SERVE?

Joshua 24:15

When my husband accepted a position with a company out of town we looked forward to a move we thought would be very positive for us. He went on ahead of me to begin his new job, but once he got there he began receiving instructions from his new boss that went against his strong code of ethics.

Finally my husband went to his boss and told him he was uncomfortable with that way of doing business. His boss responded with something similar to: "That's tough. I've paid my dues and no one is going to tell me how to conduct my business."

That's when my husband took a stand and made the decision not to continue working for this person.

His actions reminded me of Joshua when he took a stand in front of his people. Joshua said,

"Choose for yourselves this day whom you will serve..." Joshua 24:15.

Now my husband had the choice to be on the side of honor and truth or on the side of deceit and lies.

He chose honor and truth.

He quit the next day, retaining his integrity and code of ethics. You see he knew something else that his now ex-boss had never considered.

All we need to do is to choose for ourselves to serve the Lord.

Jesus has already paid our dues!

MAKING IT SPECIAL

Isaiah 29:13

While I was in high school my family had a cocker spaniel named Butch. It was usually my sister's job to feed him each night while I did the supper dishes.

So, I became very familiar with the "supper routine" she invented.

My sister would talk to Butch while she was preparing his food. She would let him see her stir and fuss over the dish. Butch would get so excited that he would nearly fall over in anticipation. The longer she fussed and talked the more excited Butch became. Finally, she would place his dish on the floor in front of him. (I really don't think it mattered too much to Butch what was in that dish. I think if it had been sliced tomatoes with vinegar and salt Butch would have eaten it just as eagerly!) Although Butch always received exactly the same food each night (plus any appropriate table scraps left on our plates), my sister always managed to make him think that he was getting a special treat.

Pretty soon Butch was turning his nose up to any food offered to him in any other way.

Sometimes we get that way with Jesus. We experience a moment of spiritual high and decide that Jesus should always come to us in that fashion. However, the longer we run after the moment the more it becomes our focus.

Pretty soon we are turning our noses up to Jesus offered to us in any other way.

The Lord warns us about that in Isaiah 29:13. He said,

"These people come near to Me with their mouth and honor Me with their lips, but their hearts are far from me."

To put it simply: We end up worshipping the moment instead of Jesus.

DOING AS JESUS DID

Mark 14:60-61

Could I stand silent and confident in the face of my accusers, as Jesus did?

When I think about that, I remember a time our middle daughter called to relate an incident that had happened to her. A person we both knew well had entered her work place and created an ugly scene – attacking her verbally with false accusations.

My heart went out to her.

"How awful!" I exclaimed. "And in front of all your co-workers too. I would have just died! What did you do?"

"Nothing." She replied. "We all have choices and that person chose to engage in that type of behavior. I simply chose not to be responsible for it."

As I hung up, I thought. "What a healthy attitude!"

I suspected that I might have responded very differently – matching fire with fire. But she didn't.

I think without being aware of it she had modeled the attitude of Jesus when He was brought before the Sanhedrin with false accusations. Mark 14:60-61 tells us,

"Then the High Priest stood up before them (the whole Sanhedrin) and asked Jesus, 'Are you not going to answer? What is this testimony that these men are bringing against you?' But Jesus remained silent and gave no answer."

Our daughter's silent response paralleled our Lord's silent response. Like Jesus, she knew that the truth needed no words. The truth remains the truth, no matter what.

BE STILL

Ruth 3:18

When I was young my mother would brush my hair every night before bedtime and again each morning before she braided it. More often than not I'd become impatient and complain especially when she found stubborn tangles that had to be worked out.

I'd wiggle and jerk, make faces and whine. Often she would tell me to be still and let her finish.

The other day I was thinking about this and the thought crossed my mind that I'm also that way with God.

When He brushes out the details in my life I often become just as impatient with Him as I used to be with my mother. Especially when He begins to work on those stubborn tangles I've left in my life. I become reluctant to let Him finish, complaining every inch of the way.

I still wiggle and jerk, make faces and whine – anything to try to make Him stop.

I can just hear God telling me, as my mother told me and as Naomi told Ruth:

"Be still my daughter until you find out what happens." Ruth 3:18

So, what usually happens?

Once the tangles in my life have been worked out, like the tangles in my hair, the brushing becomes relaxing, soothing and rewarding.

THE KIND THAT STICKS

Proverbs 18:24

It's really frustrating. Plastic wrap, that is.

Actually there are two kinds of plastic wrap. There's the kind that sticks and there's the kind that won't.

The kind that sticks seems to always stick when you don't want it to. Actually there are times I can never get it untangled enough to use.

Yet, I can't get the kind that won't stick to work for me either. It will never stay in place at all.

I guess if I had to make a choice, I'd choose the kind that sticks. It might be frustrating to work with, but once it's in place it will stay.

Interestingly enough the characteristics of plastic wrap can also be applied to people.

There's the kind that sticks with you in any situation and there's the kind that won't. And like with the plastic wrap, if I had to make a choice I'd choose the kind that sticks.

Better to have one friend that sticks with me through thick and thin than to have lots of casual acquaintances that won't.

There's a proverb about that:

"A man of many companions may come to ruin, but there is a friend who sticks closer than a brother." Proverbs 18:24.

There's one thing we can be sure of. Jesus will always be that type of friend who sticks closer than a brother will. Because once Jesus is in place in our hearts and our lives, He's there to stay.

Jesus is the kind that sticks.

PULLED APART

John 21:18

When our oldest daughter died, a part of me died with her. I prayed for God to help her find the peace she in life had so desperately sought.

In a special memorial service designed to free her, her ashes were released over the lake she had lived near in her youth. Except, as her ashes were released a handful was captured to be planted elsewhere. Something inside me ached as I watched her being pulled apart in death as she had been in life.

The service of releasing her ashes over the lake, symbolizing our prayers of unity and peace for her, was really a service for those of us still living to tangibly release her and let go. It was a service of saying goodbye.

Yet, the words Jesus spoke to Peter in John 21:18 kept resounding in my head.

"I tell you the truth, when you were younger you dressed yourself and went where you wanted; but when you are old you will stretch out your hands and someone else will dress you and lead you where you do not want to go."

Our oldest daughter's life was cut short so she would never see old age or be able to watch her young sons grow. I will always believe the act that took her life led her where she did not want to go. Someone else led her to her death.

However, like it did Peter, that act also led her safely into Jesus' arms.

Although she was pulled apart in life and in death, she will never be pulled apart again.

DID YOU PRAY FOR ME?

Romans 8:26

One of the first jobs I had after moving to New Mexico was working for the Dean of Engineering at New Mexico State University so I got to know the engineering students well.

One of the engineering students was running for president of his class and as I wished him luck he asked me if I would pray for him. I said, "Yes, of course." After the election he stopped by my office but before he would tell me the outcome he asked, "Did you really pray for me?" Even though I said, "Of course I did" I felt I really hadn't. Or had I? I began to look for the ways I did pray. I hadn't dropped to my knees or spent the day isolated and secluded in prayer. Yet I had gone through the day with a prayer in my heart. Most of the day my prayer had no audible words, but it had a hope, a dream and a vision.

It reminded me of the passage in Romans 8:26:

"In the same way, the Spirit helps us in our weakness. We do not know what we ought to pray for, but the Spirit Himself intercedes for us."

I was intrigued. As I searched my heart that day these words came to me:

DID YOU PRAY FOR ME?

"Did you pray for me?" he asked.

Did I pray for him?

I voiced a hope...I visioned a dream...

And placed him there.

Did I pray?

I sent a thought...I said his name...

And waited with care.

"Did you pray for me?"

Ah, yes. A thousand times.

jhk-1965

MARCH 14

OUR PAST AND OUR FUTURE

Isaiah 43:10

There was a scene in the movie "Step Mom" toward the end that really gave me food for thought. Isabel, the step-mom-to-be, met with her finance's ex-wife, Jackie. They were talking about a future for the children in which there would only be Isabel, because Jackie would not live to see them grow up. In this scene she was releasing that responsibility to Isabel.

Jackie told Isabel: I will always live in (my children's) past but it will be you they remember in their future. I hold their past. You hold their future.

We all have experienced this to some degree in our lives.

There are those whom we have had to let go and there are those who have had to let us go. We will be those in the past for some and we are the ones in the future for others.

However, there is One who will always be in our past and our future: Jesus. We never have to let Him go and He will never let us go.

God Himself told us that in Isaiah 43:10.

"You are my witnesses, declares the Lord. And my servant who I have chosen, so you may know and believe Me and understand I am He. Before Me no god was formed nor will there be one after Me."

God makes it very clear. He is the Alpha and the Omega. The beginning and the end. He is our past and our future.

In this world of doubts and fears, isn't it assuring to know there will always be One who will always be there?

One who will never let us go?

AN OLD IRISH BLESSING

Isaiah 49:16

The year one of our church activities fell on St. Patrick's Day my husband led us in trying to recall the words of an Old Irish blessing:

May the winds be always at your back
May the sun shine warm upon your face?
And the rains fall soft upon your fields
And until we meet again
May God hold you in the palm of His hand.

As I listened to the words, I was struck by the thought of God holding us in the palm of His hand.

Instantly I was reminded of Isaiah 49:16,

"See, I have engraved you on the palms of my hands..."

Sometimes when I need to remember a phone number, a name or something important and have no paper handy I find myself writing on my hand. It stays there for when I need to recall it.

Isaiah tells me that our names are forever engraved on the palms of God's hand.

They are. With nails, driven in deep by Roman soldiers!

We are etched so deeply into His palms He could not ever forget us or let us accidentally slip from His grasp.

ST. PATRICK'S DAY

Ephesians 6:13-17

My family celebrates St. Patrick's Day as big as, if not bigger than other occasions. The name Heffern is Irish, which gives us the excuse to follow all the customs of St. Patrick's Day.

We send and receive St. Patty cards and never would dream of not wearing green on that day. After all, green, which is the Irish national color, is their symbol of protection from evil and is suppose to ensure the luck o' the Irish.

Jesus also has symbols for us to wear to protect ourselves from evil and help us to take our stand against the devil's schemes.

We find them listed in Ephesians 6:13-17.

"Therefore put on the full armor of God, so that when the day of evil comes, you may be able to stand your ground, and after you have done everything, to stand. Stand firm then, with the belt of truth buckled around your waist, with the breastplate of righteousness in place, and with your feet fitted with the readiness that comes from the gospel of peace. In addition to all this, take up the shield of faith, which you can extinguish all the flaming arrows of the evil one. Take the helmet of salvation and the sword of the Spirit, which is the Word of God."

It's fun to wear green and recognize our heritage, but it's life saving to wear the full armor of God and to recognize Jesus as the Lord of our lives.

A COMPLETE BLESSING
Matthew 16:26

There's an Irish blessing someone once e-mailed us:

"May there always be work for your hands to do,

May your purse always hold a coin or two.

May the sun always shine warm on your windowpane,

May a rainbow be certain to follow each rain.

May the hand of a friend always be near you,

And may God fill your heart with gladness to cheer you."

Yet, as I read it I felt something was missing. It seemed complete: A prayer for work for your hands, prosperity, fortune, happiness, friendship and a heart filled with gladness. So what could be missing?

Then I realized what it was. It assumed that if we have a job, some money, a bit of luck, a true friend and we feel good we're complete. It ignored the most important human aspect: Our souls. Our souls are the only part about us that are everlasting.

Sometimes jobs don't last and the money won't stretch. Often things don't go just as you would have them. Friends can get too busy to notice while our health can fail without notice. Only our souls stay constant. It reminds me of what Jesus asked His disciples:

"What good will it do for a man if he gains the whole world, yet forfeits his soul? Or what can a man give in exchange for his soul?" Matthew 16:26

To make this Irish blessing complete it needs to include asking God to watch over our souls as well as our physical needs.

MARCH 18

PRESS ON

Philippians 3:13-14

One Saturday night as we were returning from a special Emmaus service it started lightning. It soon became apparent that we were in the midst of a lightning storm.

Then it happened. Lightning flashed directly in front of us, hitting a transformer off the road to our right. We watched the transformer sputter and spark, flare and die.

At that exact moment the rain started. Big hard drops that pounded across our windshield so hard I asked my husband if it was hailing. Just as he told me no, it did begin to hail, hitting our hood, roof and windows with a damaging force. All through this the rain continued like waving sheets, instantly flooding the highway. A flash flood had started.

I prayed for God to place a hedge around us as we pressed on in the storm. Then, just as the hail stopped, without warning our vehicle hydroplaned. As my husband fought to control it, I continued to ask God to keep that hedge around us – to press us on to safety and leave the storm behind.

And He did so, for as we exited off the highway and turned into our neighborhood, the storm ceased just as suddenly as it had started. As I thanked God, the urgency of Philippians 3:13-14 came to my mind:

"Forgetting what is behind and straining toward what is ahead, I press on toward the goal to win the prize for which God has called me heavenward in Christ Jesus."

We had pressed on in the storm toward home and, through the protection and Grace of our Lord Jesus Christ; we arrived home safe and sound.

GOD'S BRAND OF PEACE

John 14:27

In our neighborhood there are two major grocery chains – Albertsons and H.E.B. Although I generally shopped at H.E.B., I do go occasionally to Albertsons for a few things. So I really related to a life lesson a friend of mine e-mailed me.

He wrote:

"I went to Albertsons to pick up a few basics. While I was there I thought I would get chips for lunch. So I looked and looked. Then I realized why I couldn't find my brand of chips. Albertsons doesn't carry H.E.B name-brands!"

I thought, that's just like when we look and look for peace but can't seem to find it. Sometimes it never occurs to us that the place we are looking in doesn't carry the brand of peace for which we are searching.

Still, we keep searching the world over looking for that peace.

So where do we find the peace for which we are searching?

In Jesus. God sent His Son, Jesus, to us so that we could bring us peace.

Jesus said:

"My peace I leave with you; My peace I give you. I do not give to you as the world gives. Do not let your hearts be troubled and do not be afraid." John 14:27

The world doesn't carry God's brand of peace.

BITTER OR BETTER

Proverbs 14:10

Life does not allow us to choose to do only the things we want. There are just some things we must do whether we want to or not.

Sometimes we simply have no choice.

We could grumble, complain and resist. Most of us often do, even though we realize that doesn't help. It only delays the action we need to take.

You see, that in spite of having no choice in some things we have to do, we do have a choice in how we do them. The difference is in our attitudes.

When we grumble and complain and put off the action we need to take, we only make all those around us and ourselves bitter.

However, when we tackle the things we must do quickly and cheerfully we make those around us and ourselves better.

In other words, we can make those around us and ourselves bitter or better.

Proverbs 14:10 says it this way:

"Each heart knows its own bitterness and no one else can share its joy."

So, no matter the situation our choice is easy. We can decide to stay bitter or we can decide to get better!

JELLYBEANS

Psalm 139:16

Are you a sequential person? I didn't think I was until someone pointed out the way I eat jellybeans.

Now, there are lots of ways to eat jellybeans, ranging from popping handfuls into your mouth all at once to eating them one by one, by colors, or in some other kind of order.

A non-sequential person will eat jellybeans by the handfuls, mixing colors and favors randomly without thought.

A sequential person will always have a definite pattern. And I do. So, I have to admit that when it comes to jellybeans I am a sequential person.

Did you know that our God is a sequential God?

Just look at the creation story. God created the earth and all that is in it (even down to you and I) in a definite pattern. In spite of man being completely unpredictable, God is completely in control of his sequence of being.

In fact, David emphasized that in Psalm 139:16 when he said:

"All the days ordained for me were written in Your Book before one of them came to be."

Without a doubt God keeps our world and all of mankind in perfect order. Nothing is mixed randomly without thought or left undone.

Everything God created, and is creating, works in a sequential pattern – even to this day.

It makes me wonder if God would eat jellybeans that way too....

LET'S GO PLAY!

Isaiah 11:6

When we go to see our grandchildren in Dayton, Texas I know that soon after we arrive I will be putting puzzles together, reading stories and participating in play time with our granddaughters.

As soon as they see me they say, "MiMi, let's go play!

It is my privilege to do just that.

I get to let two little girls lead me into being a child again.

All through the Bible God tells us over and over and over how very precious children are. Jesus said that unless we come to Him like a little child we can never enter the gates of heaven.

Unfortunately, as we grow most of us tend to forget how to be children.

We tend to lose the unquestioning faith and trust we had as children. We become more reserved in love due to past hurts or painful memories.

Our world becomes something we must endure instead of a special place in which to play.

We simply turn our playgrounds into prisons. We treat our jobs like prison sentences and create deadlines instead of joys and songs.

So, when our granddaughters say, "MiMi, let's go play." I eagerly follow them.

For Isaiah 11:6 says:

"And a little child shall lead them."

THE LAMB OF GOD

Romans 5:8

My husband and I were invited to join the deaf church planning retreat at the Methodist Mission Home in their worship service last spring. This was to be the two of the deaf clients' first official performance of "The Lamb of God" and since we had trained them we were really looking forward to the service.

As we gathered for the worship service I noticed near the front of the room one little three-year-old girl sitting on her father's lap. I could tell both the father and the little girl were hearing but the mother sitting next to them was not. The little girl was silent as she watched "The Lamb of God" performance unfold. She was fascinated, as were we all, by the re-enactment of God's greatest gift to us – His Son – and the work Jesus did for us on the Cross. So as the nail was driven deep into the bread held on a cross by a crown of thorns, everyone held his or her breath. Not a sound was heard.

At that very moment the little girl stated in a hushed, awed tone that carried throughout the room, "Daddy, the baby died."

Those hearing, including my husband and I, caught our breath. Her simple but profound statement caught us off guard. For wasn't Jesus still as innocent and pure as a babe when He died for our sins?

I, for one, will never witness or perform "The Lamb of God" or go forward for Communion again without remembering her simple words.

"But God demonstrates His own love for us in this: While we were still sinners, Christ died for us." Romans 5:8

innocent as a baby.

CHRISTIAN SYMBOLS

Mark 16:2-4

I heard an interesting statement the other day on the radio. The speaker was exploring the meaning of our symbols in Christianity, particularly the Cross.

Many Christians, including myself, wear a cross on a chain around our necks representing a symbol of hope, the promise of life resurrected.

However, the speaker went on to say that's not what the Cross really represents.

Jesus went willingly to the Cross to die for our sins. And die He did. Even the Apostles and the women who were the closest to Him thought His death was final. It was only when the stone was rolled away from the tomb that they began to realize that maybe Jesus was still alive. That maybe everything He had told them was true. That just maybe there was hope.

Only then did they begin to recall Jesus' promise of life resurrected.

"Very early on the first day of the week, just after sunrise, they [the women] were on their way to the tomb and they asked each other, 'Who will roll the stone away from the entrance of the tomb?' But when they looked up, they saw that the stone, which was very large, had been rolled away." Mark 16:2-4

Our sins were nailed on the Cross with Jesus. The Cross reminds us He died to take them away.

The stone, however, because it was rolled away, reminds us Jesus did not stay dead. He lives so we can live.

So what is the true symbol of hope and represents the promise of life resurrected? The stone. So, shouldn't the Christian be wearing a stone on a chain around his or her neck instead of a cross?

STRUNG TOGETHER

Titus 2:11-12

The other day I looked out our kitchen window and noticed my neighbor hanging clothes on her outside line to dry. I stopped to watch her for a minute as she hung different articles of clothing, penning them together so they strung out along the line.

It reminded me of an illustration I had heard recently. The speaker had compared the common clothesline to God's Grace line upon which all the parables of the Bible are strung.

My neighbor penned together a pair of jeans to a T-shirt to a blouse to a towel, to a sheet, etc. along her clothesline.

Jesus penned together the parables of the prodigal son to the lost coin to the lost sheep to the sower to the mustard seed, etc. along God's Grace line.

My neighbor used a clothesline so her articles of clothing could dry in the breeze.

Jesus used God's Grace line so His parables could bring salvation to man.

"For the Grace of God that brings salvation has appeared to all men. It teaches us to say 'No' to ungodliness and worldly passions, and to live self-controlled, upright and godly lives in this present age." Titus 2:11-12

Jesus strung together the parables in the Bible so we might understand the whole Grace line of God and be eager to accept the salvation God is offering us.

CRISP AND SHARP

II Peter 3:13

Think about it.

In the beginning the world looked clean – crisp and sharp. You know, like it does sometimes after a good rain.

But especially with the dryness in most of Texas, it can look blurred, faded, grayed out. We blame it on everything that affects the quality of air – from no rain to the exhaust fumes of traveling vehicles, from a mysterious hole in the ozone layer to factories spilling out waste products.

There are thousands of more things that affect our earth, water and air and we never tire to list them as the reasons why the world does not look as crisp and sharp as it once did.

I'm reminded of the man who complained to his friend about how blurred and grayed everything was becoming around him. His friend looked around and then assured him nothing had changed. Everything was still as crisp and sharp as ever.

"All you need," he commented dryly, "is new glasses."

Perhaps the way we view the world is dependent on through what we are looking. Instead of looking for reasons why the world looks blurred and grayed, we might instead look for ways to keep it crisp and sharp.

Maybe we need new glasses.

When we use Jesus as our glass piece and look at the world through Him we will see it as He sees it – crisp and sharp – for

"... In keeping with His promise we are looking forward to a new heaven and a new earth, the home of righteousness." II Peter 3:13

IT DOESN'T MATTER THE WORDS

Matthew 11:28

Shortly after I had served as a team member of a deaf walk, one of the deaf walkers I had come to know came up to me and very excitedly began to sign. Now, my signing ability is very limited and this young man was signing at a high rate of speed, so I had no idea of what he was trying to tell me. However, I kept watching his hands hoping that I could pick up a sign or two while nodding and smiling to keep encouraging him.

It wasn't too long before one of the interpreters came up and asked me if I knew what the young man was saying to me. She went on to explain that he was telling me about his mother who died just a short while ago and the pain he was going through being separated from his family. My heart sunk. He had been pouring out his hurt to me and I had just sat there, nodding and smiling!

I had been so busy watching his hand signs that I had completely ignored his facial expressions and his body language, which would have all given me clues as to the nature of his message.

I learned a valuable lesson that day. Sign language is more than hand signs. It's also body and facial signs – the same as it is in any language. If you can feel what is being said, it doesn't matter the words. Jesus said,

"Come to Me, all you who are weary and burdened and I will give you rest." Matthew 11:28

Jesus didn't say, "Come tell Me…" He just said, "Come to Me…" Jesus can feel what you are trying to say, even when it makes little sense because it doesn't matter the words.

MEANT TO BE

Jonah 1:1-2

Have you ever noticed that when something is meant to be, it happens? It doesn't matter what you do or don't do.

You can't stop it or prevent it from happening.

Take Jonah for instance:

"The Word of the Lord came to Jonah, Son of Amittai: 'Go to the great city of Nineveh and preach against it because its wickedness has come up before me.'" Jonah 1:1-2

You know the story.

Jonah didn't want to go, so he ran away and boarded a ship sailing in the opposite direction. But God chased after him and caused a violent storm to arise, which threatened the lives of everyone aboard that ship. By now Jonah realized that trying to run away from God was futile – not to mention, life-threatening! So, to save the ship, Jonah had his shipmates throw him overboard. Except he no sooner hit the water than a great fish swallowed him up!

Amazingly, Jonah lived inside that fish three days and three nights before the fish "up-chucked" him onto dry land.

Then the Word of the Lord came to Jonah the second time. And guess what? This time Jonah listened and was quick to obey God, going to Nineveh as God commanded.

It was meant to be.

Jonah couldn't prevent it or stop it from happening, although he tried.

So it happened.

Even though Jonah's stubbornness caused him a "fishy" detour of three days and three nights before his arrival.

BE COMPLETE

John 16:23-24

There was a young lad who lived near a busy street in a large city. On this particular day his mother wasn't home and he wanted to go play with his friends in the park located across that busy street. However, the young lad was not allowed to cross the street alone, so he stood at the curb looking toward the park where his friends were playing.

How was he going to get there?

Standing near the lad was an elderly gentleman. He had just traveled across the country to visit his daughter he hadn't seen in years. In his hand was her address, however he had no idea which direction he should turn to find her street.

How was he going to get there?

Now the lad was familiar with the area and knew which direction the elderly gentleman needed to take in order to find his daughter's street, and the man was of sufficient age to accompany the lad across the street to the park to play.

Each had a problem the other could solve.

We all at one time or another have been in the shoes of that young lad and/or that elderly gentleman, and we too have been left at the curb because we failed to ask for help when it was standing right next to us.

Jesus cautions us to be diligent in asking for help. He said,

"I tell you the truth, My Father will give you whatever you ask in My Name. Until now you have not asked for anything in My Name. Ask and you will receive and your joy will be complete." John 16:23-24

OUR PERMANENT HOME

John 14:2-3

Shortly before we move from one city to another I received the renewal notice from our local newspaper.

Our subscription would be expiring in less than a month before our move date.

For a moment I debated about the renewal but then decided that once we moved we would probably want to subscribe to that local paper instead. After all, we were leaving the area.

It was not to be a permanent home for us.

Then it struck me that, as Christians, the world is not a permanent home for us either. No matter where we live we are just living there temporarily until our heavenly move date.

So although we naturally subscribe to earthly traditions while living here on earth, we should be renewing our efforts to read and study about the place in which we will one day reside forever.

After all, it will be a permanent home for us.

Jesus said,

"In My Father's house are many rooms; if it were not so I would have told you. I am going there to prepare a place for you. And if I go and prepare a place for you, I will come back and take you to be with Me that you also may be where I am." John 14:2-3

APRIL FOOL

CHANGE

Matthew 18:2-3

I love being a clown! It's so liberating and freeing. When I paint my face, dress in a clown suit, wear white gloves, and don rainbow hair I'm no longer Jeanne.

I'm Cary, a fool for Christ!

Jeanne has to follow all the accepted social rules but Cary is free to skip over those boundaries and be a child at heart. Jeanne must do what is expected of her but Cary is expected to do the unexpected. Jeanne is dependable. Cary is refreshingly spontaneous. Jeanne must excel and always finish what she starts. Cary is free to play the fool and flit from one thing to another.

So when I'm a clown I change.

Actually, change can be good. Jesus talked about the need for us to change.

Of course, He wasn't speaking of playacting or clowning around as a pastime. He was speaking of genuine, permanent change.

"He called a little child and had him stand among them. And He said: 'I tell you the truth, unless you change and become like little children you will never enter the Kingdom of heaven.'" Matthew 18:2-3

It almost sounds like Jesus is trying to tell us to let the clown we have inside come out, doesn't it? Every one of us has a clown inside but most of us never find a way to let him/her out. Playing a fool is not a real common pastime!

Maybe we should change that.

INSTINCTS

Proverbs 3:5-6

I believe that one way the Holy Spirit works in our lives is through instincts. It's like the Holy Spirit spiritually taps us on the shoulder – so's to speak – and gives us a pull into the direction we should choose. I can't begin to count the times I have had that spiritual tap on my shoulder pulling me to go in a certain direction or to say something, but I resisted. I usually found later that if I had paid attention to my instinct, it would have made my life or another life touching mine less complicated.

For example: One time when I was trying to drive to an unfamiliar location I became hopelessly disoriented. As I came upon a crossroad my first instinct was to make a left turn. Yet, as I tried to logically diagram in my mind my current location in relationship to where I should be, my common sense told me I needed to turn right. Of course, I followed my common sense, wouldn't you?

Later I discovered that had I followed my first instinct I would have found a familiar street just one block away that would have put me back on course. As it was, it took several hours before I recognized my surroundings. You see I failed to listen to the little spiritual tap on my shoulder when I dismissed that first instinct. By doing so I made my life more complicated than it should have been.

Proverbs 3:5-6 has words of wisdom we should write on our minds for when we become confused as to the direction we should take:

"Trust in the Lord with all your heart and lean not on your own understanding; in all your ways acknowledge Him, and He will make your paths straight."

APRIL 2

VIBRATION

Ephesians 4:12

I love the definition I recently heard describing a vibration:

"A motion that can't make up its mind which way to go!"

Sometimes circumstances in our lives call for us to take action, yet often we have no idea what that action should be. We might start off in one direction to find it ineffective. So we pause and try another direction. If that direction doesn't work either we begin to search in all directions, hoping to find the right one.

So I guess one good definition for an indecisive action could be the same as for a vibration:

"An action that can't make up its mind which way to go!"

However, there is a way to stop a vibration and to even halt an indecisive action. Each must be put into contact with a firm base or a solid atmosphere that does not support the slightest movement.

For a vibration to be stopped it must be anchored in a solid atmosphere. Without support of movement the vibration will slow down and finally disappear.

An indecisive action can only be halted if it is guided into a firm base of action. God supplied us with a firm base on which we can rely. He gave us His son, Jesus, who can stabilize every action in our lives for us. We know this for a fact because we are told that once we establish Jesus as our firm base

"Then we will no longer be infants, tossed back and forth by the waves, and blown here and there by every wind of teaching and by the cunning and craftiness of men in their deceitful scheming." Ephesians 4:12

FOR MY OWN SAKE

Isaiah 43:25

Isaiah, the greatest of all writing prophets, unveils the full dimensions of God. He points to the Redeemer – a Messianic King – Jesus. Over and over Isaiah records the words of God as God reveals them to him. Isaiah helps us to understand that although God is always the same and His nature never changes He tends to forgive us over and over for our sinful ways. He points out that its not because we deserve forgiveness.

In fact God, Himself, said:

"I even I, am He who blots out your transgressions, for My own sake, and remember your sins no more." Isaiah 43:25

"For My own sake." That means forgiveness belongs entirely to God.

God created man to be in relationship with Him but through sin man broke that relationship. Nothing man can do will ever repair that brokenness.

But God can and forgiveness is His way of mending that brokenness.

When I fail, I ask God for forgiveness. And He gives it to me. I have the benefit of His forgiveness but only to cover what needs to be covered. That means I will never receive His forgiveness in such an abundance that a supply of it will be left over for me to use as I see fit every time I mess up.

No, when I mess up, as I usually do, I need to ask again for forgiveness. (Not because I deserve it – I never will.) But since it belongs to Him and He loves me, God wants to share His forgiveness with me.

So I ask for and receive forgiveness simply because God desires to share it with me – for His own sake.

NO PLACE TO HIDE

Matthew 10:26

Our new home has Pergo® flooring in all the major living areas. Coming from a home whose major living areas were all carpeted; I have noticed a major difference.

Our home actually stays cleaner!

For instance, when I have been working in the yard and track in dirt onto the Pergo® flooring, it is quite noticeable. But a simple swipe quickly removes all traces.

However, if that same amount of dirt had been tracked onto our former carpeted area, it would have never been noticed it at all. The dirt would have remained there, hidden in the carpet fibers, building up over a period of time.

Looking back, I am sure that the weekly vacuuming I use to give the carpeted areas could have never fully removed all traces of dirt as effectively as the more frequent swipes I give my floors now.

Dirt has no place to hide on bare floors like it does in carpeting.

Sin in our lives can be like that also. We can choose to live our lives cloaked in deceit and secrecy – like carpeting over a bare floor – trapping and hiding undetected sin in our lives within it's fibers. Or we can choose to live our lives open, bared and polished – like wood flooring – removing all traces of sin in our lives as it occurs.

I know Jesus would like us to choose to live our lives open, bared and polished.

In fact He warns us:

"There is nothing concealed that will not be disclosed or hidden that will not be made known." Matthew 10:26

THE WRONG TERRITORY

Hebrews 4:12

Some dear friends of ours had a house warming recently and the invitation we received included a brief hand drawn map with directions to their new home. Using their map we had no trouble finding our way.

However, two other friends who had been invited were not as successful. On the map was a hand written notation identifying the distance between two points. It read:

[- 2 B l ks -]

My husband and I interpreted it correctly to read, "Go 2 blocks", but our friends thought it indicated "I-281", which is a familiar Texas Interstate. So naturally, after searching the immediate vicinity and failing to find "I-281", they stopped at a nearby gas station for directions.

The attendant there candidly informed them: "Honey, if you're looking for I-281 you're in the wrong territory!"

Isn't it amazing how differently we can interpret the written word? That's one reason we come together in Bible study – to help us interpret the right meaning. It is very important that we find the true way

"For the Word of God is living and active. Sharper than any double-edged sword, it penetrates even to dividing soul and spirit, joints and marrow; it judges the thoughts and attitudes of the heart." Hebrews 4:12

When we know we are on the right path we can always be sure that we are not in the wrong territory!

APRIL 6

MY PRAYER STOOL
Genesis 9:20

I have a stool I keep by my bedside that is very special to me. It's a genuine prayer stool.

I didn't buy it. You might say I came by it.

Actually it's really not a stool at all but an old wooden chair whose back had (at one time or another) been sawed off. It has a seat of woven jute that just hints now that once it had been green in color. In other words, it was already well worn and slightly tattered before I acquired it.

Yet, to me it is beautiful – filled with the forever presence of God. It is my special spot where I come to spend time face to face with the Lord.

The idea of having a special place dedicated to God is not new. Most of our churches, synagogues and congregations have for centuries featured altars dedicated to the presence of God.

In fact one of the first mentions of an place dedicated to the presence of God was by Noah as he, together with his wife and his sons and his sons' wives, came out of the ark once the waters had dried up from the flood.

"Then Noah built an altar to the Lord and, taking some of all the clean animals and clean birds, he sacrificed burnt offerings on it." Genesis 9:26

We no longer use our special places for sacrifice since Jesus became the ultimate sacrifice for us all. Today we use our altars and special places to help us come into the presence of God. Special places for where each of us can come face to face with our God.

My prayer stool is my place to do just that.

THE MASTER WILL APPEAR

Matthew 24:30

I once had a boss that had been a college professor before becoming the C E O for the company where we both worked. He lived by the rule:

"The student is only as good as the teacher."

So, when someone failed to perform up to expectation he would go back over the instructions until that person possessed the tools he or she needed to do the job. He never made anyone feel guilty for making mistakes. Quite the contrary, because of his support everyone always strove toward excellence and took pride in his or her work. He taught us to care.

One of my daughters and I were talking about this other day. Her comment to me was that not only is the student as good as the teacher but:

"When the student is ready the master will appear."

I had not heard that before. I've often heard we must be ready for the Master's coming because we know not the day or hour. However, I had never considered that maybe my life was a series of steps preparing me for that coming. It's comforting to think God is preparing me to be ready for when my Master appears.

Jesus Himself tells us that we

"...will see the Son of Man coming on the clouds of the sky with power and great glory. And He will send His angels with a loud trumpet call, and they will gather His elect from the four winds, from one end of the heavens to the other." Matthew 24:30-31

We must prepare our lives for His coming. For when it is time – whether we're ready or not – the Master will appear.

MANIPULATING THE STRINGS
Psalm 100:3

Some years ago a co-worker showed me a novel way to recycle those little plastic tubes that are left over when the adding machine tape runs out. Being somewhat of a pack rat, I hated to see them go to waste.

She told me to collect them until I had ten tubes to string together to form the body of a marionette. It takes two tubes for its body, two each for its arms and two each for its legs. Use a large wooden bead for its head. String them all together, then add personality. For a scarecrow, paint a face and add yellow yarn for hair, hands and feet. Dress the marionette in small doll size clothing appropriately. For a scarecrow, dress in jeans and a plaid shirt. Finally, attach strings from the marionette's head, legs, arms and joints to two wooden hand pieces – one controlling the head and arms and the other controlling the body and legs.

With a little practice the strings can be manipulated to make the marionette imitate human movements.

Actually, humans may be more like that marionette than we think. We like to think we're the masters of our own souls – brilliantly self-made. Yet, although we think we're in control, there's always someone manipulating the strings.

Now, that could be good or bad, depending whom it is manipulating the strings. When we allow the world to manipulate the strings, sin engulfs our lives and our movements are crooked.

However, when we allow Jesus to manipulate the strings, Grace fills our lives and our paths are straight:

"Know that the Lord is God. It is He who made us, and we are His; we are His people, the sheep of His pasture." Psalm 100:3

Who is manipulating your strings?

GOD'S BEAUTY OF THE PATTERN

Proverbs 15:5

I recently read a very thought-provoking quip from Corrie Ten Boom. She said:

> *"I once visited a Weaver's School where the students were making beautiful patterns. I asked, "When you make a mistake, must you cut it out and start it from the beginning?" A student said, "No. Our teacher is such a great artist that when we make a mistake, he uses it to improve the beauty of the pattern."*

That is exactly what Jesus, our Teacher, does with our mistakes! He takes the mistakes and blunders we make and weaves them into our lives so perfectly that our flaws do not stand out. He uses them to improve the beauty of the pattern of our lives!

In fact many times we would fail to see the beauty in our lives if it was not set against the background of our flaws. The contrast is what makes the pattern stand out so bold and perfect.

Proverbs 15:5 says:

"The eyes of the Lord are everywhere, keeping watch on the wicked and the good."

And so He weaves our lives together to be more beautiful and useful in His own designs.

We need to give Him praise for the bad as well as the good we have experienced, because we are beginning to realize that one could not exist without the other.

We would never be able to tell if something was sweet if we had never tasted anything bitter. God can weave the bitter and the sweet of your life together into a perfect pattern.

APRIL 10

PRAYING PSALM 20
Psalm 20

I've been reading the Book of Psalms and have been stuck by the beauty and simplicity.

One Psalm I keep coming back to over and over is Psalm 20. It asks God for His protection and support in times of distress. It inspired me to take the quality of its mercy and grace and revise it poetically into a prayer for you:

In times of trouble may the Lord answer you: May His name proceed your way and protect you.

May the Lord answer you in your distress: May the Lord grant you all your requests.

May He send, through angels, the protection you will need and grant you His support with fertile ground for His seed. May the Lord always read the truth in your heart and accept the work your willing hands impart.

May the Lord answer you in your distress: May the Lord grant you all your requests.

May the Lord give to you the desires of your heart, those that establish His plans so they never fall short.

May the Lord answer you in your distress: May the Lord grant you all your requests

* Amen*

Psalm 20 concludes with

"Some trust in chariots and some in horses; but we trust in the name of the Lord our God."

God will answer us in our distress.

OBEDIENCE

John 2:1-5

"On the third day a wedding took place at Cana in Galilee. Jesus' mother was there, and Jesus and His disciples had also been invited to the wedding. When the wine was gone, Jesus' mother said to Him, 'They have no more wine.' 'Dear woman, why do you involve me?' Jesus replied. 'My time has not yet come.' His mother turned and said to the servants, 'Do whatever He tells you.'" John 2:1 – 5

Now, in this event we learn that Jesus' mother, Mary, asked for and expected obedience, even though what she asked for was her will – not God's will – for Jesus at that particular time.

Jesus could have refused His mother and would have been right in doing so. It was not yet the time for Him to make Himself known as the Son of God.

He even as much told His mother.

But then He obeyed His mother – not against God, but for God! Because even while it might not have been right for Mary to ask Jesus to do what He did, Mary was His mother and therefore Jesus was counted righteous in the eyes of God, His Father, for His obedience.

We are given the perfect example of obedience in this story by observing how Jesus honored His mother. It is good for us, through Jesus, to be reminded of this.

For even though our mothers (and fathers) may sometime make mistakes, obedience is the greatest honor we can give them.

It is in the obedience that God will count us righteous also.

WHEN GOD CALLS

I Peter 3:12

A while ago the phone rang while we were watching T. V. after supper. My husband jumped up to get it, but when he answered, whomever it was hung up. So, he looked to see who it was on our Caller I. D. We sometimes have problems with telemarketers placing our number on a rote dial and not answering when we pick up.

However, this time it was one of our daughters.

Wondering why she would call and then hang up, her Dad immediately called her back and said, "Yes? You called?" He was all set to tease her. But she said, "No, I didn't call. But I caught Chyann playing with the phone. She must have called."

Our granddaughter who was only 19-months old at the time had activated our speed dial number! We were delighted. How about that?

Chyann had made her first phone call and it was to her Pop! It's a call Pop will never forget. (And I doubt if anyone could ever convince him that Chyann hadn't called him on purpose!)

When God calls us, sometimes we wonder if He really did. We expect to hear His voice; yet, He's silent.

So we call Him back in prayer to ask Him what He wanted. We know He hears us.

I Peter 3:12 tells us,

"And His ears are attentive to their prayers."

And when God calls I doubt that anyone could ever convince us He didn't call us on purpose!

A CONDITION OF THE HEART

Matthew 27:5

None of us ever have a problem of remembering that it was Judas who betrayed our Lord Jesus Christ. But often we forget that Jesus had been betrayed twice. The second time by Peter, immediately after Judas.

Judas betrayed Jesus with a single kiss for thirty pieces of silver.

Peter betrayed Jesus with a denial that he ever knew Him, not once but three times!

Why is it then that we condemn Judas for his one kiss but exonerate Peter for his triple denial? Why was Judas lost but Peter saved?

I believe the main difference was in direct proportion to their hearts. We know Judas, when he realized what he had done, took his own life. I think he was convinced in his heart he could never be forgiven, for the Scriptures say in Matthew 27:5:

"So Judas threw the money in the temple and left. Then he went away and hung himself."

On the other hand, Peter, when he realized what he had done, went out and wept for forgiveness. He was convinced in his heart he could be forgiven.

Two betrayals: Two responses. It helps us realize that Jesus was really betrayed by a condition of the heart.

Perhaps Judas could have had the same chance as Peter to rise above his betrayal, to repent, and to become a great Apostle. I suspect if Judas had believed in his heart that Jesus would forgive him, he may have repented and chosen life. After all, it was Judas himself who chose death. If he had chosen life in Christ instead, the Scriptures certainly would have recorded an entirely different account.

It reminds us that we must all watch the condition of our hearts.

MARGINS

John 13:15

On my way to work the other morning I was listening to Dr. Dobson. He had a guest on his show talking about our need of margins in our lives. He stated that we schedule one activity after another, however we sometimes fail to build adequate margins around those activities.

Just like yesterday.

I had an appointment with our CPA for income tax preparation. As I turned off the freeway onto the feeder road next to my CPA's office, I glanced at my watch. My timing was perfect. Then, as I looked for her building I realized that I had just passed it! My timing was no longer perfect.

I had failed to build an adequate margin that would have allowed for this.

Jesus is our perfect example of margins.

When Jesus sent the 12 out to preach the message and they returned, He didn't say, "Are you back already? Get back out there and get busy! Time is short. We need to save the world." Instead, Jesus took the 12 and withdrew.

He led them to a quiet place for rest and renewal. See? Jesus knew the importance of margins. No where is it recorded that He ever was in a hurry. There are simply no cases cited of Jesus running or rushing around anywhere!

In John 13:15 Jesus tells us,

"I have set you an example that you should do as I have done..."

Jesus showed us where the margins should be by living His life within them. We need to follow His example and make sure our days always contain proper margins – and Jesus!

THE MAN

Matthew 19:14

She was barely noticeable in the crowd. She was no bigger than a minute hesitating fleetingly in time. She strained forward to perhaps get a glimpse of the Man everyone was talking about. She had, of course, seen Him before because she was the one He had looked at when He said,

"Let the little children come to me and do not hinder them, for the Kingdom of heaven belongs to such as these." Matthew 19:14

She had felt strangely warmed as His eyes had met hers, though she had been shy and had not come up to Him with the rest of the children. But as she watched Him walk away she knew she would forever be one with Him.

Even now, in the sea of people, she could still feel His eyes, hear His voice.

They were singing. She looked up at a radiant face glancing down at her as she continued to push forward. Neither of them said anything. They didn't have to.

Yet she knew, just from that glance, that person was also forever one with the Man too.

He was almost here!

The hosannas rang out. The palm branches waved. The people danced in unbelievable bliss. She was almost at the edge of the road. She could hardly wait...

Here He comes!

His eyes met hers and He smiled.

She understood. He had to go. It was time.

She smiled back and watched Him ride out of sight. One day He'd be back.

THE SWORD

Luke 22:36-38

Our Sunday school class has been studying the book of Luke. Right now we are in chapter 22, taking another look at the Last Supper.

As the Passover meal ended Jesus asked His disciples if they had a sword.

"He said to them, 'But now if you have a purse, take it, and also a bag; and if you don't have a sword, sell your cloak and buy one. It is written: "And He was numbered with the transgressors" and I tell you that this must be fulfilled in Me. Yes, what is written about Me is reaching its fulfillment.' The disciples said, 'See, Lord here is two swords.' 'That is enough,' He replied." Luke 22:36-38

In our class there was a lively discussion about the meaning of the sword. With the threat of war hanging over us we all wondered what Jesus, the Prince of Peace, would say for us to do.

Some said not to fight, but other pointed out the conquering history of the Lord throughout the Scriptures. Or could it be that the real answer is somewhere in-between?

Maybe the sword itself holds the answer.

A sword is double-edged. So perhaps one edge stands for the one to whom the sword is welded against, pouring out his/her life unto death. In that case, the other edge would stand for the one who is welding the sword to conquer and capture the riches of a great victory.

One sword: Two sides.

Throughout this Holy Week of Easter we have seen this one sword fulfill two meanings for us. One edge shows Jesus pouring out His life unto death for our transgressions. Then as Easter dawns the other edge shows Jesus rising up as the Conquering King reaping eternal rewards.

PILATE

Matthew 27:19

Several Sundays ago the message focused on the trial of Jesus and how Pilate washed his hands and handed Jesus over for execution while appearing not to have condemned Him.

Our pastor has such exceptional insight and this Sunday was no different. Yet, what caught my attention was not Jesus or Pilate; it was Pilate's wife.

"While Pilate was sitting on the judges seat, his wife sent him this message: 'Don't have anything to do with that innocent Man, for I have suffered a great deal today in a dream because of Him.'" Matthew 27:19

Perhaps Pilate's wife was a follower or maybe God purposely gave her a dream of warning, knowing she would pass that warning on to her husband.

Pilate knew that it was out of envy that the Chief Priests and Elders had handed Jesus over to him (Matthew 27:18). However, just knowing the Chief Priests and Elders were trying to manipulate him into executing Jesus, innocent or not, may not have convinced Pilate to seek the release of Jesus. Ruling in favor of the Jewish leaders' requests probably was a common practice for Pilate. You know, under that ageless theory of "one hand washing the other" (no pun intended). Maybe it was because his wife asked him – *"...not to have anything to do with that innocent Man"* that he made a half-hearted effort.

Still, it really makes you wonder how Pilate could have looked into the face of pure innocence and then announce, "I wash my hands of this. Do with Him as you will." (Paraphrased)

It's like many people still do today in the face of popular unchristian beliefs: When forced to take a stand, Pilate went along with the crowd.

APRIL 18

BARABBAS OR JESUS

Matthew 27:21-23

Chuck Swindoll presented a wonderful mini-series of messages leading up to Easter.

One particular message was focused on Barabbas, a notorious prisoner destined for crucifixion for his crimes. It just so happened that Barabbas was awaiting crucifixion at the same time that Jesus was being tried before Pilate.

It was the custom in that day for a prisoner chosen by the crowd to be released at the feast. So Pilate asked the crowd which of the two they wanted him to release – Barabbas or Jesus. It happened like this:

"'Which of the two do you want me to release to you?' asked the governor. 'Barabbas!' they answered. 'What shall I do, then, with Jesus who is called Christ?' Pilate asked. They all answered, 'Crucify Him!' 'Why? What crime has He committed?' asked Pilate. But they shouted all the louder, 'Crucify Him!'" Matthew 27:21-23

That whole interaction might have been a relief to Barabbas, except for one thing. Barabbas probably was held in a detention facility close by – close enough to hear the roar of the crowd, yet not close enough to hear the single voice of Pilate. What Barabbas probably heard was the crowd shouting, "Barabbas!" And then them chanting, "Crucify him! Crucify him!"

Can't you just imagine his sense of doom when the guard marched up to take him from his cell? Imagine his total disbelief and confusion when they told him he was free to go!

It really brings home Paul's words *"While we were yet sinners, Christ died for us."* Barabbas was the first, for Jesus literally took Barabbas' place on the cross.

THE LAST SUPPER

Luke 22:8

My husband and I went grocery shopping one night for a few things we needed when we decided to purchase some special items in order to share a special meal. Over the weekend He would be attending a three-day Advanced Lay Speaker training event so we decided that that the night before he left we would share a special meal together.

As we selected fresh salmon, fresh vegetables and cabbage for slaw it occurred to me that our preparation was not unlike that of the Apostles as they prepared for their Last Supper together with Jesus.

"Then came the day of Unleavened Bread on which the Passover lamb had to be sacrificed. Jesus sent Peter and John saying, 'Go and make preparations for us to eat the Passover.'" Luke 22:8

Can't you just imagine the planning and flurry the Apostles went through to make sure that all the proper preparations were done?

I'm not sure, but I think that they might have sensed that this Passover would be different. After all, hadn't Jesus lately accelerated His teachings? Hadn't He even hinted at the events that were to come? There had to have been a bit of expectancy in the air.

Just as my husband and I prepared the last meal we would have together until he returned, so did the Apostles prepare the Last Supper they would have together until Jesus returned.

The only difference is that my husband and I continue to dine together daily. We are still waiting for Jesus.

PASSOVER

Luke 20:40

A year ago my husband and I were blessed with the opportunity to attend a Sedar. Sedar is a Jewish Holiday, celebrating the first Passover when Moses delivered the Israelites out of Egypt.

This particular Sedar was even more special as it was sponsored by Messianic Jews – Christian Jews who hold all the Jewish traditions sacred while embracing Jesus as their Lord and Master.

As the Rabbi led us through each tradition of the feast, much like the one Jesus must have led His disciples through at the Last Supper; he said something that intrigued me. The Rabbi was re-telling the Passover story as found in Exodus 12 where God told each household to choose for themselves a lamb and examine it to be sure it was free of defects before it was slaughtered at the appointed time for their salvation.

Immediately the Rabbi turned to Luke 20 where the Chief Priests and the teachers of the Law together with the Elders came to Jesus, questioning His authority. He compared Jesus to that first Passover Lamb, complete here in Scripture with the examination to be sure he was free of defects! For after examining Him, the teachers of the Law along with the Priests went away from Jesus because as Luke 20:40 states:

"And no one dared to ask Him any more questions."

Only after this examination was Jesus slaughtered on the Cross at His appointed time for our salvation.

Because He who was found perfect died for us God still 'passes over' our defects and imperfections today.

THE OTHER CRIMINAL

Luke 23:39-42

Remember the Crucifixion story?

Jesus was hung on a cross between two criminals who had also been condemned to death. The main difference, of course, was that the two criminals had been justly condemned while Jesus had done no wrong.

But perhaps the biggest difference was between the two criminals themselves. So big, in fact, that Jesus told one of them that he would, that very day, be with Him in paradise.

It happened as Jesus hung on His Cross between the two:

"One of the criminals who hung there hurled insults at Him: 'Aren't You the Christ? Save Yourself and us!" But the other criminal rebuked him. 'Don't you fear God,' he said, 'since you are under the same sentence? We are punished justly, for we are getting what our deeds deserve. But this Man has done nothing wrong.' Then he said, 'Jesus, remember me when You come into Your kingdom." Luke 23:39-42

What is so amazing about that whole interaction is that never once did the other criminal question who Jesus was! You see, he knew. Even though he had not obeyed the law and he had deliberately sinned against both God and man, the belief of this other criminal in God was pure and strong. His punishment for his disobedience was death, which came to him that day through crucifixion. He paid for his crimes.

Yet life was restored to him, not in light of his deeds, but in light of his unwavering faith.

Therefore, on that first Easter, as Jesus rose the other criminal rose with Him to paradise.

IT IS FINISHED!

John 19:30

Luke reports that Jesus said from the Cross, *"Father, forgive them for they do not know what they are doing."*

It wasn't long after that, John tells us, Jesus said,

"It is finished!" *With that, He bowed His head and gave up His Spirit.* (John 19:30)

What happened in that space between the time Jesus asked God to forgive us and the time He said, *"It is finished"*?

I truly believe that during that space of time the actual supreme sacrifice of Jesus took place. That is when Jesus offered Himself in place of our sins by asking God to place all sin for all time upon Him.

But, for God to take away our sins and place them on His Son, He had to turn His Back on Him. God cannot bear to look upon imperfection. How Jesus must have hung in agony all during the time it took for God to accept Him as our ultimate sacrifice. We get a glimpse of how agonizing that was when Jesus cried out, *"My God, My God, why have You forsaken Me?"* I believe that pierced Jesus deeper than any nail could.

You see it wasn't any ordinary nails that held Jesus to the Cross, it was His love for you and me.

Only when the work had been done and God was able to turn His Face back to His Son could Jesus tell us, *"It is finished."*

To me it is so awesome to realize that between the time Jesus asked God to forgive us and the time He declared that it was finished all the work for our salvation had been done. There is not one other thing we could ever do. It has been done for us for once and for all.

Jesus spoke and sealed our salvation. Then from the Cross He presented it to us as His gift, free of charge. It became ours with those three little words. *"It is finished."*

HE HAS RISEN
Matthew 28:5-6

My Birthday is exactly one week before Christmas, which to me is the most inconvenient time for anyone to be born. Not only having a birthday celebration that close to Christmas impossible, people seem to take the golden opportunity to give me combination birthday/Christmas gifts. I remember growing up feeling somewhat cheated.

There's one such occasion I'll never forget.

My Grandparents had hinted for months about the surprise they had for me for my birthday. When they handed me a small package, it seemed everyone literally held their breath while I opened it.

Inside was a cherry red apple-shaped pincushion. This was it? Somehow I had expected...more.

I think I can relate to how the Disciples felt as they watched Jesus die on the Cross. For three years He had been telling them of a wonderful day that was coming. He hinted at eternity and life everlasting.

Then He was dead. This was it? Somehow I believe they too had expected...more.

Then as that first Easter dawned, they found the tomb empty. Jesus even sent an Angel to remind them,

"Do not be afraid, for I know that you are looking for Jesus who was crucified. He is not here; He has risen, just as He said." (Matthew 28:5-6)

Only then did they realize that the Cross had just been a forerunner, symbolizing Christ's resurrection and our salvation. Just as I found under the Christmas tree that Christmas morning a Singer Sewing Machine complete with all attachments and carrying case to go with my cherry red apple-shaped pin cushion!

APRIL 24

THE CONTEST

John 19:30

Picture this: Satan is so ecstatic he can hardly contain himself! Jesus, his archenemy, is being nailed to a cross. With every hammer strike, Satan's joy heightens. Every demon crowds around him, breathlessly waiting....

Then Jesus speaks.

"'It is finished!' With that, He bowed His head and gave up His Spirit." John 19:30

Now, what more could Satan ask for? The Son of God was dead! But then, to be completely sure (Jesus had fooled him so many times before) Satan watched intently as the body of Jesus was laid in a tomb and sealed.

There: Now the contest was over. Satan won!

Satan and his mob danced with glee on Jesus' tomb...

But, as the earth picked up the tremor of demon feet pounding against it, a rumble started and the tremors increased. As the demons began to notice, they slowed their dance.

It was like the tremors had a life of their own and continued to grow, rocking the stone that sealed Jesus' tomb.

The contest was not over. It had only just begun...

Suddenly the stone broke free and rolled away, revealing the eternal truth:

HE LIVES!

As the line of night shrinks from the dawning of day, the prince of darkness shrank from the Lord of Light, defeated and powerless at last.

Now the contest was really over.

It's Easter!

Jesus wins!

EASTER MONDAY

I Timothy 4:9

Easter was the day Mary and the other women went to the tomb and met an angel who asked them, "Why do you seek the living among the dead?" Then Jesus appeared to Mary – Alive! Also, it was the day Cleopas and his friend walked with Jesus to Emmaus; then had come running back to Jerusalem shouting,

"He's Alive!"

But what about the day after that first Easter?

That was the day that the word spread. It was the day we realized the final defeat of death!

On Easter Monday everyone was talking about the resurrection of Jesus. Easter Monday was the day the news spread throughout the land to all people:

"He's Alive!"

I Timothy 4:9 says:

"This is a trustworthy saying that deserves full acceptance (and for this we labor and strive), that we have put our hope in the Living God..."

Oh yes.

"He's Alive!"

What does that mean to us today? I think it means the same as it did back then. Jesus touches us in His own way and in His own time, and once we recognize Him we too must run to spread the news.

Today we continue to spread the news of Easter Monday throughout the land:

"He's Alive!"

Praise God. "He's Alive!"

DID EASTER TAKE?

John 21:2-7

Did Easter take?

"Simon Peter, Thomas, Nathaniel of Cana in Galilee, the sons of Zebedee, and two other disciples were together. 'I'm going out to fish,' Simon Peter told them, and they said, 'We'll go with you.' So they went out and got into the boat, but that night they caught nothing." John 21:2-3

Jesus had been crucified. And by now they knew Jesus was alive. Some had even seen Him. They also knew Jesus had told them to wait.

But money was running low. They needed food to eat. And nothing was happening. They all agreed. It was time to move on. They needed to go back and do what they knew best – fish. So they did.

Of course it didn't work. Nothing does if it is in direct conflict with God's desires. They were supposed to wait. Instead they went fishing.

Now, if the story had ended there the answer to, "did Easter take?" would have been no. But Jesus, knowing the fickle nature of man,

"...stood on the shore, but the disciples did not realize that it was Jesus. He called out to them, 'Friends, haven't you any fish?' 'No,' they answered. He said, 'Throw your net on the right side of the boat and you will find some.' When they did, they were unable to haul the net in because of the large number of fish. Then the disciple whom Jesus loved said to Peter, 'It is the Lord!' As soon as Simon Peter heard him say, 'It is the Lord,' he wrapped his outer garment around him (for he had taken it off) and jumped into the water." John 21:4-7

Yes, Easter took.

THE REALITY OF CHRIST

Colossians 2:17

I heard on the radio the other day an important observation relating to the reality of Christ and how we view the work He did for us on the Cross.

The point the speaker made was that Jesus didn't die on a gold Cross placed between two white candles on a sacred altar in a serene setting with beautiful music. He died on a rough ugly crucifixion tree placed between two thieves on a barren hillside.

The setting was bloody. Instead of music, the air was filled with cries of agony and pain. Jesus died a very real death.

Yet, we tend to forget how Jesus died when we go to our houses of worship decorated with wonderful altars of beautiful Crosses set between white candles with inspirational music in the air.

We subconsciously gloss over the truth so that the Crucifixion story matches the beauty we prefer to see.

In other words, we close our eyes to the reality of Christ.

Unfortunately when we do that we are also closing our eyes to the reality of Salvation.

To lessen the work Christ did is to lessen Christ Himself. When Christ died on the Cross He made peace possible between God and man, and He did that in a very real way.

Paul in Colossians 2:17 says,

"[Our] Reality, however, is found in Christ."

So continue to celebrate the work Jesus did for us on the cross, but never forget that work was real. Remember that only the reality of Christ is our Salvation.

CHOSEN AND SET APART

Luke 19:30 & 23:53

Jesus was God on earth. That led to a lot of firsts that the world was to know.

Never had God been born of mortal woman. For that Mary was chosen and set apart. Never had God walked the earth in human form. For that Jesus was chosen and set apart. And, never had man succeeded in physically murdering his God. For that the Cross was chosen and set apart.

There are two other times that really stand out in my mind.

One was on that first Palm Sunday. Jesus sent two of his disciples saying to them,

"Go into the village ahead of you and as you enter it you will find a colt tied there which no one has ever ridden." Luke 19:30

Jesus was that colt's first rider. That was important because that meant that the colt had never been used for secular use. He also had been chosen and set apart to bear God.

The other was on that first Good Friday. Right after Jesus' death on the Cross, Joseph, as a member of the Council, went to Pilate and asked for Jesus' body.

"Then he took it (Jesus' body) down and placed it in a tomb in which no one had yet been laid." Luke 23:53

Jesus' body was the first to be laid to rest in this tomb. That was significant because that meant that this tomb had never witnessed death. It too had been chosen and set apart to bear God.

It had to be. If any other body had been laid to rest in it before Jesus, it would have made unfit to hold the One who would abolish death forever. For how can a place of death hold the living?

A SIMPLE THING

Matthew 26:13

"I tell you the truth, wherever this Gospel is preached throughout the world, what she has done will also be told in memory of her." Matthew 26:13

Jesus was speaking of an unnamed woman who came to Him with a jar of expensive perfume that she poured on His head.

Who she was we'll never know. What she did was a simple thing and seemingly of no consequence. We will never know her name or her history. All we know is that she poured expensive perfume on Jesus' head just before He was betrayed and crucified.

Jesus even said that she did it in preparation of His burial. Jesus knew that He would abolish death forever in His resurrection. So He brought this simple act to our attention, knowing we would never forget it.

Now, some 2,000 years later we still remember what this woman did, just as Jesus said we would. Isn't that remarkable?

Have you ever stopped to think about the little things you do – especially those simple things, seemingly of no consequence? Have you ever had someone come to you and say that something you said or did (that you can't even remember) made a difference in their life and that they would never forget it?

It is those things that are also of great importance to Jesus. He remembers those things, especially when we don't.

Jesus took the time to call our attention to an unnamed woman whose simple act is recorded for eternity. It makes me wonder if God has recorded any simple acts we have done and forgotten.

BLESSINGS: HIGH AND LOW

Galatians 6:9-10

One day after work I dashed in the grocery store to pick up a few items we needed for dinner. I was tired and in a hurry.

As I headed down an aisle, I saw the tiniest woman I had ever seen coming toward me. She was darling, however she could not have been much over three feet tall, for she had to reach up over her head to grasp the handle of the grocery cart she was pushing. As I approached her I could see she was anxiously scanning the upper shelves.

Our eyes met and as I matched her smile I, upon impulse, asked, "Can I reach something high for you?" Relief flooded her face as she pointed out the item she needed. Then as I turned to continue my own shopping, she thanked me and asked, "And now, can I reach something low for you in return?"

We both burst out laughing at the odd picture we'd make shopping together.

I was still chuckling when I got home. That brief exchange had lifted my weariness and refreshed my spirit. And although I never saw her again, just the thought of her brings a smile to my heart.

It seems to me that God had us in mind when He inspired Paul to write in Galatians 6:9-10.

"Let us not become weary in doing good, for we will reap a harvest if we do not give up. Therefore, as we have opportunity, let us do good to all people."

I paused a moment to help a fellow shopper and in return received more than I ever dreamed of giving.

HIS HANDS

Luke 24:30-31

Was it the shape of His hands? Did they know them so well that they recognized them right away?

Maybe it was in the way He broke the bread. Did He always hold it and break it in a certain manner?

Maybe it was simply His pieced hands themselves. Did they look at them and know?

Or was it as they lifted their eyes from His hands and met His eyes? Did His eyes look deeply into their souls, leaving no doubt of whom He really was?

All we really know is what the scriptures say:

"When He was at the table with them He took bread, gave thanks, broke it and began to give it to them. Then their eyes were opened and they recognized Him." Luke 24:30-31

Somehow these two had walked the seven miles from Jerusalem to Emmaus with Jesus without recognizing Him.

Is it that we do not see because we do not expect to see?

Something familiar about Jesus may have tugged at them as they walked along but they would have dismissed it. They had seen Jesus crucified. Deep in their hearts they thought Jesus was dead.

We are much like that today. We do not see because we do not expect to see. Yet, now and then when Jesus appears and walks with us we get that familiar tug at our hearts. It's only when we stop and allow Him to break our bread that we realize the impact of what His hands give.

He leaves us no doubt of Who He is.

RESENTMENT

Romans 2:1

I once heard,

"Resentment has been compared to making poison for your enemies, taking it yourself and hoping they will die!"

I thought of how true that statement really is. It describes what resentment does – at least to me. There are times that I can build a huge resentment out of nothing. Yet, instead of it improving the situation or me it only makes matters worse.

Suddenly a definition of insanity I once heard popped into my mind:

"Doing the same thing over and over and expecting to get different results"

We continue to nurture our resentment in the same old way, thinking that this time will be different.

It never is.

It's like we just can't wait to take our resentment poison, hoping that this time the other person will feel its effects!

But they never do.

The Apostle Paul knew that. When he wrote to the church in Rome he warned them about falling into this very trap.

"You, therefore, have no excuse, you who pass judgment on someone else, for at whatever point you judge the other, you are condemning yourself." Romans 2:1

Resentment, whether it takes the form of jealousy, anger, judgment or the like, is a poison that poisons its user.

The antidote?

Jesus.

AN INNOCENT MAN

Luke 23:47

There is a scene in the movie, The Green Mile, which transported me to the foot of the Cross and brought me face to face with Christ.

It was when Paul Edgecomb, a prison guard, was preparing John for execution. He began by saying, "I have to ask you something important now." He went on to explain. "On the day of my judgment and my God asks me why I killed one of His true miracles, what am I going to say?"

Yet, as a death row prison guard, Paul had no choice but to carry out the order of execution.

Paul Edgecomb's dilemma reminded me of another guard's dilemma long ago. The dilemma of the Centurion who stood at the foot of Jesus' Cross.

I suspect the Centurion, like the prison guard had probably entertained that same thought. How could he answer to his God for his part in the death of God's true Son?

Yet neither men had any choice but to carry out the order of execution. Both men were under orders to do a job. Both men were helpless to change the outcome. Both men knew the one dying was an innocent man.

Paul Edgecomb looked at John and said, "There's something I must ask you."

"The Centurion, seeing what had happened, praise God and said, "Surely this was a righteous man." Luke 23:47

RAINS

Philippians 4:6

While I was still in grade school I learned how some country folks predict rain. It happened during a weekend I spent with a classmate out at her family's farm.

That Saturday morning we were following her grandfather around while he did chores. He began telling us about each animal, it's history and it's personal antics. His knowledge and his wit mesmerized me. Then, during a break, he leaned back against the barn door, hooked his thumb toward the pasture where the cows were grazing and announced, "Rain's coming. You girls better git to the house."

Puzzled, we peered up at the bright sky and asked, "What rain?"

"See them cows?" he offered. "They told me. Cows know when it's going to rain so they bunch up together when it's near time. They like dry ground, so before the rain comes they stake out a spot, kneel down on all fours and wait for the rains to pass. When you see cows kneeling you can be sure there's rain ahead."

I can't tell you how many times since that day that I have made my own announcement to everyone within earshot that rain was coming.

Because now when I see cows kneeling, I know.

That is also true of those who kneel in prayer. Philippines 4:6 says

"Do not be anxious about anything, but in everything, by prayer and petition, with thanksgiving, present your requests to God."

When Christians bunch up together and kneel in prayer, showers of God's Spirit rain down on them.

When you see people of God kneeling, you can be sure there's rains of blessings ahead.

THREE THINGS

Matthew 11:11

Jesus said, *"I tell you the truth: Among those born of women there has not risen anyone greater than John the Baptist..."* Matthew 11:11

No one greater than John the Baptist? So what was it about John that made him so great?

Chuck Swindoll suggested that it was because of three things John the Baptist was called to accomplish.

John did them eagerly, joyously and without hesitation. That's what made him so great.

First, he was called to clear the way for Jesus' coming. Second, he was called to bring others to repentance and to confess their sins in baptism. Third, he was called to get out of the way. He needed to let those he had prepared turn and follow Jesus. Then, his job was done.

I think we are called much like John today. First, we are called to clear the way. We need to clear our lives of the things that separate us from God. Second, we are called to repent for those things that have separated us from God. We must work to confess and remove those things from our lives – sometimes over and over again until they are gone for good. Third, we are called to get out of the way. In order to truly be rid of those things that separate us from God we need to die to self. We must strive to have no control of our lives except to live them in the Lord.

John was called to do three things.

He was the voice crying in the wilderness so we might hear and learn how to do the three things we are called to do.

BABY BIRDS

Isaiah 11:6

My best friend and I had lunch with a close mutual friend who works for a state park. After we finished eating she took us out to her car so we could see her new "babies" – a nest of baby birds!

A camper at the park had discovered the nest in the well wheel of his camper just as he was preparing to leave. Not wanting to drive off with the baby birds, he reported his find to the park office.

I had never been that close to nestlings that small before. I was amazed at the way those baby birds responded to our friend.

She explained that they knew she was their food source. During the short time she had been caring for them they had come to associate her with food and now whenever they sensed her presence they became excited, opening their beaks and throats, flapping their tiny fuzzy wings and chirping incessantly.

As I watched her feed them I just had this feeling that God meant for us all to live that way. That He had created us to live harmoniously with all His creatures.

"The wolf will live with the lamb, the leopard will lie down with the goat, the calf and the lion and the yearling together; and a little child will lead them." Isaiah 11:6

As I watched my friend practicing this passage, I knew that a time would be coming for us to live harmoniously one with another.

My friend's little baby birds attest to that.

THE GAME
Isaiah 40:28-31

My cat and I invented this game. Well, O.K... My cat invented it and allows me to play.

She runs around the corner to "hide." I creep up to the corner and jump out at her and we "bat" at each other. Then it's my turn to run around the corner to "hide." She creeps up to the corner and jumps out at me and we "bat" at each other. Then she runs around the corner...

Thus the game continues until she or I tire of it. I must admit I usually tire before she does.

Aren't we glad that when we go to the Lord in prayer or for comfort He never tires?

In fact, He gives us strength so we never tire.

"Do you not know? Have you not heard? The Lord is the everlasting God, the Creator of the ends of the earth. He will not grow tired or weary, and His understanding no one can fathom. He gives strength to the weary, and increases the power of the weak." Isaiah 40:28-29

The game my cat and I play is all in fun and neither one of us are compelled to continue the game once we tire. We don't have to. It's not a matter of life or death for us.

Yet, in the game of life, to play the game is to live and to stop playing is to die. So we have no choice. We are compelled to continue the game. We must keep playing.

Isaiah 40:30-31 continues:

"Even youths grow tired and weary and young men stumble and fall, but those who hope in the Lord will renew their strength. They will soar on wings like eagles; they will run and not grow weary; they will walk and not be faint."

GIVING

Acts 20:35

Our grandson, David, came running into the kitchen one weekend while I was visiting and asked for a Popsicle. After checking with his mother to be sure it was O.K. I handed him one and he took off.

It wasn't but moments later he was back asking me for another. Puzzled I inquired, "David, I just gave you one. What did you do with it?"

He said, "Pop."

My heart nearly busted with pride and love as I realized what David had done. He had taken the Popsicle I had given him to his Grandfather and was now coming back to get one for his own.

Although David was only two and a half at the time, his first thought was for others before himself. Not only that. I was totally impressed with his trusting confidence. He had given away his only Popsicle and then returned, absolutely certain that another would be restored to him.

Overwhelmed, tears sprang to my eyes as I handed him another Popsicle.

I felt like giving him the whole box!

Paul in Acts 20:35 tells us to remember the words the Lord Jesus Himself said,

"It is more blessed to give than to receive."

Giving comes so naturally for our David. He does it so spontaneously that I know Jesus must have had him in mind when He said we needed to come to Him with the trusting confidence of little children.

GRACE AND DIGNITY

Ephesians 4:7

"Have you ever had one of those nights you just couldn't sleep?" It took me back a moment. It was the last thing I expected my four-year-old granddaughter to say over the phone to me that night.

(I couldn't believe how grown-up she sounded!)

As I admitted I had, I asked her if she was having one of those nights. Chyann said, "Yes. There's so many things stuck in my head and I can't get them to come out."

(I could have been talking to an adult friend!)

I wasn't sure of what to say next so I prayed for God to let me know how to respond. But, before I could, Chyann confided, "MiMi, I'm not scared of the lightning because it comes from Jesus. I know Jesus is the light."

(Now I knew. There must be a storm raging in Dayton, Texas!)

So I said, "Chyann, you're right and you know what else? Thunder is just God clearing His throat."

Chyann was quiet. Then she flatly stated, "I don't like thunder!"

(Somehow I knew we had gotten to the heart of her sleepless night.)

I thanked God for allowing me to respond to a very precocious four-year-old in such a manner it allowed her to keep her grace and dignity.

Paul in Ephesians 4:7 tells us

"But to each one of us grace has been given as Christ apportioned it."

Our responsibility is to respond to each other with the grace that Jesus has given us so that we, in turn, save each other's dignity.

"I SHOT CHERI"

Proverbs 3:5

It was one of those early spring days when everything begins to stir and everyone feels so alive. Our middle daughter, our youngest daughter and I were on our way home from some short trip to the store or school or dance lessons.

I was driving. Our middle daughter, Cheri, was sitting in the front with me while her younger sister sat in the back. We were enjoying each other's company while listening to the car radio. As the song "I shot the Sheriff" came on, the younger one started singing along with it.

As she did, her sister and I looked at each other in surprise.

Had we actually heard what we thought we heard?

Almost in unison we asked her, "What did you say? Sing it again."

To her the word "sheriff" had sounded exactly like "Cheri", her sister's name. So she was singing, "I shot Cheri but I didn't shoot no deputy!"

It had sounded right to her so she hadn't thought to question it. That is, until we brought it to her attention.

Sometimes we tend to do that when we read the Bible.

At times our misinterpretation of a passage may sound right to us. When it does, we never think of questioning it either. It may make perfect sense to us especially if we are leaning totally on our own understanding. That is, until someone questions it and brings it to our attention.

That's why Solomon, the wisest man in the Old Testament took the time to remind us in Proverbs 3:5 to

"Trust in the Lord with all your heart and lean not on our own understanding."

MAY 11

UNFORGETTABLE FEAR

Mark 15:34

Sometimes we can become so scared that we can never forget it. That's when it becomes unforgettable fear.

It happened to my sister when she was just a toddler. We were on a shopping trip downtown Pensacola, Florida with our mother and our aunt, along with our cousin. As we walked down the sidewalk, going from store to store, our mother had my sister hold onto the hem of her dress. Mother's arms were filled with packages so this manner of keeping her close worked perfectly. That is, until we tried to cross the street.

While we had waited for the light to change my sister had let go of mother's hem. Then as we began to move across the street she obediently reached out for mother's hem. Except shortly after she did, she realized the hem in her hand was not mother's!

She became terrified. She tried to turn to find mother but because she was so little she was carried forward by the surge of people crossing the street. My sister, to this day, can still recall the terror she felt, for at that moment she felt totally alone. She truly thought she would never see mother or any of us again.

She experienced unforgettable fear.

There was another long ago who could totally relate to exactly how my sister felt. He too felt truly alone, when He, hanging in agony on a Cross, couldn't find His Father.

"At the ninth hour Jesus cried out in a loud voice, 'Elio, Elio, lama Sabachthani?' which means 'My God, my God, why have You forsaken me?'" Mark 15:34

It was the most terrible cry of unforgettable fear. My sister had cried out, "Mama, Mama, where are you?" And like our Savior, who rose from the grave to save us, our mother emerged from the crowd to save her.

GENTLE SOFT RAIN

John 14:27

I love rain. Not rain storms but the gentle soft rain that mesmerizes and relaxes me. I can get lost in its sound.

There are times I want to curl up with a good book, soft music in the background and a cup of hot chocolate next to a warm fire banked to remove the damp chill rain brings out of the air. Other times I feel like playing in the rain. It energizes me. I want to run through the rain and turn my face up to the drops while splashing in the freshly collecting puddles like a little child.

There's just something about the gentleness and the sound of that type of rain that calms the spirit and fills the soul.

But I hardly ever get to enjoy that type of rain. Usually when it comes, I'm too busy to notice.

Not to mention, of course, how hard it would be to schedule rain to come at a time I would be free to enjoy it. Rain doesn't follow man's schedule!

It's a good thing that is not the true way our spirits are calmed and our souls filled. There is One who brings even deeper calmness to our spirit and more completeness to our souls and we don't even have to wait for it to rain!

That One is Jesus.

Jesus says,

"Peace I leave with you; My peace I give you. I do not give to you as the world gives. Do not let your hearts be troubled and do not be afraid." John 14:27

Jesus calms the spirit and fills the soul, rain or shine!

THE DOOR

John 14:6

As a small child I developed a vivid imaginary world in which I often played. At the center of this world was my self-created best friend, Bob. Now, Bob didn't live at our house so whenever he would come over to play I would go ask my mother to let him in. I delighted in drawing my mother into my play because she had such a special way of entering my world and sharing my imagination.

Years later she shared with me one of her fondest memories about my imaginary play stage. I had come up to her one afternoon and said, "Mama, Bosco's at the door. Will you let him in?" Now this was a new name to her. I had never mentioned Bosco before. Never the less, she went to the door and opened it with the usual greeting, reserved up to this point just for Bob. It was at this point, my mother told me, that she noticed how strangely quiet I had become. I was looking at her in total disbelief.

Then I said, "Mama, Bosco's a dog!"

Sometimes I'm afraid I treat discipling others that same way. Sometimes I tend to assume that they already know whom it is at the door of their hearts wanting to come in. My mother didn't know my new imaginary friend was a dog until I told her. Those I disciple won't know that it is Jesus at their door until I tell them. Jesus says,

"I am the way, the truth and the life. No one comes to the Father except through Me." John 14:6

My not revealing that Bosco was a dog to my mother was harmless.

But my not revealing to others that Jesus is the way, the truth and the life is serious and a matter of life or death.

MAY 14

GARDENS

Matthew 26:36

I never thought much about the significance of gardens in the Bible until my pastor brought them to my attention one Sunday morning.

The first garden, the Garden of Eden, was a perfect garden. It was this garden in which God created and placed man to live in perfect harmony and fellowship with Himself.

But man failed to honor the rules that God had set. Thus the perfect harmony and fellowship man shared with God was broken for all time.

As devastating as that brokenness was for man it must have been even worse for God because He created a way to restore that perfect harmony and fellowship. That's why He gave us Jesus. He knew that through His Son we could be restored unto Him.

That brings us to another garden.

A man-made garden called Gethsemane where Jesus went to prepare Himself on our behalf.

"Then Jesus went with His disciples to a place called Gethsemane, and He said to them, 'Sit here while I go over there and pray.'" Matthew 26:36

It was here that He who had no sin made the decision to become sin for all mankind so we could again live in perfect harmony and fellowship with God.

The Garden of Gethsemane restored wholeness to the Garden of Eden.

WITH ALL OF OUR HEARTS

Matthew 22:37

How would you describe your personal relationship with Jesus?

Poor? Fair? Just O.K? Good?

When was the last time you asked Him how He was and really took the time to listen to His answer?

Most of the time that we spend in prayer we focus on needs and ourselves. We do fine in intercessory prayer and personal prayer, yet we very seldom focus on what God might want, even though Jesus Himself told us that we are to

"'Love the Lord your God with all your heart and with all your soul and with all your mind.'" Matthew 22:37

Think about it.

It's not normal to love someone without caring how they are or what they need or what they want. No, when we love that deeply our primary focus is always on the needs and desires of the ones we adore. We put our loved ones' comfort above our own and we spend a great deal of our time trying to please them. When we are not with the ones we love, we are thinking about them. We are constantly trying to maneuver every minute of our lives in order to spend as much time as we can in their presence.

In other words, we love the one of our desire with all our hearts, minds, and souls.

Jesus is simply saying we need to love our God no less than that.

Talk to Him.

He'll teach you how.

BLEMISHES AND DEFECTS

II Corinthians 6:17-19, 21

If you want to feel good about the house you live in, never ever put it up for sale!

One of the requirements before the sale is complete is to have an inspection report done on the house. This is where the buyers with a professional inspector walk through your house, poking into every nook and cranny, pointing out every defect. That's when you begin to look at your house through someone else's eyes. All those old familiar signs of wear and tear that has become embedded in the personality of your house turn into blemishes and defects. Such as: Those special marks on the doorframe that stood testimony to your child's growth now become blights that must be erased!

So when I read the final written inspection report on our house I was horrified! It wasn't until we started to smooth out those blemishes and fix those defects that I began to feel better about my home again.

Sins in our lives are like that also. Actually one of the hardest thing for anyone to do is to go through an honest examination of conscience. Especially with those to whom you are accountable. The thought of having to crawl through every nook and cranny of your life, dredging up every blemish and defect is hard enough. Having to admit those blemishes and defects to another person is horrifying. And it's equally tough to start smoothing out those blemishes and fixing those defects in our lives.

In fact, the whole process would be impossible if our professional inspector wasn't Jesus.

"Therefore if anyone is in Christ, he is a new creation; the old has gone, the new has come! All this is from God who reconciled us to Himself through Christ and gave us the ministry of reconciliation; that God was reconciling the world to Himself in Christ, not counting men's sins against them... God made Him who had no sin to be sin for us so that in Him we might become the righteousness of God." II Corinthians 6:17-19, 21

REBECCA

Genesis 24:3-4

Friends of our just became new grandparents!

Their son and daughter-in-law adopted a precious three-year-old from China and had just arrived Stateside with her. As the proud grandparents showed us their first pictures of her, they told us that their son and daughter-in-law had always said that if they ever had a little girl they would name her Rebecca.

And now their little Rebecca had arrived!

I thought it rather appropriate.

Think back to the Old Testament story about the original Rebecca.

Remember?

Abraham sent his servant to another land to bring back a wife for his son, Isaac, which is exactly what his servant did.

"Abraham said to his servant, "I want you to swear by the Lord, the God of heaven and the God of earth, that you will not get a wife for my son from the daughters of the Canaanites, among whom I am living, but go to another land from which I came to get a wife for my son Isaac.'" Genesis 24:3-4

So Abraham's servant went out to another land and brought back the original Rebecca.

Just like our friend's son and daughter-in-law went out to another land and brought back their Rebecca.

RED FISH ISLAND

II Corinthians 4:6

One Mother's Day, while our daughters were little, we took our recently purchased new-to-us sail boat out to Galveston Bay. Then we set sail to meet some friends on Red Fish Island, which is located off the ship channel.

It was a perfect day, so it may have been our over confidence in our inexperienced sailing ability that caused us to not become alarmed when we were the last boat to leave the island. As we began to leave, the evening barges were just beginning to come in, causing large crashing waves to pound against the rocky area where our boat was anchored.

In order not to dash our boat to pieces, we had to physically hold it away from the rocks. Even though we used all our strength to hold the boat, the barges were coming in and the waves were growing stronger. We knew it was a losing battle. By now it was getting late and the island seemed deserted. Then as it got darker, we were able to see the glow of a campfire from the other side of the island.

It was our ray of hope!

So often that's what we do today. Over confident in our inexperience and our abilities, we approach our daily living with ways that are completely our own. It's only when crises threaten to crash us into life's rocks that we are willing to look for help. Sometimes our lives have to become dark before we can see the glow: The glow of Jesus who is our ray of hope.

II Corinthians 4:6 says,

"For God, who said, 'Let light shine out of darkness' makes His light shine in our hearts to give us the Light..."

Then, like the captain of that big powerboat that pulled our sailboat to safety, Jesus, as Captain of our souls, guides our lives back to safety.

MAY 19

PHOTO ALBUM

Hebrews 10:7

One night we called to see how our middle daughter and her husband were doing. We hadn't talked in a while so we were anxious to catch up. As we were talking, Chyann wanted to know who was on the phone. Her mother told her, "MiMi." Then Chyann ran and brought her mother the photo album and turned to my picture and said, "MiMi."

As our daughter shared that with me I realized that even though I can't see Chyann daily, she is growing up knowing me.

Even though it was not yet Mother's Day I felt that it was. I knew I had just received the best gift of all. The changing world of a child could mean that without frequent contact I could become a stranger to her. However, her mother uses the photo album to make sure that doesn't happen.

I had my daughter put Chyann on the phone so I could tell her how much I love her.

Jesus' disciples did the same thing for Him years ago. They wrote down all they could about Jesus so that we could look at their word pictures and know Him.

The New Testament is our photo album and the Scripture inside is our picture of Jesus. I think Jesus Himself was referring to His photo when He said,

"Here I am – [see] it is written about Me in the Scroll." Hebrews 10:7.

We use Scripture to make sure we continue to know Jesus while He is apart from us.

BE A MODEL

I Peter 2:21

When our youngest daughter was two years old she was chosen to be a model for a major clothing department store in the city where we lived. She was just the right age and size to complete their Easter layout of children's clothing.

We were delighted that she, out of all the others who had applied, was the one they chose. We were also pleasantly surprised when she was allowed to keep the outfit she modeled as compensation for her time.

As a mother my major duty to my daughters as they were growing up was to be a model for them. Now, it's true my daughters did not have the luxury of picking out a mother, like the department store did a model, who may have been a better choice and, Lord knows, I was not perfect in my role. But that in no way lowered the standards I needed to meet in order to be the model they needed.

To be the model they needed I needed to let Jesus be my model. If Jesus was my model and I modeled Him to my daughters, then they would reflect not me but Jesus in their lives.

Man's disobedience broke the relationship we once had with God. There was only one way to restore that brokenness and God knew of just the right One who could do that.

God not only sent His Son, His only Son, to restore that brokenness but to also be a model for us.

I Peter 2:21 tells us

"To this you were called, because Christ suffered for you, leaving you an example, that you should follow in His steps."

NUDGES

Psalm 16:11

I must admit that while I don't believe in physic happenings I do believe in nudges from God. For instance:

We were in the process of moving and I had been busy packing boxes. I had previously removed all items from the spare bedroom in order to tuck packed boxes in there out of the way.

One evening, I finished packing a few boxes and, as I was tired, decided to stop, grab a bite to eat, and relax a few minutes before bedtime. I deposited the boxes in the spare room of growing boxes and then went into the kitchen to fix supper.

That night as I was falling asleep I suddenly realized I hadn't seen our cat all evening. I knew she was somewhere in the house because she had kept jumping into every box I tried to pack. So I turned over, got comfortable and closed my eyes again.

But I couldn't sleep. I kept getting a mental nudge to get up and open the spare bedroom door. It was overwhelming, so finally I got up, padded down the hall and opened the door.

Out popped our cat, slightly miffed at being trapped so long inside!

As David said in Psalm 16:11

"You have made known to me the path of life."

So did God, using a mental nudge, make known to me the need for me to open the guest bedroom door and free our cat!

MAY 22

WHO WILL TAKE CARE OF ME?

John 14:2-3

A short while ago I had the privilege of delivering communion to one of our older members living in the nursing division of one of our local retirement communities. It's a service our church offers monthly.

As I was leaving, I saw a woman in a wheel chair sitting in the hall leading to the front door. As I passed her I smiled and said, "Good-bye." She looked at me and asked, "Are you leaving now?" I pause and told her that I was.

I started to continue on my way, but was stopped by her small plaintive voice. "I just can't remember. I'm so ashamed."

Without knowing how to respond I said a quick prayer, deciding to use my listening skills, then reached out to her. "Maybe I can help." I said.

"You would do that?" she responded. I affirmed her, realizing that dignity and self-respect had become all but lost to her. Then she continued, "I just don't know. I can't remember and I hate to ask them again. Who's going to take care of me when I die?"

Immediately I thought of John 14:2-3.

"...I am going to prepare a place for you and if I go and prepare a place for you, I will come back and take you to be with Me that you also may be where I am."

I knelt down to her level and took her hands.

"Jesus." I said. "Jesus is going to take care of you."

An unbelievable relief flooded her face and her whole being lit up. "Oh yes. That's right. Now I remember. Jesus will take care of me."

DAY AND AGE

Luke 12:15

This day and age has changed. People are more careful in their relationships and tend to guard their property just as closely.

In fact, today most people don't even know their next door neighbors – much less, trust them!

When I was a child growing up we thought nothing of leaving our doors unlocked and our windows opened. We knew and trusted our neighbors. We knew each other's businesses, we helped raise each other's children and we relied on each other's integrity.

We were family.

That's not the case today. Today when I forget to lock the door my husband fusses at me. And it's well that he does because we simply live in a different day and age.

Jesus taught His disciples much about being on guard against all sorts of evils, especially in the last days.

In fact, once when Jesus was speaking to the crowd

"He said to them, 'Watch out! Be on your guard against all kinds of greed; a man's life does not consist in the abundance of his possessions.'" Luke 12:15

Of course Jesus was speaking of guarding our souls not our houses. We should seek to keep safe His spiritual benefits rather than our material things.

If we lose our possessions our insurance benefits will usually replace the lost items but if we lose our spiritual benefits we lose our lives –

Regardless of the day and age!

POP'S PEAS

John 5:43-44

Our pastor one Sunday used the illustration of a family who ate their peas with a knife. As he did, I found myself remembering with fondness an early childhood memory about eating peas with a knife in my family.

Actually it's more of my sister's memory than it is mine.

When my sister was hardly more than a baby our grandfather, Pop, would feed her peas off the end of a table knife. He would mash the peas to puree them, then scoop up a baby-sized mouthful on the end of his knife and offer it to my sister. Now, my sister really did not like peas at all but she would eat her fill as long as Pop presented peas to her in this manner.

It had to be Pop's peas or no peas at all.

Isn't it funny how we sometimes latch onto certain ways of doing things and refuse to experience those things in any other way?

When the teachers of the law persecuted Jesus because of His teachings and many miracles, Jesus told them:

"I have come in My Father's name and you do not accept Me; but if someone else comes in his own name you will accept him." John 5:43-44

You see the teachers of the law were use to worshipping God within the letter of the law only.

Therefore when they came face to face with God in human form, they refused to recognize Him.

Just as whole peas on a plate and mashed peas on a knife are still the same peas, our Father God in heaven and His Son, Jesus, on earth is still the same God.

HE WHO IS IN US

I John 4:4-6

I thoroughly enjoy watching Rod Serling's old back and white Twilight Zone series on TV. Perhaps the fact that he had taken a personal interest in my writing talent and even once called me to see how I was progressing had something to do with it.

However I have always marveled in his ability to take the ordinary and weave the extraordinary around it, usually while making a moral point or two.

Like the rerun I recently saw about a storekeeper who always exaggerated everything: Aliens from outer space that believed every word the storekeeper said kidnapped him. They were convinced that they had captured one of the earth's most intelligent and accomplished beings

The moral point being, of course, not to exaggerate your importance or your accomplishments because someone might actually believe you and call your bluff.

All of us at time have stretched some part of who we are in order to build up our own importance. It's human nature. Yet the only part of whom we are that we should brag about is "He who is in us."

More to the point, John explains:

"You, dear children, are from God and have overcome the evil ones because the One who is in you is greater than the one who is in the world. The evil ones are from the world and therefore speak from the viewpoint of the world and the world listens to them. We are from God, and whoever knows God listens to us; but whoever is not from God does not listen to us. This is how we recognize the Spirit of Truth and the spirit of falsehood." I John 4:4-6

THEY HAVE NO MORE WINE

John 2:1-3

"On the third day a wedding took place at Cana in Galilee. Jesus' mother was there, and Jesus and His disciples had also been invited to the wedding. When the wine was gone, Jesus' mother said to Him, 'They have no more wine.'" John 2:1-3

The thing that really caught my attention in this particular passage was Jesus' mother, Mary, and her unwavering confidence that Jesus would correct the situation. This is in spite of the fact that we are told that Jesus and His disciples were only at the wedding as invited guests. It was unheard of even in those days for the guests to supply the wine for the festivities.

On top of that, we can be pretty sure Mary wasn't trying to send Jesus to the store. She would have known that He did not have the financial means to purchase the wine needed for a gathering this size.

From Scripture we learn that this is Jesus' first recorded miracle. But, I wonder. Was it really His first miracle? Maybe it was just His first public miracle.

I suspect that Mary knew her Child so well she expected miracles from Him. Had she witnessed previous miracles from Jesus and knew? No one knows for sure. All we do know is that Mary must have witnessed something in Jesus to be so confident that she could make this request of Him and expect it to be fulfilled.

Does Jesus expect the same steadfast faith in us that His mother, Mary, exhibited?

Maybe one reason this account of Jesus' first public miracle was included by John in his Gospel was to remind us that nothing is impossible for Jesus.

Perhaps John is reminding us that all we need to do is to state our case, like Mary did, and then expect Jesus to act.

SOME DUMB

Matthew 13:13

As I waited for the oil to be changed in my car I scanned through an old dog-eared Reader's Digest that I found in the waiting area.

I love those cute anecdotes they scatter throughout the magazine.

In this issue, the one that caught my attention was about a guest aboard an Alaskan cruise ship. He was standing out on the deck as they approached a large glacier. Turning to an attendant nearby he asked if he could tell him the name of it. The attendant looked at him and then glanced up at the glacier and replied, "Some dumb glacier, I think." Thoroughly disgusted with the attendant's incompetence the guest fumed all the way to his cabin to retrieve his guidebook and map. Tracing the map to find the glacier's location, he was amazed to find that the attendant was right. Its name was "Sumdum Glacier!"

Jesus had the habit of speaking in parables to the people so His disciples at one point came to Him and asked Him why. Jesus answered them:

"This is why I speak to them in parable: 'Though seeing, they do not see; though hearing they do not hear or understand.'" Matthew 13:13

I can just imagine the disciples looking at each other in confusion. That made little sense. Didn't Jesus want the people to see, hear and understand?

But then Jesus explained that those who believed in God would see, hear and understand. But a calloused-hearted people who had rejected God would never be able to see, hear or understand.

All they would hear would be 'some dumb' parable!

A CORD OF THREE STRANDS

Ecclesiastes 4:12

I have been a Methodist my entire life. My mother was Methodist and her parents were Methodists as well. It is my background and my heritage.

Fortunately I married a Methodist man and never had to experience the compromise some couples are faced with when each is of a different religious background.

Recently I ran across the letters that my mother had written to her parents while she was in college concerning a young man she had met and fallen in love with. In these letters my mother not only emphasized the attributes of this young man, who eventually became my father, but also his sterling character.

His faith background was Protestant, but not Methodist. However, as he pledged my mother his love he also pledged her his faith. He did this, my mother explained to her parents in her letter, because family unity in worship was of extreme importance to them both. They knew to include God in their marriage would strengthen it. Adding God to their marriage would make it a cord of three strands.

A cord of three strands is not easily broken.

Solomon, the wisest man in history recognized this. He said:

"Though one may be overpowered, two can defend themselves. A cord of three strands is not quickly broken." Ecclesiastes 4:12

My parents and their parents before them not only had a strong faith, but also a united faith.

Their strong united faith and unfailing love of Jesus is the most priceless legacy they passed on to me.

ARRESTED

Matthew 10:19-20

Our youngest son-in-law use to be a police officer. Actually he still is. He serves on the reserve force, which means he is able to still play police officer now and then. I guess its true:

Once law enforcement gets in your blood it's there for good. At least that's the case for our son-in-law and he is very good at what he does.

When an officer arrests a suspect he or she must read the suspect the Miranda warning, which tells the suspect of his legal rights. It reads in part:

"You have the right to remain silent and not make any statement at all and that any statement you make may be used in evidence against you..."

In one of our Wednesday night services several years ago the speaker's subject was about God's Grace and its effect on us. He likened our being arrested by a police officer to our being arrested by Grace. Then, in explaining the difference, the speaker made this comment:

"You don't have the right to remain silent if you have been arrested by God's Grace!"

When Jesus sent out the twelve to go from town to town spreading the Good News of the kingdom of heaven, He told them what to do if they were arrested:

"But when they arrest you, do not worry about what to say or how to say it. For it will not be you speaking, but the Spirit of your Father speaking through you." Matthew 10:19-20

We do have the right to remain silent if man has arrested us but we don't have the right to remain silent if God's Grace has arrested us.

THE FUTURE

I Thessalonians 5:11

A few years ago we had the honor of watching our eldest grandson graduate from high school. Kevin looked so wise and tall in his cap and gown, ready to take on the world. We were all so proud of him excelling in a scholastic system that had helped prepare him to move forward in today's complex world.

We were eager to hear of his plans for the future.

I remember reading somewhere that the future is in the hands of our children, and as our children (or grandchildren) grow, we need to give those hands something to hold on to.

Paul said it this way,

"Therefore encourage one another and build each other up just as in fact you are doing." I Thessalonians 5:11

Without a doubt, our task as grandparents didn't graduate with Kevin. God still expects us to encourage his growth in every way we can, even as we share our visions of him setting his goals for the future.

We must continue to cover him and his steps in prayer and to encourage him, building him up in every way we can.

We pray daily for Jesus to lead Kevin in the way he should go.

Yet, we are confident. For with Kevin's abilities and intellect, we know the future is in very good hands.

Our Kevin will see to that.

WATER

Genesis 1:1-2

A few years ago I began a study into water. I have always believed that there is more to water Biblically than we realize. Yet, in trying to research the topic I discovered that water from a Biblical point of view is largely unexplored. That just whetted my appetite for more.

Through the years I have touched on different aspects of water trying to find some common threads to help me in my research. I am finding that the more I study and the more I research a most amazing pattern is emerging.

For instance: When God created the heavens and earth in the beginning, water was already there! Scripture tells us God created the heavens and the earth – but that His Spirit only hovered over the waters.

"In the beginning God created the heavens and the earth. Now the earth was formless and empty, darkness was over the surface of the deep, and the Spirit of God was hovering over the waters." Genesis 1:1-2

I believe water was already in existence with God before the beginning because water was very actively involved with all Creation. Perhaps that is why every pivotal point in Biblical History, including life itself, is centered on water.

To cite some examples: The Creation, Noah and the Ark, Moses and the Red Sea, David and Bathsheba, Elijah and the war against idolatry, John the Baptist, and Jesus' first miracle - turning water to wine.

I am more convinced than ever that Jesus' first miracle was just a glimpse into what will one day be His last. And I believe it will definitely have something to do with water.

WATCH FOR ME
Mark 13:37

Several years ago I flew out to Las Vegas to meet my brother whom I had not seen for quite a few years. I could hardly wait to see him!

When I reached the hotel as prearranged, I called up to his room to let him know that I had arrived. I could tell he was as excited as I was. At last we would see each other again and catch up on family news.

"Watch for me," he said. "I'll be right down!"

I began to search every face coming toward me for his. As I watched, the thought crossed my mind: Will I still recognize him after all these years? I scanned the crowd anxiously.

Then I saw him. I knew him instantly! As I reached out and touched him the years melted away as if time had never passed.

Later I recalled Jesus telling His Disciples, "(Watch for me.) I'm coming to get you, so be ready! (I'll be right down!)"

Mark 13:37 tells us that Jesus said,

"What I say to you, I say to everyone: 'Watch!'"

I envision those Disciples looking up with expectation, watching for Jesus to come – much like I watched for my brother. As time passed, I wonder if they, like me, entertained that same thought of 'will I still recognize Him after all these years?'

Today every time I find myself wondering about that I simply remember my brother.

Then I know, beyond a shadow of a doubt, that when I see Jesus I will know Him instantly!

FULL CIRCLE

John 14:3

A friend of mine recently asked me what I had planned for the weekend. It just so happened that particular weekend I had a funeral to attend in the morning and a wedding to go to that night. Then I made the observation of how that would enable me to experience the full circle of life in one day.

My friend agreed, but then questioned the order: A funeral first, then a wedding?

I had never given a thought to that before, but without hesitation I replied, "Not for a Christian it isn't."

Didn't Jesus say in John 14:3

"If I go and prepare a place for you I will come back and take you with Me so that you also may be where I am."?

And didn't Jesus also say He would come as a Bridegroom to His bride, the church? What is the church if not you and me – God's people?

Jesus, through His death on the Cross, went to prepare a place for us. He intends to come back for us as our Bridegroom.

There will be great rejoicing for us in His Heaven after our earthly funeral, for that is when our true wedding will take place.

So a wedding after a funeral really does make perfect sense after all.

Remember that Christ is preparing a place for each one of us so we can go and be with Him.

Our greatest joy will be in discovering the wedding He has planned for us in our eternal life!

FILLED WITH THE SPIRIT
John 16:7

Filled with the Spirit. What does that mean?

In the Gospel of John Jesus spoke about the coming of the Holy Spirit. Jesus told His disciples

"Unless I go away, the Holy Spirit will not come to you. But if I go, I will send Him to you." John 16:7

Even as I read that I could hear the urgency in Jesus' voice: He said, *"Unless I go away, the Holy Spirit will not come..."* I imagine the disciples were dumb-founded!

They must have looked at each other and asked, "So, what's so special about the Holy Spirit?"

Well, consider this: Jesus on earth, in human form, could only physically be with those within His reach. The Scriptures record a time when Jesus was so overwhelmed with the people's needs he cried out, *"O Father, there's so many! How can I help them?"* I can just imagine our Heavenly Father's answer, *"So come home so We can send them the One who can!"*

That's exactly what Jesus did. And the Holy Spirit who came when Jesus left has the ability to fill all of us at once, no matter who we are or where we are. That's why Jesus was so excited.

We all have the Holy Spirit within us. He is our connection to God. Jesus left so the Holy Spirit could fill us. That way Jesus could be with us always. No wonder Jesus was excited as He anticipated the Holy Spirit coming into our lives.

And how excited He was! He couldn't wait for us to be filled with the Holy Spirit! He couldn't wait until He could be with all of us at the same time, forever.

LAST SHALL BE FIRST

Mark 10:31

A friend of ours had his central air system go out a short while ago and with the warmer weather coming on, he and his family was beginning to feel the heat. But he didn't have the cash available to replace it. He and his wife prayed about it and knew God would provide, but they had no idea how.

Then they were invited along with us to attend the Mission's baseball game. One of the promotions at the game was a drawing for a Carrier Air Conditioning unit. Of course our friend lost no time signing up for it even thought the odds were around 2,000 to 1 that he would win. However, much to our delight, his name was the last of the five finalists drawn!

As he made his way down to the playing field where each contestant was to choose a bag, all of us prayed that this would be the way God was going to meet his air conditioning needs.

Because he was the last contestant called he had no choice but to take the last bag. As each contestant opened his or her bag, the tension built. Again our friend, being contestant #5, was the last one to open his bag. And the winner was…our friend!

What excitement there was in our area of the stands!

Did you notice that our friend was always last? His name was the last drawn. He was the last on the field. Each contestant had the opportunity to choose a bag except our friend.

Mark 10:31 says

"But many who are first shall be last and the last first."

We should have known, but once again God had to let us know that He provides for all our needs. Down to the last detail!

For our friend was the last called, but the first to claim the prize.

A FEW GOOD MEN

Matthew 10:22

I think what impressed me the most about the movie, "A Few Good Men," was the passion the two Marines displayed for their 'code.' They were willing to die for it.

Even in the face of persecution, they put their obedience to this 'code' first before their own lives.

They never once wavered or quit.

As the movie progressed I found myself mentally comparing the dedication these men showed for their cause to the dedication Christians should show for Jesus.

God depends upon us to never waiver or quit.

We all need to catch that same passion those Marines displayed, letting nothing deter us from putting Jesus first.

That's why Jesus called a few good men to follow Him. He chose the few who would uphold the 'code' of the Way. In the face of persecution and for some, even death, these few good men would have to put their obedience to the 'code' of the Way first.

Even Jesus knew that wouldn't be easy.

In Matthew 10:22 He warned us,

"All men will hate you because of Me, but he who stands firm to the end will be saved."

That tells us that even in the face of persecution, we need to put our obedience to Christ and the 'code' of the Way first.

Even before our own lives.

TRUST ME

Genesis 6:22

Noah was not concerned with pleasing people. He didn't care what others thought. If he had, he would have never built the ark and mankind may have been permanently lost. Noah listened to God, not man.

There are several things that make this unusual, even for Noah. First of all, when God told Noah he was going to destroy all humanity by causing it to rain until the earth would be covered with floodwaters, that may have seemed to Noah like an idea straight out of science fiction. Noah probably had never heard of rain for up until this time rain had not existed. Noah may have had no concept of what God was talking about.

Then, on top of that, God told Noah to build a big boat – on dry land and miles from any large body of water! Noah must have wondered if he had heard God right.

I can almost hear God saying to Noah, "Just trust Me."

The town's people and those of the surrounding area must have thought Noah crazy. They probably laughed at him and tried to dissuade him. But Noah didn't listen to them. Instead, Genesis 6:22 says,

"Noah did everything just as God commanded him."

Sometimes God calls us, expecting us to not be concerned with pleasing people. Just as often we can't see what God is leading us to do. Now it probably won't be anything as far out as He led Noah to do, but like Noah, God expects us to do everything just as He commands. At times we may wonder if we heard God right. Others will try to tell us we didn't.

I can almost hear God telling us, "Just trust Me."

The real question is, do we?

THE THIRD DAY: A WEDDING

John 2:1-2

"On the third day a wedding took place at Cana in Galilee. Jesus' mother was there and Jesus and his disciples had also been invited to the wedding." John 2:1-2

Who's wedding?

Given Mary and Joseph's station in life, it is doubtful that they would have had friends or associates who could have afforded this type of wedding. Also, Joseph was not mentioned so he may have already died.

Therefore, they probably would not have been invited – unless one of their family members was directly involved. If this had been the wedding of a male relative of Jesus, the wedding preparation would have been in the hands of Jesus' family. We know that was not the case. Scripture says they were invited and they would not have needed to invite themselves.

However, a well-to-do gentleman, marrying a female relative, perhaps a half-sister of Jesus, would have been able to afford such a wedding as John describes and the family and friends of Jesus would have certainly all been invited.

It is also interesting to note that this wedding took place on the third day after Jesus was baptized, just before He started His ministry. It was almost as if Jesus, in His earthly father's absence, was making sure there would be someone to care for His family before He left.

An arranged marriage of this sort would have accomplished that.

Jesus didn't just lay down His hammer one day and leave without regard for His earthly family. I believe He took each family member into consideration and planned accordingly. Just as He does for each of us today.

NO MATTER WHAT

Matthew 28:20

My husband walked into the kitchen the other evening whistling a tune. He got what he needed and went back to what he was doing.

Without realizing it I began humming that same tune as I prepared supper.

Time passed. I set the table, answered a phone call, finished cooking and called my husband back in to eat.

Still, that same tune was bouncing around in my head.

Has that ever happened to you?

Some little tune or refrain sticks in your head and, like a stuck record, keeps playing over and over in your mind. It just won't go away.

No matter what.

If we let Him, Jesus can be that tune for us in our heads and hearts. His promise to be with us forever insures us of His abiding presence throughout eternity.

Jesus made that very plain, especially in the Great Commissioning when He said:

"And surely I am with you always, to the very end of the age." Matthew 28:20

Jesus will always stick in our head and our hearts with such a sweet refrain that we will look forward to Him playing His songs of salvation over and over in our minds.

When that happens, He will stick in our minds.

No matter what.

OOPS!

Isaiah 64:8

I have a friend who was telling me of an art class she once took. It was a multimedia type class. They studied a wide range of art media, from simple sketching to pottery and glass blowing.

During the time they were learning to work with clay, she chose to fashion a simple vase. She went on to tell me about the problems she encountered getting the clay to the right consistency and the frustration she had in mastering the potter's wheel. Then she said that just as she began to get the hang of it, her thumb slipped.

Oops!

Isn't it wonderful that we have a God who never has to say Oops?

It's a good thing since we are told that

"Yet, O Lord, You are our Father. We are the clay, You are the Potter; we are all the work of Your hand." Isaiah 64:8

Just think, if God's thumb had slipped when He first formed man from the dust of the ground, none of us would be here today.

No, God doesn't make mistakes. No where is it recorded that God ever said Oops!

So the next time you find yourself saying Oops remember the One who fashioned us to be perfect. And because He knew we would have to say Oops now and then, God supplied us with the means to even overcome that.

He sent us His Son who came to cover all our Oops with salvation!

ONE MATCH FIRES

John 17:22

One summer after beginning high school I attended a two-week Girl Scout camp. Now, I usually attended Scout camp most summers but this was the first year I was old enough to attend the exclusive, sought after "Pioneer Camp."

I was so excited.

Armed with bug spray and a bedroll I set out with 14 other girls to brave the elements and conquer the wilderness. However, the most lasting thing I learned that summer was how to build one-match fires.

To build a one-match fire is quite an art: First, a small pile of dry twigs and leaves is accumulated. Then progressively larger twigs are placed in teepee style around it. Next, logs are laid out in log cabin style close around the teepee. If the wood is properly dry and has been properly placed, one match is all that is needed to ignite that small pile of dry twigs deep inside the teepee. That small protected flame will easily feed out to the larger twigs and then finally ignite the logs.

Soon you have a one-match roaring fire!

It's no different with the fire we all have within ourselves. When Jesus prayed for all believers He said,

"I have given them the Glory [fire] *that You gave Me, that they maybe one as We are One."* John 17:22.

If our souls have properly prepared, we can receive God's Glory (fire) and become one with Him.

That means that Jesus, who is matchless, lights our internal flame.

That makes His a No Match Fire!

WANNA TALK

James 4:8

Our middle daughter called us the other night. Her father answered the phone and talked with her a while before handing the phone to me.

I had not been on the phone more than a few seconds when she told me that my granddaughter wanted to talk to me.

When she came got on the phone I said, "Hi, Chyann. I love you."

Chyann said, "I wanna talk to my Pop."

As I handed the phone back to my husband my heart overflowed at the joy that simple request gave him.

I imagine that is the type of joy our Heavenly Father must feel when we go to Him in prayer. James 4:8 says,

"Come near to God and He will come near to you."

Like Chyann we must be determined in our goal and persist until we get to talk to God directly – even if it's only for a few minutes.

The attention span of a young child is extremely short. Yet those few intimate moments Chyann shared with her Pop will warm his heart forever.

Let us never fail to make it a point to warm the heart of the Supreme Father of all.

Take a few minutes and be persistent.

Be determined in your goal and say, "I wanna talk to my God."

MY STORYTELLERS

Luke 10:38-39

One of the pastors I worked with collects Southwest Indian Storytellers. He and his wife are building a wonderful unique collection. Each piece has significant meaning and I understand no two are exactly alike.

I have two Storytellers of my own that are not like any others. One of my Storytellers has children at her feet, knees, lap, hands and head all intently listening to her wonderful way of weaving a story. Her gift was so spellbinding that the children always clambered for her to "tell it again" and listened just as intently each time she did. I know. I was one of those children, for that Storyteller was my mother. When she was a child her mother had enrolled her in a diction class where she learned to speak so well that through the years she was often called upon for public dissertations. Through these performances she developed her beautiful talent of weaving stories. She had a unique way of unfolding new life into old tales that left her listener spellbound and hungry for more.

It was my mother who introduced me to my other storyteller, the greatest Storyteller of all, Jesus Christ. It was at my mother's knee that I learned the stories of Jesus. Then she taught me how to sit at the feet of Jesus like Mary to hear His life saving stories.

Luke 10:39-39 tells us:

"As Jesus and his disciples were on their way, He came to a village where a woman named Martha opened her home to Him. She had a sister called Mary, who sat at the Lord's feet listening to what He said."

When we hear the words of Jesus we join Mary at His feet. It's this greatest Storyteller that has us all at His feet, knees, lap, hands, head and heart spellbound by His every word.

FOREVER LOVE OUR COUNTRY

II Chronicles 7:14

I will forever love our country even though she is like an errant child at times, filled with warring factions that lead her astray: Sometimes in body, Sometimes in mind.

Sometime she succumbs, sometimes not.

Still, she keeps on fighting to keep her sons and daughters safe and free!

Lift her up to God and pray with me that He continues to bless her and keep her strong enough to withstand the warring factions she daily faces.

Pray with me,

"O God, help her people to turn back to You so that we will remember. Remember what this country first stood for and how You are still using her today – sometimes in spite of herself! God, You said,

"If My people, who are called by My name, will humble themselves and pray and seek My face and turn from their wicked ways, then I will hear from heaven and will forgive their sin and will heal their land." II Chronicles 7:14

"Lord, help us turn back to you. Help us to do it in Your Holy name. Amen."

Come fellow-patriots, let's join hands and seek His face and pray. Let us turn back to God.

It's time for healing. And as we do, we shall remember Your promise, Lord. It's time for You to hear from heaven, forgive our sins and heal our land.

I shall forever love our country. Come my brothers and sisters, come love her with me.

THE FRIEND OF THE BRIDEGROOM

John 3:29

John the Baptist said in testimony of Jesus:

"The bride belongs to the bridegroom. The friend who attends the bridegroom waits and listens for him, and is full of joy when he hears the bridegroom's voice. That joy is mine and it is now complete." John 3:29

I never fully understood that testimony of John's until someone explained to me the importance of the bridegroom's friend and the role he played in the wedding ceremony.

Back then it was the friend of the bridegroom who guarded the bridal chamber the day of the wedding and kept it secure for the newly wedded couple.

(I suppose much like how we try to guard the honeymoon vehicle today from the pranks of the wedding guests!)

It was the custom of the bride to signal the bridegroom and then try to slip out unseen during the wedding feast and enter the bridal chamber. When the moment was right, the bridegroom would slip out to join her.

When bridegroom arrived, he would check with his friend to make sure the bridal chamber was secure and his bride was waiting for him inside. Once the bridegroom entered the bridal chamber the duties of the friend were complete.

John the Baptist was sent ahead of the Christ as the friend of the bridegroom. The church is the bride and Jesus is the bridegroom. John was the friend posted to guard the way.

So, John waited and listened until he heard Jesus' voice. When Jesus came and sought him out, John was filled with joy because knew his job was done and his duties were now complete.

MISSING THE POINT

Proverbs 19:2

Sometimes it's easy for us to miss the point and when we do, it could have a serious impact on the lives of others around us.

A very dear friend of ours used the following illustration to emphasize that point.

'A certain young man, traveling in an isolated area, stumbled across an old abandoned well and fell in. The old well began to narrow about half way down so the young man became stuck.

No matter how he tried he couldn't free himself and no one heard his cries.

'Finally, in desperation, the young man turned to God. "Lord," he prayed, "please send someone to help."

Almost immediately he heard a voice calling down to him. "Hello? Is someone down there?"

'The young man had no doubt that God had sent him a deliverer, for within minutes he was freed. In fact he was so moved by the whole experience that it changed his life forever. Right then and there, the young man vowed that even if it took him a lifetime he would share with everyone he could God's incredible love and saving grace.

'So, in order to make sure everyone would have the same chance as he to experience God's saving grace, the young man spent the rest of his life...

'...Pushing others into the well!'

Proverbs 19:2 cautions us:

"It is not good to have zeal without knowledge, nor to be hasty and miss the [point]."

WHAT WILL YOU DEDICATE?

Luke 14:35

What will you dedicate to God out of your life, the chicken or the egg?

First let's consider the egg. The egg is unique in that it has a dual function. An egg that has been fertilized and properly incubated contains life. From it another life emerges. An egg not fertilized but properly retrieved from the roost sustains life. Most of us eat eggs in some form or fashion daily.

If we dedicate the eggs of our lives to God, we set-aside for him that portion of our lives filled with good works and compassion.

Now, let's consider the chicken. The chicken is also unique. And it also has a dual function. It is the chicken that actually lay the fertilized eggs that contain life. From the chicken all other chickens come. The chicken also lay the non-fertilized eggs we eat to sustain life.

So, taking all things in consideration, without the chicken there would be no eggs in our lives. When we dedicate the chicken of our lives to God we are giving Him our all.

When Jesus talked about the cost of being a disciple in Luke 14, He said we must give everything to Him if we want to be His disciples.

"In the same way, any of you who does not give up everything he has cannot be my disciple." Luke 14:35

The eggs of our lives are but pieces that can be replaced. However, the chicken is our entire being.

So, what will you dedicate to God out of your life –

The chicken or the egg?

DO IT AGAIN, DADDY

Luke 1:37

Max Lucado led us in prayer as we each interceded with prayers of our own. We had just learned earlier that day that Archbishop Patrick Flores of the Catholic Diocese was being held hostage and we feared for his safety.

It hit real close to home for my husband and me. Archbishop Flores had worked closely with a committee of which we were members just a few years prior. Together we had planned the Cursillo/Emmaus Fiesta de Colores fifty-year Celebration which successfully united all three-day movements, such as the Walk to Emmaus, with their predecessor, the Roman Catholic Cursillo movement, for a day of mutual celebration.

As Max prayed he reminded God that all things work to His glory. Through out history so many things Satan earmarked for evil God snatched away and used for good. Max ended his prayer by expecting God to allow that to happen in this situation.

It reminded me of that cute orange juice commercial. You know the one where the little boy is sitting under a tree with his father waiting for the sun to come up? Every time the father takes a sip of orange juice, the sun would come up a bit more until, with his last sip, the sun was completely risen. The boy, watching his father sip and the sun rise, turns to his father in awe and exclaims, "Do it again, Daddy!" That little boy has no doubt. He knows his father can do anything.

This was exactly how Max Lucado ended his prayer.

That is the way we always should turn to God. Our prayers need to be filled with that same unfailing trust and complete faith that little boy and Max Lucado showed. Our Father God can do anything and will

"For nothing is impossible with God." Luke 1:37

THE POINT

I John 2:14

A little league football coach was going over the latest game strategy with his junior team before their first big game. He needed to instill in them the drive to never give up. To get them to see exactly what he wanted he used an illustration.

"Suppose," the Coach said to the boys, "a play is called and a player is knocked down and when he was hit he didn't get back up."

One of the boys commented, "That's not the one you want us to be like, huh Coach?" "Nope." Said the Coach. "But suppose in the play a guy is hit and gets back up and is hit again and doesn't get back up..."

The same boy interjected, "That's not what you want us to be like either, huh Coach?" "Nope." Said the Coach. "Now, suppose a guy gets hit and gets back up and is hit and gets back up and is hit and gets back up...."

One of the boys in the back of the room chimed in, "THAT'S who you want us to be like--the one who keeps getting back up!" The Coach slowly shook his head and said, "No, no, no! You're missing the point. I want you to be like the guy who keeps knocking those guys down!"

This is a good lesson to remember in our own lives. When we allow Satan to hit us we've also missed the point. We know Satan will never win and Satan knows it also. We must remember that no matter how many times he seems to overtake our lives we need to keep knocking him back down. The Apostle John made reference to that when he said in I John 2:14,

"I write to you fathers, because you have known Him who is from the beginning. I write to you – because you are strong and the Word of God lives in you and you have overcome the evil one."

YOU DO YOUR FATHER PROUD

Matthew 5:16

Father's Day is the day that we nationally honor our fathers with cards, gifts, and other special considerations. It is the day we nationally stop and take time to let our fathers know we love them and to tell them that we appreciate all that they have done for us.

If you could choose any gift in the world for your father, what would it be? Do you know which gift, above all others, would make your father the happiest?

Well, as you may have guessed, it might not be anything material.

The truth is that material things do not make even fathers happy. So what could it be that would make your father so proud of you that it would fill him with complete happiness?

Matthew 5:16 gives us a clue:

"Let your light shine before men that they may see your good deeds and praise your Father in Heaven."

This is what would make your father so proud of you that it would fill him with complete happiness:

Living your life in front of God and men in such a manner that would bring honor and respect to your father.

It is the best gift we possess that is ours to give.

Then, as others witness your life they will say, "You are such a blessing to your father. You do your father proud!"

CHASING RABBITS

Isaiah 65:24

"Oh, look! Was that a rabbit on the side of the road?"

We were in the car. Our husbands were in the front and us girls were chatting in the back. We were talking about a subject close to my heart and I had been sharing some of my deepest feelings with her.

In fact, I was right in the middle of a sentence when she directed this question to her husband. Obviously she wasn't listening to what I was saying.

So I stopped talking.

It took her a few minutes to realize I was silent, so it may have been more out of courtesy than interest that she asked, "I'm sorry, were you saying something?" I simply stated, "That's O.K." and then changed the subject to another topic I was sure would be of interest to her.

She was oblivious to the whole interaction.

Later, as I thought about how that had made me feel, I exclaimed, "Oh, Jesus, isn't that the very thing I do to You all the time? Is that how You feel when I act like I'm not interested or I don't listen to what You are trying to tell me? You only want to offer me eternal life and salvation while I prefer to go off chasing rabbits!"

Isn't it comforting to know that Jesus will never do that to us?

No matter when, where or how often we go to Him He will always be there and He will always listen. To put it in God's own words, as is recorded in Isaiah 65:24

"Before they call I will answer; while they are still speaking I will hear."

WEEDING OUT

Colossians 3:8-10

After repainting our master bedroom my husband and I began weeding through years of "stuff" we had accumulated over the years. We went through books that were no longer useful or worth keeping. We collected all types of scattered family photos and mementos from every nook and cranny and put them in one place to go through more thoroughly later. We hauled out bags of useless trash and non-wearable clothing.

The end result was a cleaner, better-organized room with a lot more space and a lot less "stuff".

Just as we weeded out our bedroom we need to weed out our lives. We tend to fill our lives with all sorts of "bad habits", giving them a place in our lives by using the excuse that they are a part of our humanness. However, Colossians 3:8-10 tells us

"Rid yourselves of all such things as these: Anger, rage, malice, slander, and filthy language from your lips. Do not lie to each other, since you have taken off your old self with its practices and have put on the new self, which is being renewed in knowledge in the image of its Creator."

The end result is a lot more productive and moral life and a lot less "bad habits."

I don't know which is harder: Weeding out our bedroom or weeding out our lives. Both require turning loose and letting go of things we, down deep, really want to keep.

On one hand, it's easier to weed out "stuff" instead of "bad habits" because it doesn't require a lot of personal change. On the other hand, weeding out "bad habits" is life saving and prepares us for salvation.

It may take little more work to accomplish but the rewards are ever so much greater!

A STRAIGHT LINE

John 14:8-9

My father was killed when I was just two years old so I grew up hearing stories of him. It was the only way my sister and I came to know him, who he was and what he did. My grandparents and my mother would delight in telling my sister and I all about his endearing charms and his special mannerisms and characteristics. Everything that made our father the man he had been.

One of his most unusual and unique characteristics was his habit of arranging everything into straight lines. My mother would tell us that no matter how she artistically arranged her knickknacks and pictures, she would eventually find them all lined up together in a straight line or in rows. I had never heard of anyone else with this particular characteristic so I always embraced it as a special trait that only my father possessed.

Until now.

Now I see that same trait coming to life in our youngest grandson. In his play he also arranges everything into straight lines or in rows – exactly like I had been told his great grandfather use to do before him!

It's proof that we all inherit characteristics and traits of our forefathers and, through those traits, our forefathers will always be alive in us.

Even Jesus emphasized this fact when

"Philip said, 'Lord, show us the Father and that will be enough for us.' Jesus answered, 'Don't you know Me, Philip, even after I have been among you such a long time? Anyone who has seen Me has seen the Father. How can you say, 'Show us the Father? Don't you believe I am in the Father and that the Father is in Me?'"

HOW BEAUTIFUL ARE THE FEET

Romans 10:15

When our youngest daughter graduated from college cum laude we were so proud! We took the video recorder in order to document the entire commencement exercise. As we waited for the ceremonies to begin, her father recorded a quick prelude of the stage area. Then he spanned the fast filling coliseum area before setting the recorder aside to use later.

We were seated in the second tier section in aisle seats. When the processional began my husband resumed his filming. We didn't want to miss a single detail!

Later, as we viewed the tape we discovered we had gotten a bonus. In his excitement my husband had forgotten to turn off the recorder when he had set it aside after spanning the coliseum area. As it so happened, the recorder had been placed on the floor directly facing the aisle and the steps leading in and out of our section. What we had done was to record over a half-hour of feet entering and leaving!

Now, that may sound boring to you, but we managed to create an amusing game of it. Together we picked out the best, the worst, the ugliest and the most beautiful feet of those that we had recorded.

Isaiah talked about feet also. In fact, Paul quoted him in Romans 10:15.

"How beautiful are the feet of those who bring Good News."

Isaiah was referring to those who brought the exiles the good news of their imminent release from captivity in Babylon. Paul applied it to Gospel preachers who bring the Good News of our release from captivity to sin. We, of course, used it as a symbol of beautiful feet bringing the good news of our daughter's formal release from her captivity to study!

SPEAK OUT FOR JESUS

Luke 23:39-41

3-2-1.   Three crosses – Two thieves – One King.

Most of us have studied accounts of the physical aspects of crucifixion. The victim dies, usually not from being nailed to the cross, but from asphyxiation. The unnatural position of the arms extended out and nailed down forces the victim's body to sag downward. As the body sags the air is forced out of the victim's lungs. To force air back into the lungs the victim must push up with his feet which, of course, are nailed down also. This continual up and down motion in order to breathe is exhausting, not to mention, excruciating. When the victim becomes exhausted to the point he can't push himself back up, he asphyxiates.

Think, then, of the effort it must have taken for one of the thieves, in spite of all this, to speak out for Jesus:

"One of the criminals who hung there hurled insults at [Jesus]: 'Aren't You the Christ? Save Yourself and us!' But the other criminal rebuked him, 'Don't you fear God,' he said, 'since you are under the same sentence? We are punished justly for we are getting what our deeds deserve, but this Man has done nothing wrong!'" Luke 23:39-41

How many of us, in a similar situation, would be tempted to conserve our energy in order to prolong our own lives instead of expending it by exerting the effort to speak? Sometimes we are moved to speak out in someone's behalf, but for one reason or the other we fail to make the effort. Even when it requires no effort on our part we sometimes let our chances pass.

So the next time you are moved to speak out for another but are tempted to hold back, remember the thief who spoke out for Jesus in spite of the consequences. It just may save your life too.

STIRRED ANEW

Luke 24:25-27

Cleopas and his friend had just reached Emmaus after traveling the seven dusty miles from Jerusalem. They were weary and worn, physically as well as emotionally.

Not surprising, considering the events surrounding Passover. Their beloved Lord and Master, Jesus, had been crucified.

But they had hoped…

Now a Stranger, traveling in their company, had gotten them stirred anew.

"He said to them, 'How foolish you are, and how slow of heart to believe all that the prophets have spoken! Did not the Christ have to suffer these things and then enter His glory?' And beginning with Moses and all the prophets, he explained to them what was said in all the Scriptures concerning Himself." Luke 24:25-27

Oh, how many of us do that?

We hear without hearing. We even believe without believing.

We say Jesus is alive. And we believe it.

Do we believe it as a matter of fact, the way we believe day is day and night is night?

Or, are we more like Cleopas and his friend than we like to admit?

Like Cleopas we are all traveling some road in our lives looking toward home. We have all experienced hardships and tragedies along the way. We are all weary and worn physically as well as emotionally.

But we had hoped…

Would Jesus entering our lives get us stirred anew?

SNAPSHOT IN TIME

Song of Songs 4:9

Over ten years ago at our youngest daughter's wedding there was one isolated snapshot in time that I will never forget.

It's forever embedded in my memory as if it only happened yesterday.

During the reception, after the ceremony, shortly after the bride and groom's first dance, a little girl around three or four in age came up to the bride. Now all my daughters are beautiful and our youngest is no exception and her wedding dress and veil really framed her beauty well, especially with the flushed cheeks, sparkling eyes and radiant smile dancing with her new husband had given her. The little girl just stood there in front of the bride transfixed.

Her face was a classic study of pure adoration.

I caught my breath as I realized that my daughter in her bridal gown was possibly the most beautiful thing that child had seen so far in her young life. The breathtaking wonder that shone in her eyes echoed the beautiful haunting verse found in the book of Song of Songs 4:9:

"You have stolen my heart, my sister, my bride; you have stolen my heart with one glance of your eyes…"

As the little girl's eyes took in the beauty of the bride I could almost see it being embedded in her heart forever. It was a magical moment, like gazing at a fairy princess! I guess my daughter recognized the little girl's awe for she leaned toward her and softly said, "Go ahead. You may touch it."

Slowly the little girl stretched out her hand and touched the wedding gown, smiled and then, as the snapshot in time faded, skipped away to play.

ONE PERFECT BEING

Genesis 2:18 & 22

The perfect man.

That would have to be Adam, before the fall, right?

After all, God created man in His own image. That gave Adam an absolutely unique relationship to God. The Scriptures reveal that God put Adam, the perfect man, in a perfect Garden and everyday, in the cool of the day, God would come and walk with him. The perfect God walking with the perfect man in the perfect garden.

End of story, right?

Not quite…Remember?

"The Lord God said, 'Its not good for man to be alone. I will make a helper suitable for him.'" Genesis 2:18

Now, if Adam were so perfect, why would God have thought he needed a helper?

"Then the Lord God made a woman from the rib He had taken out of the man, and he brought her to the man." Genesis 2:22

God looked at the perfect man and found him incomplete. He then supplied him with what would make him truly perfect: Woman.

So when man is joined to woman, man not only gets a suitable helper, to use God's words, but together, man and woman, they form one perfect being. Man alone is lacking. Woman alone is lacking. Only joined together do they become perfect.

This is the month of June, known as the wedding month. More couples marry in June than in any other month to form this inseparable union.

When they do they become one perfect being in the eyes of the Lord.

FILL US BACK UP

Acts 2:1-4a

This has really been a rainy season for Texas and we are predicted to receive even more moisture before it's over.

I decided to take advantage of it. So I set out several small buckets on our back patio to catch the rainwater. Then I took the water that had collected and used it to water my indoor plants. They never have the chance my outdoor plants do to be watered by God. Then I set the buckets back out on the back patio just before it began raining again.

It wasn't long before I noticed that the water I had used had already been replaced!

I emptied the buckets of God's water on my indoor plants so God filled them back up.

God can do the same thing in our lives. Just like He filled my buckets with rainwater, God can fill us with His Holy Spirit.

Sort of like that first Pentecost. Pentecost is the fiftieth day after the Sabbath of Passover week (Easter) and signifies that day and hour when the Holy Spirit first came and filled man.

"When the day of Pentecost came [the Apostles] were all together in one place. Suddenly a sound like the blowing of a violent wind came from heaven and filled the whole house where they were sitting. They saw what seemed to be tongues of fire that separated and came to rest on each of them. All of them were filled with the Holy Spirit..." Acts 2:1-4a

God rains His Holy Spirit into our bodies when we set our lives before Him. Then as we pour out the Holy Spirit He gave us into the lives of others, we will discover that, like my buckets on the back patio, God will fill us back up.

THE SECRET OF A LONG LIFE

Matthew 7:28-29

Recently while browsing through the card section looking for appropriate birthday cards for our family and friends, we came across a cute one that had a perfect touch of humor for a very dear friend of ours.

It stated on the front something to the effect of: "I went to the mountain and asked the wise man there the secret of a long life, and for your birthday I'd like to share his words of wisdom…"

(Open the card)

…"Keep breathing as long as you can."

We laugh because its message is so simple and true, yet totally unexpected.

Just like Jesus' message. The words of wisdom He gave His first followers were so simple and true, yet totally unexpected. Especially in light of what the teachers of the law were telling them:

"When Jesus had finished saying these things the crowd was amazed at His teaching, because He taught as one who had authority, and not as their teachers of the law." Matthew 7:28-29

The messages the people were use to hearing were of elaborate laws and rules. They demanded strict, if not impossible, obedience if one wished to live in accordance with what the teachers of the law had determined was God's will.

But Jesus' message was simple and easy to understand. It freed the people from the bonds of unnecessary laws and rules and showed them how easy it really was to live within God's will. Jesus' message revealed to the people the secret of a long life.

I think Jesus might agree with the words of the wise man on the mountain with one major modification: "Believe in Jesus and you'll keep breathing forever!"

WATER TO WINE?

John 2:7-8

At the wedding at Cana in Galilee Jesus changed water to wine which was the first of Jesus' miraculous signs. Listen to John 2:7-8

"Jesus said to the servants, 'fill the jars with water'; so they filled them to the brim. Then He told them, 'Now draw some out and take it to the master of the banquet.' They did so."

As I thought about that, a question arose in my mind. Think about it…water to wine. Jesus told us that one day He would changed us. Since our bodies are upwards to 80% water that might mean His first miracle just might be a forerunner to His last.

Will Jesus change us into something so glorious when He comes again, that the final miracle of changing us will really be the completion of this, His first miracle?

All of us are submerged daily in water – from the droplets of moisture in the air that we breathe in to the blood that course through our veins.

Jesus, while in earthly form, was no exception. When Jesus was carried in the womb of His mother, Mary, He was submerged in water. Then, in Baptism, Jesus was again submerged in water. Just like we are today.

However, Jesus carried it one step further. As He hung from the Cross, and as He was pierced for our transgressions, from His side flowed blood and water.

We need to remember that nothing Jesus does is by accident. Nothing is without meaning.

Perhaps in the changing of water to wine Jesus was actually showing us of a much greater change still to come.

FIREWORKS

Psalm 16:11

As we near the fourth of July, I automatically think of fireworks. Not the destructive type we've all experienced at times, but the glorious displays of festive splendor. Displays of fireworks that explode across the sky and erupt into thousands of brilliant little lights.

We gasp in delight and eagerly wait for the next spectacular display.

Christians, however, don't have to rely on a festive occasion to experience incredible fireworks. Christ's own Spirit who is the Master of our very souls supplies a Christian's type of fireworks. Our fireworks explode across our souls and erupt into continual inner joy.

You see that's the difference between believers and unbelievers.

The difference is in the type of fireworks.

The unbeliever's fireworks erupt outside his being and are seasonal in nature. His joy is dependent solely upon outside influences.

The believer's fireworks erupt continually within his being, regardless of the season. Unlike the unbeliever, the believer's joy is constant and independent of any circumstances.

King David alluded to this in his powerful prayer for safe keeping when he described the joy of God's continual display in his soul.

"You will fill me with joy in Your presence, with eternal pleasures at Your right hand." Psalm 16:11

Our joy is the fireworks that continually display within our souls.

FIREWORK ISSUES

Luke 5:8 & 10

Thinking of the 4th of July always brings thoughts of fireworks.

Yet fireworks are not just confined to the 4th of July. They are experienced in all phases of life: Sometimes not always in enjoyable ways.

Scandals, human error, misconduct, revenge, and similar firework issues all have the same explosive effects on our lives.

As far as I know, all the Apostles came to Jesus with firework issues from their private pasts. Simon Peter's firework issues were raised when he said,

"Go away from me, Lord. I am a sinful man." Luke 5:8

Jesus' response?

"Don't be afraid." Luke 5:10

You see Jesus did not talk much about His Apostles' pasts.

Their personal firework issues were never exploited. All firework issues in the background of the twelve were downplayed, buried in redemption.

This is encouraging to us who have spiritual and moral resumes' that are regrettable. We know Jesus will do for us as He did for His Apostles. He took that first group and turned them into Kingdom champions. We need to remember that no one is beyond redemption, beyond the possibility of life changes.

Jesus always begins right where we are. Shallow character, questionable reputation, and pessimistic perspectives will not stop Him.

Jesus can take the firework issues of our lives and with a kind breath, blow them away!

PEACHES

Proverbs 8:33

It was such a mixed-up dream. I was standing amid the peach trees listening to the peaches sing!

No. It wasn't anything I ate before I went to bed. It was a series of events I had experienced a few days before – all relating to peaches.

First, in our weekly staff meeting, as we were going over the calendar events, someone mentioned that Peaches (a Christian singer) was coming to sing for one of the planned events. I was intrigued, as I had never heard of anyone named Peaches before.

Later that same day, a dear friend of mine called to invite my husband and I over to her house to celebrate the Fourth of July and her birthday. As we chatted she told me her family was going to pick peaches that weekend. It was an annual event they always did together every year.

Then that Sunday at church another friend began telling me the fun she had. She had gone with my friend and her family to pick peaches. She told me that this year had been a particularly good year for peaches.

On the Fourth of July, when we arrived at my friend's house, we found we were in for a wonderful treat. She had made the most wonderful peach cobbler from freshly picked peaches!

So, it was no wonder I was standing amid the peach trees listening to the peaches sing a few nights later!

When God wants to get our attention His message will often repeat itself over and over until we get it. It usually bombards us from all directions until we take notice.

In fact, God tells us,

"Listen to My instructions and be wise; do not ignore it!" Proverbs 8:33

JULY 4

EXPLOSION OF GLORY

John 10:10-11

After the resurrection of Jesus Christ, Christianity exploded across the Roman Empire.

Its very beginnings demonstrated that Christianity was not a mere work of man. It was the reconciliation of man to God through the life, death and resurrection of His Son.

Jesus came to earth so we could come to know our God. He willingly went to the Cross so we could come to know forgiveness. He rose from the grave in an explosion of Glory so we could come to know everlasting life.

Jesus Himself told us:

"...I have come that they may have life and have it to the full. I am the Good Shepherd. The Good Shepherd lays down His life for His sheep." John 10:10-11

What a wonderful explosion of joy this is for us! There isn't really any work we need to do. Jesus did all the work for us. All we need to do is to confess Jesus as our Savior and turn each day into a testimony of that fact.

As we tell others the story of Jesus' reconciliation of man to God they too will experience that wonderful explosion of joy. We share the Good News of Jesus Christ with someone and they share the Good News with another who shares it with still others. The list goes on and on and the explosions of joy grows.

The magnitude and the power of Jesus keep spreading and growing in continual explosions of the Glory He started.

CLOWN COMMUNION

Ephesians 1:11-12

We were called to do Clown Communion for several Chrysalis' over the Fourth of July weekend. We didn't hesitate even though we had already committed to do Clown Communion for a local Methodist church that same weekend. My husband and I were delighted, as clown ministry is one of our favorite ministries.

However, we did wonder about our instant popularity after receiving another call for a third Chrysalis the following weekend.

It wasn't until we arrived to do the second Chrysalis Clown Communion that we got our answer. When we arrived on the site, a friend of ours met us and explained how God had planned all this.

Some time ago we had given this friend one of our ministry cards, which he had placed in his wallet and then promptly forgot. However recently, while on vacation, he accidentally dropped his wallet into the lake. After he had fished it out he spread the contents out to dry. That's when he found our ministry card, wet, smeared and faded, but still legible.

Shortly thereafter he was contacted by the Chrysalis community looking for clowns to do Clown Communion. He was able to give them our names and phone number.

As we acknowledged God's hand in our presence, we knelt and gave Him thanks for allowing us to serve Him. As we did Ephesians 1:11-12 came to our minds:

"In [God] we were also chosen, having been predestined according to the plan of Him who works out everything in conformity of His will."

God used our friend's mishap with his wallet to make sure we would be remembered when it came our time to serve.

FROZEN IN TIME

Hebrews 13:8

One Fourth of July weekend my husband and I met my sister and her husband at the home of our aunt in Pensacola, Florida, the place of my birth.

As we neared the section of town where my aunt lived, I grew excited. There was Palafox Boulevard! I remembered the brick streets and the faint humid salt smell in the air. We turned on Cervantes Street. Yes, there's 15th Avenue.

I was almost home!

Oh, my! There's the corner tree we use to climb, and there's my aunt's house. My grandparents used to live next door...but wait! Somebody built a house between my aunt's present home and my grandparents' former home! Gone was my grandfather's beautiful flower garden where we use to walk in the cool of the evening long ago.

Part of my heart was vested in that garden, and now it was gone.

"Why do things have to change?" I thought. Immediately the words from Hebrews 13:8 came to my mind.

"Jesus Christ is the same yesterday and today and forever."

Some things will always be subject to change. We grow and as we grow we change. We move and new people come and take our place. Streets are widened and renamed, new houses are built, trees are cut down and planted back again. Gardens disappear and new ones are cultivated.

Some things will always be frozen in time.

Our memories of loved ones, of hometown homesteads, and even of its gardens. The bonds of family and friendship will always remain the same.

As will Jesus.

BLESSING

Romans 8:28

When I was younger and still living at home with my parents and siblings, we children would take turns saying grace at the dinner table. One particular day had been a hectic day in which we seemed to just naturally not be able to do anything right. We had gotten in trouble all day, much to our mother's distress.

It was my sister's turn to say grace at the dinner table that evening so she prayed, "Thank you God, for our food..." She paused and then continued. "...And thank you God, for our troubles, because they keep our feet on the ground."

I have never forgotten that. It reminds me that in all things I need to give thanks. God's blessings are showered upon us every day, if we only look for them. Sometimes they come in the form of trouble.

(I have often wondered if our mother choosing to "ground" us as punishment was really God's way of inspiring my sister to add that note to her prayer!)

I know we have a delightful God that sometimes smiles at us in our trouble because He knows what blessings we will receive from it.

He never promised we'd be free of troubles and I don't believe that He purposely directs trouble our way. After all, we seem to do nicely in that department all by ourselves. But He does promise that He will be with us in troubled times as well as in prosperity.

It's almost like a promise of desert if we just finish a small helping of some undesired food. That's how short our time of trouble is in the light of God's promised blessing!

"For we know that in all things God works for the good of those who love Him who have been called according to His purpose!" Romans 8:28

HIDDEN TREASURES

Matthew 13:44

Recently I heard a story about two boys playing marbles in a vacant field. As they played a passing traveler noticed how the marbles sparkled as the boys played. So he stopped to investigate. He noticed that the marbles the boys were playing with were actually rough, uncut diamonds that they had found in that same field. So the traveler immediately left and sought out the owner of that field, making arrangements to purchase it but keeping his discovery of the diamonds to himself.

That little story reminded me so much of Matthew 13:44 where Jesus said

"The Kingdom of Heaven is like treasure hidden in a field. When a man found it, he hid it again and then in his joy went and sold all he had and bought that field."

The traveler hid his discovery of the diamonds in his heart just as Jesus wants us to hide His Word in our hearts. Jesus expects us to turn aside and investigate His Word so we can recognize its priceless value.

Then we will know its worth and have to have it at any cost.

You see the boys who first found those uncut diamonds never knew their value. They carelessly used them for their own entertainment and enjoyment. Those diamonds were worthless to those boys, but to the traveler?

He saw their value and knew he had to have them at any cost.

The Words of God found in the Holy Bible are our diamonds – sometimes rough and uncut – but with study, His Word become polished and priceless! When that happens we will, in our joy, give all we have to possess all that Jesus has promised us.

We have to have Jesus at any cost.

LOVE OR LIKES?

Isaiah 11:6

The little granddaughter of my best friend just may be wise beyond her years. I remember a time when at a function we attended together someone complimented a particular food dish, exclaiming, "I just LOVE this!"

Promptly my friend's granddaughter announced (in her most grown-up voice) "No. You don't love that. It's just food. It can't love you back. You can't love anything that can't love you back. You can like it but you can't love it."

Wow! The really put my perspective in line. I had never considered how I was using the word love before. Since we only have one word in the English language for love, it really does make sense to reserve it for those things that really count. The things that can love you back.

Isaiah 11:6 ends by stating:

"...And a little child will lead them."

Jesus used a child to lead me to this simple truth as only a child could. She opened my eyes and allowed me to examine my heart to separate the loves of my life from the likes.

Today, every time I start to exclaim, "I just love (this or that)" I find myself mentally stopping and asking myself: "Can it love me back?" Then I adjust my compliment or statement accordingly. I can only "like" chocolate, ice cream, my car, my house or a good movie – things like that. But I can love you and I can love Jesus because both you and Jesus can love me back!

It's not often that I allow the simple message of a child to lead me into a truth coming straight from the Heart of Christ.

I hope you, like me, will reserve your love for the things in your life that really count.

CHANGE OF HEART

Hosea 11:8

One night while serving as a team member on the Walk to Emmaus, I experienced a change of heart.

A young lady had wandered onto the campgrounds and into our sleeping quarters as we were preparing for bed. She had a terrible fight with her husband, and she had been drinking. Concerned for her safe being, we offered her water and some fresh cookies we had just received.

However, as she began sharing her story, it became evident she needed more time and help than we had to give. We knew we needed sleep for the next day activities, yet we could not in all decency send her away. So, one of our team members went to wake our Spiritual Director who had already retired for the night.

As we waited for him to arrive, I found myself becoming impatient with her. I recall thinking; "She has no business here...."

Yet, the next morning when our Spiritual Director spoke of the incident, the picture he painted was quite different than the one from my impatience. He told us of a young lady with many complicated problems. She had just needed someone to hear her pain and she had reached out to us because she had no other place to turn. And, because we had taken the time to listen, he had been able to guide her into returning home.

I was amazed. I had hardened my heart toward this young lady, but our Spiritual Director softened his and in the process aroused my compassion.

Even though Hosea 11:8 tells us,

"...My heart is changed within me; all my compassion is aroused"

But I had to experience a change of view before I could experience a change of heart.

IN THE LIGHT

Colossians 2:8

As children, my sister and I kept a Praying Mantis during the summer months in the bedroom we shared. It was our way of keeping mosquitoes and other insects from bothering us while we slept. Sometimes the Praying Mantis would be somewhere on my bed when I woke, so I developed a habit of trying to locate it before I rolled over. However, usually it would be hard at work at one of our window screens.

One particular morning I woke earlier than usual, so everything was still in that black and gray pre-morning cast. I automatically looked toward the window nearest my bed for the Praying Mantis.

However, another movement caught my eye. I saw a headless man running in our neighbor's yard just outside our common chain-linked fence! He was jumping around and flapping his arms.... I could scarcely breathe or move and I dared not to take my eyes off him! I had to keep watching to make sure he didn't notice me or start towards me. Then, as the light grew stronger and color began to pierce my black and gray world, the headless man began to come into focus. He was a pair of our neighbor's long johns pinned to the clothesline, flapping in the stiff morning breeze!

Satan does that to us all the time. He jumps around and flaps his arms, trying to scare us into submission. But Paul tells us in Colossians 2:8,

"See to it that no one takes you captive through hollow and deceptive philosophy, which depend on human tradition and the basic principles of this world rather than on Christ."

Christ is that light that grows strong within us, piercing our black and gray world so that we are able to see Satan for what he really is.

GOD'S WORD

Psalm 23

When my mother died I agonized over not being with her at her moment of death. My sister and I had left the hospital to go home to eat and rest.

As we arrived home we got a phone call from the nurse assigned to attend our mother. What was her favorite bible verse? As I said Psalm 23, I knew I should return. But I didn't.

The next time the phone rang it was to inform us that she had died. That time I did return, but now she was no longer there.

I cried, "God, I should have been there."

Then God said gently, "And what would you have done for her if you were?" Shocked in receiving the impression of God's voice, I just repeated: "I should have been there." "So, since you weren't there, what happened?" asked God. I thought about the nurse who called. "The nurse read Psalm 23 to her." "So then, the last thing your mother heard before she died was My Word?" persisted God.

By now I could scarcely breathe as the impact of that question hit me!

"Yes, Lord." I whispered. But God was not through. He asked. "Would your mother have heard My Word if you had been with her instead?"

I just hung my head. During that period of my life it would have never occurred to me. As it was it took me almost five years later to see the Hand of God.

I praise Him for caring so much for my mother that He made sure that the last earthly sounds she heard was His Word.

As His word was spoken He caught her up to Him. She entered into Heaven with the Angels picking up where the nurse left off.

THE LONGEST WALK

I John 1:9

I don't remember how old I was, but I must have been around four or five when I thought I'd surprise my grandmother by washing her kitchen floor. I knew exactly what to do. I had carefully watched my grandfather hose down the back porch!

So, while the rest of the family was out visiting under the front pine trees, I dragged the hose into the kitchen. Just as I turned on the water my mother came in...

...I don't remember exactly what she said, but I do know she ended by telling me I had to go out and tell my grandmother what I had done and then come back and clean it up.

That walk from the back door down the drive to the front yard was one of the longest walks I can ever remember taking.

When I reached my grandmother and she noticed me, I volunteered in a very small voice, "Mamaw, I washed your kitchen floor for you." When she smiled at me and said, "Why, thank you, Jeanne. That was so sweet of you." I felt eternally relieved.

As my heart and step lightened, I skipped back up the drive to tell my mother. However, I felt so full of joy that I paused a moment to respond back to my grandmother out of the bubble in my heart, repeating her favorite phrase to me: "And it was cute of me too, huh Mamaw?"

I believe Jesus responds to us like my grandmother did. I John 1:9 says,

"If we confess our sins, He is faithful and just and will forgive us our sins."

Sometimes when I've done wrong or when something turns out wrong that I meant for good, I feel reluctant to go and confess my sin until I remember that longest walk down the drive and the unbelievable relief and joy I felt when I received unconditional forgiveness.

A SIGN

Isaiah 7:10

Earlier this year my husband and I made an emergency trip to New Mexico to check on my older cousin who was in questionable health.

What we found there was appalling. We knew then that the nagging feeling we had to make this trip was well founded. I found myself wishing I had come earlier.

The day after we arrived, her sons arranged for her to be admitted to a hospital for observation. We were there to follow her to the hospital, talk to the doctor and establish a good network to keep the family informed of her progress. They even gave me an eight hundred number so I could check in with the doctor and talk to my cousin every day. There was not much more we could do.

As we left to go home I prayed to God for her safety. I felt as if there should be more that I could do but I didn't know what. That's such a helpless feeling.

Then I remembered reading in Isaiah 7:10,

"Again the Lord spoke.... 'Ask the Lord your God for a sign, whether in the deepest depths or in the highest heights.'"

So I prayed again and this time I asked God to give me a sign that the little I was able to do was enough.

It wasn't five minutes later that I looked up toward the mountains in the north and witnessed the most glorious rainbow spanning across those highest heights. It was the most unusual rainbow because it was created out of minute dust particles in dry air!

I instantly knew that this was God's answer. He placed a rainbow in the highest heights where no rainbow should have been.

Just for me!

DYING TO SELF

Romans 14:7-8

One of the first things we learn in Christian Clown training is to die to self. I practice this each time I white my face. As I apply the white base, I pray for God to help me put aside my agenda for His agenda. It is a very tangible way for me to put aside self and put on God. I physically white out me until only He is left. What I am striving to do is to become what He needs me to be.

Those close to me often comment that I become a different person when I am in clown. Perhaps this deliberately dying to self frees me to become a non-threatening caring presence with no agenda of my own.

Recently I heard that dying to self actually frees us to accept God.

I think that's true because that's exactly what I strive to do each time I white out my face to put on His. God can't work in me unless I get myself out of the way and give Him room to work.

"For none of us dies to himself alone. If we live, we live to the Lord; and if we die, we die to the Lord. So whether we live or die, we belong to the Lord." Romans 14:7-8

Dying to self is easy for me when I am transforming into clown. I do become a different person.

It's when I'm not in clown that I have the most difficulty.

I must practice getting myself out of the way in my daily life and giving Him room to work.

His agenda should always be my agenda whether I'm in clown or not.

THE HEART OF THE AUTHOR

Psalm 119:27

In high school I took a year of journalism. Although I loved to read and my paternal grandfather and I occasionally exchanged poetry, this type of communication just didn't seem to work for me. Yet, just when I had decided that journalism wasn't for me an incident occurred that changed my life.

My teacher, realizing the struggle I was experiencing, took the time to work with me on my next assignment. He was the one who opened my world to the power of imagery and symbolism that has never left me. He taught me to look beyond the written word into the heart of the author.

I find that one of my greatest assets today.

My God, Creator of heaven and earth, is also the Master of imagery and symbolism. I feel a special closeness to God, knowing we share that love.

It's like we share a secret delight that I constantly uncover on each page anew. The Bible is full of His wonderful symbolism. It comes alive for me and I never tire of His power and wit. Sometimes I can't wait to see what His Word reveals next.

My daily prayer echoes Psalm 119:27:

"Let me understand the teaching of Your precepts then I will meditate on Your wonders."

How I delight in searching the Scriptures for the endless revelations His Word has for my life.

For I am eagerly looking into the Heart of the Author.

THE FINISHING TOUCH

John 1:3-4

I remember the story of a famous artist who was finishing a remarkable painting featuring a beautiful bird poised for flight. But as he applied the last stroke of the brush and stepped back to view his work, something seemed to be missing. It was a suburb painting that promised to be the artist's best, but it needed something.

After reflection, the artist picked up his brush and added just a speck of white in the bird's eye. It only took that finishing touch to bring the bird to life and change an ordinary painting into his greatest masterpiece!

As we traveled to Dayton, Texas to visit our middle daughter, her husband and our grandchildren I thought of that story. I told my husband it made sense. To get the whole picture we must apply more than one stroke. Yet it only takes one stroke for the picture to become real.

Still, the whole picture could be missed without that finishing touch.

Then my husband made the observation that it's also true within our lives. Our lives are composites of all the strokes we have applied to it since birth. But only our Master's finishing touch can change the whole pictures of our lives from the ordinary into masterpieces!

"Through Him all things were made; without Him nothing was made that has been made. In Him was life, and that life was the light of men." John 1:3-4

Only when we allow Jesus to apply His finishing touch to our lives, will we receive eternal life.

That speck of light Jesus gives us will change us into His greatest masterpieces.

IN A ROW BOAT

Matthew 14:29

While we were still young enough believe courting danger was fun, my sister, my cousin and I took an old rowboat out in Pensacola Bay to "Alligator Cove." Our objective was to sneak up on the alligators lining the banks to sun themselves. Our plan was to get close enough to slap our oars on the water in imitation of their warning sign. We wanted to see if we could make them move.

It took three of us to do this because the old rowboat had a rather large hole in its bottom. My sister, as the youngest, got stuck with the job of bailing while my cousin and I rowed.

We were in a rowboat going after alligators armed with just an oar and a bailing can!

A few years ago a dear friend and I went to hear Tim Hansel, author of "Eating Problems for Breakfast," and "You Gotta Keep Dancin'," among others. He emphasized how we as Christians should never give up spreading the good news no matter how hard it gets.

"Sometimes," he said, "it's like going after Moby Dick in a rowboat armed with just a harpoon and a jar of tarter sauce!"

My memory flashed back to our "alligator hunt."

I think the early disciples could have related to Tim's reference also. In fact, Matthew tells us about Peter's experience.

"Then Peter got down out of the boat, walked on water and came toward Jesus." Matthew 14:29

Peter stepped out of the rowboat, going after Jesus, armed with just a prayer and a touch of faith!

PLAY-ON-WORDS

Acts 8:30-31

Recently a good friend shared with me a humorous play-on-words that had occurred to her some years ago.

She was giving someone who had called her for information another telephone number to call. (She explained to us that this was back in the day when the first two digits of all telephone numbers designated their depot or station point. Such as: CA for Capitol, HE for Hemlock, ME for Metro, etc.)

In this instance, she was telling the person to write down the number (for example), Capitol 2 – 3210. When the person paused, evidently confused, she inquired to see if she needed to repeat the number. The person hesitated a moment more, then tentatively ventured, "No... But...um...How do you make a capital two?"

Just the thought of this innocent play-on-words still makes me giggle.

Sometimes, even when we think we're making ourselves perfectly clear, the ambiguity of our subject can catch us off guard.

Our study of the Scriptures can be like that too. The meaning we glean from what we study may not be right. So we need to come together to study and learn by inviting others to help us understand.

It is just like when Philip met the Ethiopian on the road outside of Jerusalem:

"Then Philip ran up to the chariot and heard the man reading Isaiah the Prophet. "Do you understand what you are reading?" Philip asked. "How can I," he said, "unless someone explains it to me?" Acts 8:30-31

With so many parables, analogies and play-on-words in our lives, we are likely to not understand everything we see, hear or read unless someone explains it to us also.

FORGIVE AND FORGET

Isaiah 43:25

My husband and I were talking the other day about forgiving and forgetting. He made a very interesting point.

Forgiving someone doesn't necessarily mean forgetting. Sometimes forgetting is not humanly possible. God is the only one who can truly forget when He forgives.

In fact, God Himself tells us:

"I, even I, am He who blots out your transgressions for My own sake and remember your sins no more." Isaiah 42.25

To illustrate this, He told me about a study he recently read in one of his devotions concerning bees:

When an outsider (such as a wasp) invades a beehive, the bees sting the invader to death. Then, since they can't remove the invader from the hive, they simply wrap its remains in layers of wax so thick the features become blurred.

Thus the invader becomes part of the hive.

The point my husband was trying to made was simply this:

We are not God. We find it hard to forget.

Usually we can't remove hurtful encounters when they invade our lives. So, what we need to do is to wrap them in layers of forgiveness and prayer so thick that they become vague and blurred in our memory.

Thus they become part of our lives, building character instead of pain.

THE STONE

John 8:3-7

"The teachers of the law and the Pharisees brought in a woman caught in adultery. They made her stand before the group and said to Jesus, 'Teacher, this woman was caught in the act of adultery. In the law Moses commanded us to stone such women. Now, what do you say?' They were using this question as a trap. But Jesus bent down and started to write on the ground with His finger. When they kept on questioning Him, He straightened up and said to them, 'If any one of you is without sin, let him be the first to throw a stone at her." John 8:3-7

Many interpretations have been assigned to this story. Yet, the other day I heard of yet another that could have taken place.

The teachers of the law and the Pharisees had obviously set up this whole incident as a trap to discredit Jesus. The Scriptures themselves tell us that. Perhaps this unnamed woman's partner in adultery helped them stage the incident and purposely lured the woman into the situation.

If so, perhaps he was there also, among those in the crowd that day, holding a stone, preparing to throw it at her.

When Jesus straightened up He just might have looked deep into the eyes of this man as He said, *"If any one of you is without sin, let <u>him</u> be the first to throw a stone at her."*

Immediately the man would have known that Jesus knew!

Maybe, having been thus exposed, he would have dropped his stone and walked away.

Then the others, realizing their scheme had been uncovered, may have had no choice but to turn and follow...until there were none left to accuse her!

JULY 22

SPRING INTO BEING

Isaiah 42:9

Did you know that my mother was actually the first one to discover the Pillsbury® Doughboy™?

As a young girl she had a recurring dream about little "puffy" men tumbling and dancing around. In her dream there were hundreds of them in all different colors.

When Pillsbury® first came out with their doughboy, my mother immediately recognized him.

He was one of the little "puffy" men (the white one) who danced around in her dream!

My mother delighted in telling this story. In fact, I think my mother was halfway serious when she told us she always wondered how Pillsbury® got him out of her dream. How were they able to pick one of her little "puffy" men to be the one to spring into being?

Isaiah had a recurring dream also. His vision concerned the coming of the Son of God, the Messianic King – Jesus. In recounting his vision he described Jesus perfectly long before He sprang into being.

God didn't ask Isaiah to understand his vision any more than he allowed my mother to know the significance of her "puffy" men.

However, God did acknowledge that Isaiah's vision was true.

God told Isaiah in Isaiah 42:9:

"See, the former things have taken place, and new things I declare; before they spring into being I announce them to you."

CHOCOLATE CHIP COOKIES
Luke 24:20-21

After my family moved to Michigan we continued to spend every summer in Florida with our relatives. We would have the car packed and on the last day of school as soon as we were released, we would jump in the car and take off. It was in preparation for one of these trips that my sister decided to bake us a batch of her chocolate chip cookies to take with us.

You have to understand that my sister makes the best chocolate chip cookies in the world! So it was so hard for us to wait. We could almost taste them. It was no surprise that we had hardly left town when one of us asked if it was time for cookies yet!

However, as we bit into them we made a horrible discovery. They tasted terrible! How could that be? We had hoped to feast on the best chocolate chip cookies in the world only to find them unedible.

I wonder if that was how the two on the Road to Emmaus felt that day as they were traveling from the crucifixion toward home. They had hoped Jesus was the true Son of God, only to watch Him die on the Cross like a common thief.

Cleopas, one of the two, in expressing his despair, said,

"The Chief Priests and our rulers handed Him over to be sentenced to death, and they crucified Him; but we had hoped that He was the One who was going to redeem Israel. And what is more, it is the third day since all this took place." Luke 24:20-21

It wasn't long until we discovered that using the wrong type of shortening had ruined the best chocolate chip cookies in the world for us. We had to throw them away because they couldn't be salvaged.

Yet this was not the case for Cleopas and his friend. They discovered the Stranger who joined them on the road as they traveled was Jesus resurrected!

And in Him their hope was salvaged.

KEEPING US FROM ALL HARM
Psalm 121:7-8

When I was a child visiting my grandparents in Pensacola, Florida a special treat each summer was for us was to take a trip across the three-mile bridge to the Santa Rosa Island on the Gulf side. There we would spend the day playing in the white sand, getting sunburned while swimming in the Gulf of Mexico.

How we loved to leap out into the crashing waves, allowing them to wash us back to the shore. In fact, we'd get so carried away in our play that our mother, along with our aunt, uncle and grandparents had to establish ground rules designed to keep us from harm.

The surge of the waves crashing into the shore while being pulled back out to the deep created a natural undercurrent that could be very dangerous. So about every three to five minutes, whichever family member was on guard would call for a "stand up" check. We would have to stop our play and raise our arms to show the guard on duty that we were still able to stand and the swell of the water was not surging over our heads.

If we began to drift out too far we were instantly called back in, and if we even looked like we were in danger, someone was immediately by our side encircling us with his/her strong arms, keeping us from all harm.

That's how I feel God is with us today. He knows the dangerous undercurrents of this world and He has established some ground rules designed to keep us safe, for

"The Lord will keep you from all harm – He will watch over your life; the Lord will watch over your coming and going both now and forever more." Psalm 121:7-8

When we begin to drift away God instantly calls us back and if we even look as though we are in danger, He will encircle us in His strong arms keeping us from all harm.

THE RIGHT CONNECTION

James 4:7-8

The phone was ringing almost as I walked in the house. It was my husband. His car wouldn't start and he was stranded. I snatched up a few tools I thought he might need and headed out to rescue him.

When I got there, he had already determined that it was the battery, so making use of the inadequate tools I had grabbed, he removed the old battery. Then, using my car we went to the nearest store, purchased a new battery, and returned to install it. However, once the new battery was installed and he tried to start the car, everything electrical was still dead. Something was still wrong. Perhaps it wasn't the battery after all.

Our only option at this point would be to have the car towed to our mechanic for repair. Still, my husband kept coming back to the thought that it had to be the battery! So before he called for help he began to retrace the battery connections again. That's when he discovered the bolt on the positive connector of the battery was still slightly loose.

You see the tools I had grabbed were not the proper tools to use for this type of job, so although he had thought all the connections were solid, this one bolt had fooled him. So once he tightened that bolt, it made the right connection. It worked!

That's how it is with God also. When our relationship with God falters we look for ways to reconnect it. We snatch up a few tools we think will work. However, when we try to renew our relationship we may find it still broken. Our self-made tools and ways simply won't work!

James, the brother of Jesus, wrote a letter to early church Christians to help them find a way to keep their connection to God strong. To keep our connection strong we need to remember what he told them to do:

"Submit yourselves, then, to God. Resist the devil and he will flee from you. Come near to God and he will come near to you." James 4:7-8

BUMPS IN THE ROAD

Matthew 10:34

The other day I heard a very common complaint:

"I should have known! It never fails. Just when things are going right, they fall apart. Why must there always be bumps in my road?" As I thought about that I realized that is exactly what the ups and downs of life are – bumps in our road.

If life was always a smooth, straight, sleek road and we all went down that road in perfect harmony, motor humming, with clear sailing, we'd all be lulled to sleep. We need bumps in the road to jolt us back and alert us to life. We need to be stimulated and energized to keep moving forward.

We need bumps in the road to remind us that we are alive.

When we decide to follow Jesus we often find that instead of perfect harmony in our lives we encounter more bumps in the road.

In fact, didn't Jesus Himself tell us?

"Do not suppose that I have come to bring peace to the earth. I did not come to bring peace but a sword." Matthew 10:34

Maybe Jesus was trying to say that His coming was suppose to create bumps in our road.

Just think. Before Jesus came in our lives we were traveling down the smooth, straight, slick road of apathy, moving comfortably further and further away from God.

Then, ** bump! ** Jesus arrived, jolting us back to salvation.

Jesus is the bump in the road that truly says, "I am life!"

FERTILIZER

Romans 6:1-2

When we moved into our new home, one of the things that needed our attention was the condition of our lawn. It hadn't been watered in some time and brown spots were beginning to materialize in a random pattern.

Immediately we began watering while checking into lawn treatments that might be effective in reviving the grass. We started by applying a recommended fertilizer to our lawn and giving it a good watering. It wasn't too long after we fertilized that God sent us a good long soaking rain. So now, although we still have a ways to go before our lawn is in good condition, it's now well on its way.

See how God works?

The sermon subject at the church we visited that Sunday focused on the fertilizer in our lives. The pastor made the point that sometimes God uses our sins – big and small, intentional and unintentional – to be our fertilizer. Just as fertilizer on lawns, flowers and gardens help make the plant roots strong and healthy, so can our sins help us grow in grace and make us strong and healthy.

Whoa, you say!

"What shall we say then? Shall we go on sinning so that grace may increase? By no means! We died to sin; how can we live in it any longer?" Romans 6:1-2

The point is not to keep on sinning because it's good for us. Of course it isn't.

The point is that our sins (for we all sin and fall short) can be used as building blocks, if we allow those sins to be fertilizer and not stumbling blocks. They can help us to grow stronger in the Grace of God.

INTO ONE

John 17:21

Early one morning, just before dawn, I woke up, which is a miracle in itself. (I don't do mornings well.) However, this particular morning I got up, poured myself a cup of coffee and walked down to the lake.

Our lake house was only a few blocks from the launch and camping site. After settling into a comfortable spot to watch the sun come up, I set my coffee cup down beside me.

It was one of those beautiful crisp calm mornings you read about. The birds were just beginning to stir and dive for fish. Their song joined the sound of the water gently lapping at my feet while the sky prepared itself for the sun to burst forth in splendor and glory.

I gave a sigh of deep contentment as I reached for my coffee, but in the process, tipped the cup over.

As I watched, the dark liquid of the coffee ran into the clear water of the lake, staining it, then mingling together until I couldn't tell where the coffee ended and the lake water began.

They blended into one.

It suddenly occurred to me that is how Jesus wants us to be. He wants us to run to Him and allow our lives to mingle and blend with His until we can't tell where we end and Jesus begins.

In fact that was Jesus' most fervent and precious prayer for us:

"...that all of them [us] may be one, Father, just as You are in Me and I am in You. May they also be in Us so that the world may believe You have sent Me." John 17:21

We need to blend into one with Jesus.

THE GIFT IS THERE

Jeremiah 29:11-14a

Luci Swindoll, sister to Chuck Swindoll, in an excerpt from one of her books, tells about a delightful dream she once had.

She dreamed someone in a white robe presented her with a gift-wrapped box. But inside was another box, and another, and another... Each box was beautifully wrapped, but empty. So Luci said to the white-robed figure, "There's nothing in the boxes."

The white-robed figure replied, "The gift is there. Keep looking."

...Isn't that just like life seems to be for us sometimes?

The more we do; the more we try; the more we unwrap our lives; the more we seem to find nothing there.

The more we seek God the more illusive He seems to become.

That's when God replies:

"'I know the plans I have for you, plans to prosper you and not to harm you, plans to give you hope and a future. Then you will call upon Me and come and pray to Me, and I will listen to you. You will seek Me and find Me when you seek Me with all your heart. I will be found by you,' declares the Lord." Jeremiah 29:11-14a

Sometimes we are tempted, like Luci, to stop looking and announce "There's nothing there."

But God keeps telling us "The gift is there. Keep looking."

THE LIE OF OMISSION

Genesis 3:1

There is a form of lying that is done without a word. It's the lie of omission. Recently I witnessed it in action.

During a meeting in which the members present were being asked to approve a plan, a question was raised as to the wisdom of one of its aspects. The presenter of the plan offered a weak defense. The committee, knowing that a mentor had been appointed to the presenter previous to forming the plan, assumed the presenter and his mentor were in agreement with what was being presented. So after a few more minutes of hesitation, the committee reluctantly voted to approve the plan as presented.

Later I learned that the presenter and his mentor were not in agreement. Not only that, but the presenter deliberately misled the mentor as to the time of the meeting so that when he arrived, the vote had already been cast.

You see the mentor had raised the very same question the committee did, and the presenter knew he was intending to let the committee know before the vote. So instead of saying, "You know, my mentor asked me the same thing..." the presenter, by his silence, allowed the committee to think there was no problem.

This lie of omission has to be one of Satan's greatest inventions. He certainly uses it a lot, beginning in the Garden of Eden when he

"Said to the woman, 'Did God really say you must not eat from any tree in the garden?" Genesis 3:16

Satan's question was designed to mislead Eve just long enough to plant a seed of doubt in her mind. It worked. You know the rest of the story.

If Eve had come to Satan later and challenged him, Satan probably would have said, "Hey, all I did was ask a question. I never told you to eat it, did I?"

STAND OUR GROUND

I Corinthians 15:58

The day the movers loaded our furniture on the van the inside door to the garage stayed open all day. The men were moving all the boxes and furniture out through that door. I was in the computer room packing some last minute items when I heard a commotion. Our petite 4-½ pound cat was growling and hissing and the movers were yelling.

I couldn't imagine what was happening so I hurried out into the hallway just in time to see our cat, hair bristling, trying to back down a full-grown Doberman that had wandered into our house through the open door!

This Doberman was almost as tall as I was so I know he could have swallowed our petite cat in one bite, if he'd had a mind to. However, size meant nothing to our cat. She stood her ground. Then under the barrage of our cat's threatening demeanor, the Doberman tucked his tail between his legs and with one last frightened glance at the cat, put his head down and ran from our house as fast as he could.

I got to thinking. If a petite little cat could stand her ground to a full-grown Doberman, we should be able to stand our ground to Satan and his wiles.

We sometimes might feel that we are too little to stand up to big evils and bad temptations but as Paul assures us in I Corinthians 15:58

"Therefore my dear brothers, stand firm. Let nothing move you. Always give yourselves fully to the work of the Lord because you know your labor in the Lord is not in vain."

So if we stand our ground, we will always be on the side that wins. Satan will tuck his tail between his legs, put his head down and run from our lives as fast as he can.

RECOGNITION

I John 4:7

One Saturday night my husband and I attended a special worship service. Near the end of the service, one of the people attending caught my eye and excitedly waved at me. I smiled and waved back, thinking that she sure looked familiar. But as hard as I tried, I couldn't place where I knew her from or who she was.

Several days later I received e-mail from a former colleague. She had been the person who had waved at me. However, since I hadn't expected to see her, I hadn't recognized her.

We all have had instances like this in our lives when we see someone we know but we just can't place them.

A good example of this is perhaps running into one of the waitresses from your favorite café in the grocery store. Or, like I did, running into a former work associate at a church service. In both cases she would look familiar but since they would be out of their usual environments, they would become harder to identify.

John, the Apostle and author of the Gospel of John and Revelation, knew that. He didn't want that to ever happen to us concerning God, so in I John 4:7 he emphasized:

"Dear friends, let us love one another, for love comes from God. Everyone who loves has been born of God and knows God."

You see John wanted to make sure that we would never have any difficulty in recognizing God.

We need to be able to recognize Him in every setting and in every situation.

GOD'S FINGERPRINTS

Matthew 28:16-20

There are a few people each of us knows that God always works through.

One of those individuals came into our lives as we began to look for a home to buy. This person had been called by God to enter the ministry and, as a result, was selling her home.

As soon as we walked into her home we could feel the power of prayer and God's presence. We found God's fingerprints in every room.

She is one of those individuals who when you are in her presence you know you are also in the presence of God. She is not afraid to let God shine through her life and because of that she leaves God's fingerprints behind in every life she touches.

She is among the ones who take seriously the words of Jesus in the Great Commission:

"All authority in heaven and on earth has been given to Me. Therefore go and make disciples of all nations, baptizing them in the name of the Father and of the Son and of the Holy Spirit, and teaching them to obey everything I have commanded you. And surely I am with you always, to the very end of the age." Matthew 28:16-20

God counts on us all to go and make disciples because He has no hands on earth to use except ours. So the only way His fingerprints can materialize in our lives is if He shines through us and uses our hands.

It's only when we touch others for Jesus that we can leave behind God's fingerprints in the lives of others.

ENCOURAGEMENT

Psalm 145:8-9

My paternal grandfather and I always exchanged the poetry we wrote. He continually encouraged me in my writings, which helped me to cultivate and nurture my budding ability.

It also developed in me a love for creative writing. So soon after I moved to New Mexico I decided to continue trying to improve my writing skills. So I applied to one of those creative writing courses by mail, "The Famous Writers' Course".

To my delight I was accepted and received my books and a detailed syllabus. I set right to work. I completed my first set of assignments in record time! One evening, several months into the course I received a phone call from one of the instructors. He was traveling and was happen to be at the El Paso airport waiting for his next connection. Since he had a few minutes to spare he called me to offer me encouragement and to compliment me on my progress so far.

Imagine my amazement and awe as I realized I was actually speaking to Rod Serling, author, screenwriter, and creator of 'The Twilight Zone!' I just couldn't believe he had ever seen any of my work, much less made a special point to call me to encourage me in it.

God is like that also. And it's just as amazing to me that He would be interested in my life, much less make a special point to listen to my amateur prayers and offer me encouragement.

It's like we read in David's psalm of praise:

"The Lord is gracious and compassionate, slow to anger and rich in love. The Lord is good to all; He has compassion on all He has made." Psalm 145:8-9

DIAGRAM

Ephesians 4:25

A pastor I consider being a mentor to me as well as a wonderful friend had us dissect a verse of Scripture during our Bible study in order to understand it better.

"Therefore each of you must put off falsehood and speak truthfully to his neighbor, for we are all members of one body." Ephesians 4:25

Therefore: Usually when you see a *"therefore"* or a *"wherefore"* in the Bible you need to look at the verses prior to this statement for clarification.

Each of you: The subject of the sentence is *"you"* and, in this case, *"you"* is plural. It pertains to us all.

Must: A directive. We have no choice but to comply.

Put off falsehood: Describes how we are to speak; that is by *"putting off falsehood."*

Speak: "Speak" is the verb and means to verbalize our thoughts.

Truthfully: "Truthfully" is an adverb that describes the way we are to *speak.* Jesus tells us in John 14:6 that He is the Way and the "Truth" and the light. So the way to speak *"truthfully"* is to speak of Jesus.

To his neighbor: The object of the sentence is the phrase *"to his neighbor".* Here again, as in the case of *"you"*, *"his neighbor"* is also plural.

We are all members of one body: This is the entire theme of the sentence: *"We are all members of one body."*

So this verse is saying:

"We are to speak of Jesus to everyone since we are all of the same body."

KING OF THE MOUNTAIN

Luke 21:27-28

Of the time each summer my family would spend in Florida each year half of it we usually spent at my aunt and uncle's summer Bay House located on the Santa Rosa Island off Pensacola Bay. One particular summer, while at the Bay House, we spent delightful hours playing on a raft that we had anchored out into the bay a short distance. Our favorite game that year was playing "King of the Mountain". In this game one person stands in the middle of the raft while the rest of us try to get up on the raft and push him/her off. The one who manages to push the "King" off becomes the "King of the Mountain".

That summer one of our older cousins usually became the "King of the Mountain". So pushing him off the raft became our common goal, even though trying to move him was almost as impossible as moving a real mountain! No matter how many times we would try to push him off, we would only end up being dunked for our troubles. But we kept coming back again and again, never tiring of trying.

Today Jesus is my "King of the Mountain". And He maintains that same steady unmovable presence in my life that our older cousin did for me on that raft.

No matter how many times I try to push Jesus out of my life, He always stays, letting me know He can't be moved and He will never leave me. So I never tire of coming back again and again to Jesus.

In Luke 21:27-28 Jesus tells us

"At that time we will see the Son of Man (our "King of the Mountain") coming in a cloud (His "raft") of power and great glory. When these things begin to take place, stand up and lift up your heads, because your redemption is near."

Our "King of the Mountain", Jesus, can never be moved and never will He leave us. He is with us always, even to the end of time. Because Jesus is King our faith is constantly renewed and our mountains become molehills.

Jesus is King of all Mountains!

AUGUST 6

PICTURES

Matthew 7:7-8

When I was a child and my family would take family drives or Sunday trips or travel by car on mini-weekend vacations, I would curl up in the back seat by the window (when it was my turn) and watch the sky.

My sister, brother and I would play a game we called "guess the animal" seen within the billowing clouds in the sky. It was fun describing a rabbit or an elephant or a long-tailed dog to my siblings, trying to get them to see it. Sometimes the picture would change before I could get them to recognize what I saw. Then I'd have the added joy of describing a new or sometimes different animal.

Once either my sister or brother saw what I was seeing, it would be their turn to point out the animal he or she saw.

Recently I realized that our search to know Jesus is quite a bit like that game.

We listen to others describe their walk with the Lord. Then we take those pictures, trying to see what they see. Then as we study God's Word, trying to complete our own picture, sometimes the picture we have of Jesus changes. We begin to see more completely as we give others a turn to find and point out to us what they see. And so, as we give of ourselves and receive from others, we continue growing closer in our search for Jesus.

Yet we can always be sure that we will find Him. How do we know?

Well, Jesus Himself promises us that. Jesus says in Matthew 7:7-8

"Ask and it will be given to you; seek and you will find; knock and the door will be opened to you. For everyone who asks, receives; he who seeks, finds; and to him who knocks, the door will be opened."

ILLUSIONS

James 1:16-17

Not so long ago I was sitting in Burger King eating a quick breakfast with my husband before we headed out to one of those all day meetings. From where I was sitting I could see the cars as they pulled up to the drive-through window.

Suddenly I noticed a car pulling up in the opposite direction – directly in front of a car that was just pulling away from the window! I pointed it out to my husband, stating if neither car stopped there was going to be an accident. While I was still speaking, both cars continued to move toward each other in a head-on crash position.

I caught my breath! Then, as they met head-on, the car moving in the wrong direction melted into the other car...

In reality there had only been one car. The other vehicle I had seen had been a optical illusion, a reversed reflection of itself. It had been just a shadow, yet, for a moment it seemed so real.

Suddenly I knew that this was how Satan works in our lives. He creates shadows for us so he can get us to move away from the Truth. When this happens, it might be easy to, like I did, think that shadow real.

It's interesting that James, the brother of Jesus, know this and warns us about it.

"Don't be deceived, my dear Brothers (& Sisters). Every good and perfect gift is from above, coming down from the Father of the heavenly lights, who does not change like shifting shadows." James 1:16-17

Our God is not a God of shadows. He does not present the Truth in optical illusions that melt away. His Word is always lasting, solid and true.

HARMONY

Psalm 51:10

A musical instrument cannot play itself, but in the hands of a master musician, it can come alive with beautiful, soul stirring music.

We ourselves are also instruments through which God can produce beautiful music, songs of peace and harmony, for those around us to enjoy. As His instruments we are continually sharing the blessings of God's love that lives in our own hearts and minds.

Then in harmony with the peace of God within us, within others and all around us, we bring every person on this earth into the harmony of our song:

> *"Make me an instrument, and instrument of worship as I lift up my heart to the Lord.*
>
> *Make me a symphony, a symphony of worship as I lift up my heart to the Lord.*
>
> *Make me a love song, a love song of worship as I lift up my heart to the Lord."*

Psalm 51:10 starts out

"Create in me..."

And He does. The love and peace of Jesus are waiting to be played through our lives in an uplifting harmony of prayer, thoughts, words, worship and action.

As instruments of God, we can finally begin to understand that we are eternally one in the harmony of God.

MERCY

Psalm 31:16 & 57:1

This morning as my husband was doing his devotions he shared with me a special insight God had given him on "forgiveness."

It was all about that little word, "Mercy."

When God forgives He instantly forgets. However, we can't forget that easily. We ask God for forgiveness and we even receive it, but we always continue to feel guilty until we remember to ask God for His mercy.

Once we receive God's mercy that's when our guilt goes away. Only then are we truly freed.

The reason we struggle with forgiveness is because we forget that we need mercy to make the guilt go away. So we often fail to ask God for it. David knew that. That's why he cried out to God in Psalm 57:1:

"Have mercy on me, O God, have mercy on me."

David knew that in order for him to feel the forgiveness that he had already received, he needed God's mercy.

Forgiveness is like an outer layer with mercy the inner layer. You can't have freedom from guilt unless both layers are present in your life. You always have forgiveness when you ask for forgiveness, but until you ask God for His mercy you can't receive freedom from guilt.

So don't forget to ask God continually for His mercy. It's ours just for the asking.

We don't have to ever feel guilty about anything God has forgotten!

"Make Your face to shine upon Your servant: Save me for Your mercies' sake." Psalm 31:16

DISCOVERING THE BANQUET

Psalm 119:35-38

One summer day at my grandparents' home when I was young I decided to eat my lunch on the front porch. As I sat on the steps munching on my sandwich, I noticed a line of ants crossing the walk in front of me. All the ants were busy scurrying along to some appointed designation back and forth, pausing only to touch antenna now and again before moving on. I decided to make their day.

I broke off a crumb from my sandwich and dropped it on the sidewalk near them, but they continued to scurry on their way, ignoring the feast I had set for them. So I picked up a stick lying nearby and began to gently corral one of the ants toward it. Every time I got an ant to move in the right direction he would turn and scurry back to his friends. But I was determined. You see I could see the banquet waiting for him even though he couldn't until I forced him to run smack dab into it!

I thought, how much like that ant we are. God provides us a banquet but we keep going our own way, following the crowd and ignoring His direction. He has to patiently keep steering us over and over again back to the point of His diversion every step of the way. Like that ant, we are mindless of anything except our own self-conceived direction.

I think David realized this. That's why he offered this request to God in Psalm 119:35-38:

"...Direct me in the path of Your commands, for there I find delight. Turn my heart toward Your statutes and not toward selfish gain. Turn my eyes away from worthless things..."

God can see the wonderful bounty waiting for us, but we can't until we run smack-dab into it. Then we are surprised at what we consider an unexpected blessing!

GOD'S PRESENCE

Romans 12:2

Have you ever felt like something that had never happened before was now happening again? Where just the impression of it came into your being and everything seemed to be in soft focus?

And, as you watched, in a dream-like state, you could see it unfold before you exactly as you somehow knew it would.

Something unexplainable was happening – something you knew – and yet, you didn't.

Some call it déjà vu. Some call it transformation. What ever it is, it has happened to me several times in my life.

The times I remember most are during the times I have entered a sanctuary or chapel alone in its stillness. There is something about the quietness within that causes me to hold my breath in anticipation and expectation, for I've been there before – in God's presence.

There is an instant in which the impression of His presence comes into my being and I feel His hand on my head. It is a familiar feeling and it unfolds just as I knew it would.

Something wonderful is happening. Something I've experienced before, and yet -- maybe not.

I remember reading in Romans 12:2,

"Do not be conformed any longer to the pattern of this world but be transformed by the renewing of your mind."

It's like I know I know yet I don't.

So I am transformed by God's presence each time for the first time – again.

EYE OF A NEEDLE

Mark 10:25

Our high school's computer teacher came into my office a few days before school started while she was preparing for the first day of class. She showed me an amazing picture of a tiny microchip so small it could easily pass through the eye of a needle.

It naturally reminded both of us about the eye of the needle mentioned in the Bible.

Jesus was telling a rich young man,

"It is easier for a camel to go through the eye of a needle than for a rich man to enter into the Kingdom of God." Mark 10:25

Now, in the day of Jesus, the back gates in the wall protecting a city were purposely small. This made it easy for a city to protect itself against attacking armies. Any opposing force coming through these gates would be forced to enter into the city one man at a time. Therefore, these back gates were often referred to as the "eye of a needle". Also, for a merchant to get his camel through the "eye of a needle" back gate, he would have to dismount and unload his camel of its burdens. Then he would have to squeeze the camel through the narrow opening and reload him on the other side.

Most merchants entered through the main gate of the city because to use the back gate was hard – very time consuming and difficult – but not impossible!

Then the computer teacher shared with me an insight I had never considered.

She said that we are all like that camel at the gates of Salvation. We need to unload the burdens we carry to get through the door of Salvation. Yet, unlike the camel, when we pass to the other side we must never pick up those burdens again.

Impossible?

No. Just very difficult.

SPOT OF SHAME

Hebrews 9:14

In most high school college level literature classes one of the required parts of the course is studying the Shakespearean plays. One of the ones I studied was "Lady McBeth."

Now Lady McBeth was a very troubled soul that had been driven mad by her participation in a murder. Of course I don't want to give away the story line in case you want to read it later, but she tried everything to rid herself of that guilt. She kept washing her hands over and over, repeating that famous line: "Out, out damn spot!" But no matter how hard she scrubbed her hands, her bloodguilt remained.

She could never wash out her spot of shame.

You see there was something Lady McBeth had not learned. You can't wash guilt away by yourself no matter how hard you try. Imaginary or real, her guilt kept her in its power with no relief, no forgiveness, and no mercy.

Lady McBeth had no hope of salvation.

But we do. There's only One who can wash all guilt away and that is Jesus. Hebrews 9:14 says,

"How much more, then, will the blood of Christ...cleanse our consciences for acts that lead to death?"

None of us may have committed murder like Lady McBeth, but we all have committed sins that seem to hold us in similar bondage. All of us, at times, have also tried to wash out our own spot of shame to no avail.

However, when we call on Jesus, He will take our spot of shame and with His blood wash us as white as snow.

For Jesus is the only One who can do it.

THE FIG TREE

Matthew 21:18-19

Among my favorite memories is the fig tree in my Grandparents' back yard. When I was young it became a symbol of stability in my life. I knew that, short of cutting it down, it would always be there.

It was familiar and comforting to me.

Although it was hardly a climbing tree, I managed to find a way. I use to climb up into it and allow it to cradle me during some of my more unstable times.

It was my secret healing place. One that no one ever knew about.

Therefore, when I first heard the story about the fig tree in Matthew 21:18-19 it really caught my attention.

"Early in the morning, as He (Jesus) was on His way back to the city, He was hungry. Seeing a fig tree by the road, He went up to it but found nothing on it except leaves. Then He said to it, 'May you never bear fruit again!' Immediately the tree withered."

I remember thinking, "That wouldn't have happened if Jesus had come to my fig tree! My tree would have fed Him."

I felt a special connection with Jesus in knowing He and I shared the same taste in figs. I even entertained the thought that maybe He, as a boy, climbed up into a fig tree like me.

I wondered that as He did, did He know that someday there would be a me?

I think He did.

AUGUST 15

WE WERE WILLING

II Corinthians 8:12

Not so long ago my husband and I were driving home from a meeting when we were caught in a sudden downpour. Just ahead of us was a city bus. As we passed it, I noticed a young woman exit the bus and dash up the street, unprotected in the heavy rain.

On an impulse, I said, "O poor thing. Let's turn around and help her." So we turned around at the next corner and doubled back. Though we looked and looked the young woman had disappeared.

I was disappointed. I had really wanted to help her but we hadn't been quick enough. We didn't catch her before she reached her designation or found some other shelter from the deluge.

As we continued on our way, my husband told me, "That's O K. We were willing and that's what counts."

As I thought about that I knew he was right.

Jesus cares more for what's in our hearts. Our hearts had gone out to that young woman and we had turned to help her. It didn't matter that we were unable to do so. All that mattered was that we were willing.

In fact, II Corinthians 8:12 says:

"For if the willingness is there, the gift is acceptable according to what one has, not according to what he does not have."

Willingness is the motive of true generosity.

Jesus can look into our hearts and know if our desires to act are compatible with His Word. And if the willingness is there, no matter the final outcome, He will accept the deed as complete.

FOOTPRINTS

I Peter 2:24

It's wonderfully strange how God leads us.

I was driving our youngest daughter to school one rainy morning. We were passing through an elementary school zone when the crossing guard stopped us. As we waited for the children to cross we saw a small boy in a yellow slicker and red boots walking along the curb less than a block away.

He was on a mission. He was making sure that he didn't miss a single puddle of water in his path! At each puddle he would stop and jump square in the middle of it.

After watching him a short while, my daughter made the comment that it seemed to her that he was trying to stomp hard enough to make his footprint stay in the water. We laughed and I made the observation, "You know, that would make a great country-western song: 'I found your footprints in the water of my heart.'"

Little did I realize that years later I would pick up that theme and dedicate it to Jesus in a song I entitled "I Found His Footprints in the Water of My Heart."

I took my memory of that small boy dedicated to his mission and added the example Jesus left us in I Peter 2:24:

"To this you were called, because Christ suffered for you, leaving you an example that you should follow in His step."

Then, inspired with the special time and laughter my daughter and I had shared, the music and words flowed from me.

To follow His footsteps we must first see them. As Jesus lives in my heart that's where I need to begin looking for them.

That's how I found His footprints in the water of my heart.

THE REWARD

Luke 5:4

I always gain such wonderful insights Sunday mornings during our pastor's sermons. Sometimes I find myself taking notes so fast I can hardly read them later.

The sermon a few Sundays ago focused on Luke 5:1-11, and the story of Jesus using Simon's boat as His pulpit to teach the people.

"When He had finished speaking He said to Simon, 'Put out into deep water and let down the nets for a catch.' Luke 5:4

Now, Simon had worked all night fishing without success, but out of respect for the "Teacher" (who knew nothing about fishing!) he agreed. So Simon put out the nets and caught such a large amount of fish that two boats were literally filled to overflowing!

Isn't it amazing?

Simon, who would be called Peter, allowed Jesus to use His boat and because he did, Jesus rewarded him.

Here is where God spoke to me through my pastor, for suddenly I noticed something I never had before:

Even though Jesus abundantly blessed Simon, Simon had to work for it! If Simon hadn't put out into the deep and let down the nets, or pulled them back in, he would have missed the reward Jesus intended for him.

It's the same today.

When we give Jesus our time, talents or possessions to help Him reach others He will reward us too. But to receive our reward we too may have to work for it.

MY PILOT

Psalm 48:14

To update myself on latest Windows applications one year, I attended a seminar our school offered. The instructor began in light banner designed to put us at ease.

"Look at it this way." He said. "A computer is just a machine. It only does what you tell it to do."

In the same light banner, someone in class challenged, "Then how come my computer does weird things on its own every time I touch it?"

We all laughed, fully understanding her dilemma.

"Well, I think what we have here," the instructor responded, "is pilot error."

Automatically I thought of my Pilot. Psalm 48:14 says

"For this God is our God for ever and ever; He will be our guide (our Pilot) even to the end."

What God does in my life is perfect. It's only when I try to take the control away from Him that my life goes on "error alert." When God is my Pilot my life runs smoothly. Without my Pilot my life hits turbulence and sometimes crashes out of control.

So I suppose a more accurate statement would be "user error" instead of "pilot error."

I spoke up and said, "No, it has to be 'user error.' I know my Pilot and my Pilot is 'error-free'!"

STAIN

I Peter 4:8

One fairly bad storm recently caused our roof to leak just enough to leave a water stain on the ceiling in our family room. Once it dried an ugly brown ring appeared around the stain. It was quite noticeable.

After having the roof replaced, my husband decided he could easily repair that interior stained area himself by simply repainting that part of our ceiling. However, as the paint dried, that ugly brown ringed stain bled through, now looking even worse than before!

It was obvious that a stain like that required a stronger solution.

So he applied a strong primer sealer stain killer solution directly to the stain. That permanently sealed the damaged area and prevented that ugly brown ringed stain from bleeding through again.

Now we can't even tell where the stain once was.

Just as the primer sealer stain killer covered our water damaged area on our ceiling so does love cover a multitude of sins in our lives. If we try to blot out our sins any other way we only manage to repaint those areas of our lives temporarily. Like that ugly brown ringed stain on our ceiling the ugliness of the sins we try to cover up will bleed through.

It is obvious that sin like that requires a stronger solution.

Remember what Paul tells us:

"Above all, love each other deeply, because love covers over a multitude of sins." I Peter 4:8

Love is the primer sealer sin killer we need to apply to our sin stains so that they will be erased forever.

SHIFTS

John 3:16

I think the young man, who would years later become one of our son-in-laws, was sixteen when our youngest daughter and I went for a ride with him in his dad's truck. He dearly loved that truck so it surprised me when he asked if I'd like to drive. I was hesitant because it had been years since I'd driven a stick shift. However, with a bit of coaxing I took the wheel and he talked me through the shift changes.

Although I was rusty at first, I began to regain the knack of coordinating the clutch with the shift. I was encouraged and started to think that maybe he might not be regretting his offer. With his help I was able to relax and enjoy this special treat. I knew then that one of this young man's special attributes was to share without reservation what he loved with those he loved around him.

That popped into my mind the other day as I was telling someone of the "shifts" that my husband's and my lives have taken over the years. Sometimes it's these little things – like the genuine willingness of our future son-in-law to give of himself – that make the most memorial impact in our lives' shifts. All of us need someone to guide us through the shifts of life.

Today for me that someone is Jesus. Even when I'm hesitant and faced with yet another difficult shift, Jesus takes the time to talk me through it. I think that's because one of God's special attributes is to share without reservation everything He loves with those who belong to Him. In fact, John 3:16 tells us,

"For God so loved the world that He gave His one and only Son, that whoever believes in Him shall not perish but have eternal life."

Our future son-in-law, at a very early age, taught me that I could conquer shifts.

And with Jesus' help the lesson he taught me will carry me through all shifts of my life.

LOST KEYS

Matthew 28:20

The other morning as I started to leave the house for work I suddenly realized my keys were not where I normally kept them.

I began to backtrack through the house to areas where I might have left them. I searched and searched without success. I just couldn't find them.

So I went back to the area I normally kept them to do a more thorough search. I just couldn't imagine where they were. If I didn't find them soon I'd be late to work.

They had to be somewhere.

Imagine my disbelief as I set down my purse and glanced at my hand.

My keys were in my hand all along.

What I had thought was lost was actually always with me.

Jesus said,

"And surely I am with you always to the very end of the age." Matthew 28:20

Even when we think we're lost and there's no hope in sight, Jesus is still there. He is like the keys that were in my hand when I thought they were lost.

Jesus will always be with us, especially when He senses we need Him the most.

But, sometimes it's not until we set down the burdens we carry that we notice.

AUGUST 22

BEE STING

Psalm 10:14

One Sunday in a small church in Robertsdale, Alabama I was sitting on the front row with my family. I must have been around six, not quite seven, years old at the time.

It was summer because the church windows were all opened wide in hope of catching a breeze to cool the sanctuary. The pastor had just begun the sermon when my baby brother fell asleep with his head in my lap.

Suddenly a bee flew in one of the windows, buzzed down and stung me on the leg. I was in agony yet I didn't know what to do. If I moved I'd wake my brother. He might cry and, besides, my mother had always taught me to never interrupt the pastor. No one seemed to notice my distress. Except for one of the choir members.

I guess it was because she was facing me that she noticed the tears of pain flowing down my face, so she quietly slipped down to my side to ask me what was wrong. I told her about the bee. She then gently moved my brother's head from my lap, took my hand, and led me out of the sanctuary. She took me to the kitchen area, removed the stinger and applied a soothing paste of baking soda to my already swollen leg.

I don't remember that lady's name or even what she looked like, but I'll never forget what she did. She saw my distress and came to my aid. But I think God was the first to notice my distress and sensed my inability to help myself.

The Psalmist in Psalm 10:14 declares:

"But You, O God, do see trouble and grief; You consider it to take it in hand. The victim commits himself to You. You are the helper of the fatherless."

God saw my distress and sent another to be His hands and feet. God allowed that choir member to become aware of my situation.

AUGUST 23

WHO'S IN YOUR DRIVER'S SEAT?

Psalm 143:9-10

Last Sunday, on our way to church we passed a marquee that asked, "Who's in your driver's seat?"

I remarked to my husband that Jesus was in my driver's seat…even though I kept trying to push Him out.

So he asked me, "If you keep trying to push Jesus out, then who is really in your driver's seat?"

That made me think.

If I'm busy trying to push Jesus out of my driver's seat then I'm surely not paying any attention to where I'm going. And Jesus surely can't lead my life in the way it should go if I'm constantly pushing at Him! That certainly leaves my life out of control, ready to crash and burn.

I had to confess. "I guess there's no one in my driver's seat."

I need to pray as David did in Psalm 143:9-10:

"Rescue me…O Lord for I hide myself in You. Teach me to do Your will for You are my God; may Your good Spirit lead me on level ground."

To get on level ground I need to give Jesus full rein of my life and allow Him be the only driver in my driver's seat.

Then, and only then, I will be able to answer my husband's question and say in confidence:

"Jesus is in my driver's seat."

IMPERFECTIONS

John 3:17

Who of us have not fallen flat on our faces at one time or another? Doesn't it sometimes seem that there are those who are just waiting for us to fall?

Then, when we need mercy the most, all they extend to us is callous condemnation.

Recently a person we considered a spiritual advisor in our lives took offense at something we did. In the interaction that took place because of our action, no attempt of reconciliation was offered.

Quite the contrary, this person seemed to enjoy pinpointing our imperfections.

Sadly it seems that there are those who sincerely think that when it comes to gifts theirs is pinpointing imperfections in others. They seem to get such joy from practicing this self-anointed "gift".

According to them, nothing you do could ever be good enough.

Actually, nothing anyone can do will ever be good enough. We have all sinned and fallen short. However, Jesus came to save us from the everlasting condemnation of our imperfections.

We know that because Jesus said,

"For God did not send His Son into the world to condemn the world but to save the world through Him." John 3:17

Jesus came to remove our imperfections, not to point them out. Jesus replaces our imperfections with Himself.

So, instead of looking for imperfections in self or others we should be looking for Jesus.

Because if you look close you will find Him.

JUMP-START

John 14:15-16

The heat of Southwest Texas is hard on cars, especially on the batteries. Without warning a battery can die. So it wasn't odd that a few days ago I witnessed a caring act of a driver who had stopped to offer aid to a fellow traveler stranded along the highway.

Their two vehicles were facing each other with the hoods up. A cable linking the two vehicles together was visible. Therefore I safely concluded that the problem was more than likely a dead battery. It was obvious that their intent was to try to jump-start the dead battery back to life.

Sometimes the ways of the world are as hard on our Spiritual life as heat is on car batteries. Likewise when our Spiritual lives fade or die we can be left stranded along life's highway.

However, there is always One who will come to our rescue: Jesus.

Then, as we stand facing Jesus He uses the Holy Spirit to jump-start our Spiritual lives back to life. The Holy Spirit will always be there for us.

In fact Jesus promised us:

"If you love me, you will obey what I command. And I will ask the Father and He will give you another Counselor [the Holy Spirit] to be with you forever – the Spirit of Truth." John 14:15-16

The Spirit of Truth is our Spiritual Battery Cable connecting us to Jesus. The Holy Spirit will always be there to comfort us in all things and to jump-start our Spiritual lives back to life when the ways of the world have left us stranded.

INNER BEAUTY

II Corinthians 4:7

A few summers ago our weather was so dry that for most of the season water rationing was in effect for our area. We were only allowed to water our dying grass with hand-held hoses during certain hours on certain days. But no matter how diligently we watered during our allotted times our grass remained slightly shriveled and brown.

Then the drought broke and it rained. It only rained for a short time: About the same length of time as we were actually allotted to hand water on our rationing schedule. So that means that God watered our grass about the same length of time we would have watered that day and used about the same amount of water we would have used.

Except.

When God finished His watering, our grass perked up and turned green! Our watering kept the grass barely alive. God's watering made it flourish.

The same thing is true in our lives. All types of media flood our lives with messages designed to improve it. We are enticed into trying all sorts of products created to enhance our mental and physical beauty. Unfortunately, nothing works for long.

In II Corinthians 4:7 Paul explains why. He says

"But we have this treasure in jars of clay to show that this all-surpassing power is from God and not from us."

We are the jars of clay and Jesus is our treasure inside. Man-made products may give us a temporary illusion of outer beauty for a short while. But God's true Son, Jesus Christ, is the only One who can give us that everlasting inner beauty that keeps flourishing.

SAFE SPOT

Psalm 124:7-8

The other day I was in the kitchen when I heard the most awful chattering of birds in our back yard. I looked out to witness birds of all shapes and sizes (cardinals, sparrows, blue jay, doves and a titmouse). Their racket was directed at our cat that had curled up to sleep between two large potted plants on our deck.

The cat was watching the birds as they continued to announce her presence to the world. It was very obvious none of the birds were pleased.

They wanted our cat gone!

Then the strangest thing happened. The little titmouse fluttered out of the tree down on the deck, just out of the cat's reach. Our cat, now fully awake and alert, crouched and twitched, never taking her eyes off that little titmouse. Then she poised and sprung at the little bird. In perfect timing, one of the blue jays swooped down at the cat as she leaped, while the little titmouse flew back up into the tree!

I couldn't believe what I was seeing. This was perfect bird teamwork in action!

That little titmouse purposely lured our cat out from her safe spot between the potted plants so the blue jay could "get" her. As amazing as the plan was, it didn't quite work. Our cat made it back to her safe spot but I believe, only by the skin of her teeth!

Sometimes we can find ourselves striving toward something that has been cleverly disguised to lure us away from God. Just like our cat, we can find ourselves unprotected, under attack and exposed. That's when we need to run back to our safe spot only found in Jesus.

Then, like David in Psalm 124:7-8, we can exclaim,

"We have escaped like a bird out of the fowler's snare; the snare has broken and we have escaped. Our help is in the name of the Lord, the Maker of heaven and earth."

DILEMMA

Hebrews 2:18

My husband and I are trained clowns and through the years we have met other clowns and shared stories and experiences. One of our clown friends shared with us one of his experiences at a fund-raiser.

At this particular event, in keeping with its theme, he had dressed as a large, lovable Saint Bernard dog, complete with a fully hooded facemask. The only thing was, the day was hot. It became almost unbearable inside the costume.

It wasn't long before he began to have problems breathing. As he literally panted for breath, his glasses began to fog. He knew he needed help and began struggling to loosen the furry hood. However, his paw-covered hands couldn't grasp the edges. So, trying to call someone's attention to his dilemma, he began motioning wildly with his hands.

Only everyone thought he was still performing and began laughing at him, waving back.

Doesn't that happen to all of us sometimes? We get ourselves into a bind or in a serious situation in which we need help. Only our cries are misinterpreted and no one comes to our aid. So our dilemmas remain hidden away behind our painted smiles where no one knows.

No one sees.

Except for one. Just like the man, who peered close and realized that our friend was in distress, there is One who will be there for us too.

Jesus is the One who will come to our aid when no one else notices.

"Because He Himself suffered when He was tempted, He is able to help those who are being tempted." Hebrews 2:18

SANDALS

Acts 1:8

I remember the summer my sister, my cousin and I decided we needed to make some money. We thought that maybe we could manufacture a product and then sell it door to door. We knew we needed a product everyone would use, so after many debates, we settled on sandals as the ideal product. We figured that if we took orders first we could even custom fit our prospective buyers. We got right to work. After taking several orders we began by tracing our feet, the feet of prospective buyers (and the feet of anyone else who would stand still long enough) on cardboard. After we cut out the footprints we punched holes on the sides and at the toe and attached strings to fashion straps that could tie and secure the sandals to the wearer's feet. Finally, armed with a box of our finished products we went first to our family members & prospective buyers, then throughout the neighborhood selling our product.

We had visions of becoming rich!

During the time the Apostles were waiting to be baptized with the Holy Spirit, as Jesus had promised, they must have discussed how they could witness to the people, for Jesus had said to them:

"You will receive power when the Holy Spirit comes on you and you will be my witnesses in Jerusalem, and in all Judea and Samaria, and to the ends of the earth." Acts 1:8

And when the power of the Holy Spirit came upon them they took it and went first to their family members then throughout the neighborhood into the world.

They had visions of saving everyone.

Those to whom we sold our sandals purchased them from us because they knew us, not because we had a good product. Those to whom the Apostles witnessed received the Holy Spirit from them because God is, and always will be, the best product!

THE RIGHT TOUR GUIDE

Colossians 2:13

Most of us, at one time or another, have taken a tour. No matter if we were visiting in another country, or just visiting a local historical site, we usually depended on a tour guide of some sort for our information. That's O.K. if the tour guide is reliable. But if he/she is not, we may have a problem. We could receive false information, which may impair our ability to accurately view the site being toured.

You know when we review our day before we fall asleep, Satan eagerly comes forward and volunteers to be our tour guide. Only he is not reliable.

He wants to lead us back to review every wrong in our lives hoping we will forget those wrongs have already been forgiven. That's why the touring company he works for is called "Guilt Trips, International"!

Satan is working extra hard to get us to focus on past mistakes. He wants to guide us away from the knowledge that the past has no hold on us. You see once we have asked for forgiveness we are forgiven. We won't forget the mistakes we made: We need to remember so we can learn from them. But, since we can recall the wrongs we've done, Satan counts on us forgetting that those wrongs have all been forgiven.

That's why Paul reminds us:

"When you were dead in your sins and in the uncircumcision of your sinful nature, God made you alive with Christ. He forgave us all our sins, having canceled the written code, with its regulations, that was against us and that stood opposed to us; He took it away, nailing it to the Cross." Colossians 2:13

So when we review our day before we fall asleep, the first thing we should do is to request Jesus as our tour guide. He works for "Guiltless Trips, International"!

THE BODY

I Corinthians 12:14-16

I don't know why I prefer not to wear shoes but every chance I get I ditch them! It's not that shoes hurt my feet. Most of my shoes fit well and are quite comfortable.

I just prefer to be barefooted.

Because of that, the other day as I was walking, barefooted of course, from the bedroom to the kitchen, I caught my little toe on the doorway casing. My little toe stopped right there; only, the rest of me kept going!

Oh, the excruciating pain!

You know when that happened, all of my body rushed to comfort me.

No matter what my hands were doing, what my ears were hearing, what my eyes were seeing or where my mind was, the moment I hurt my little toe all of me came together to help comfort and ease that hurt.

That's how Paul describes the members of the Body in Christ.

"Now the body is not made up of one part but of many. If the foot should say, 'Because I am not a hand, I do not belong to the body', it would not for that reason cease to be part of the body. And if the ear should say, 'Because I am not an eye, I do not belong to the body', it would not for that reason cease to be part of the body." I Corinthians 12:14-16

Not once did any part of my body express non-concern over the pain my little toe was suffering. Likewise Paul is saying, in the Body in Christ when one person hurts all of us should stop to help comfort and ease that hurt.

What affects one member of the body affects every member of the body.

BASEBALL

Acts 14:21-23a

During the time a good friend of ours was the promoter for the San Antonio Missions, he encouraged us to come to all the home games. He would tell us that any time we wanted to come out to a ball game to just let him know. So we often took him up on that offer.

Now, I had never been fond of baseball before. I thought it was slow and boring. Yet, once I took an interest in the activity – learning the rules, the players it's personality and the signals – I found myself enjoying the games and looking forward to them.

Did you know that Christianity is a lot like baseball? Just think about it.

To play baseball you must have a team. San Antonio's baseball team is the Missions. To be a Christian you must have a team. The team my husband and I belong to is the United Methodist Church.

Every team must have a leader. In baseball it is the coach. In Christianity it is the pastor. Also, whether it is baseball or Christianity we all need coaching. And, the object of both baseball and Christianity is to win. In baseball we play to win the game for the team. In Christianity we witness to others to win souls for Jesus.

In Paul's travels he and Barnabas went to Derbe, a border town in the southeastern part of the Lycaonian region of Galatia.

"They preached the Good News in that city and won a large number of disciples. Then they returned to Lystra, Iconium and Antioch, strengthening the disciples and encouraging them to remain true to the faith." Acts 14:21-23a

Paul and Barnabas were among the first coaches in early Christianity and they put together a mighty team for the Lord and won many souls for Jesus.

SAVED

Romans 10:13

During the summers we spent in Florida, we often would swim at Bayview, located in an inlet on the bay side of Pensacola just a few blocks from our Grandparents' home. Out in the bay area, a short distance from the swimming dock, was the high-dive tower. But because the water was so deep and the distance was so great we had never attempted to swim out to it.

One summer day my cousin and I talked about swimming out to the tower. I was hesitant at first because I knew I wasn't that strong of a swimmer and I had never attempted that distance before. However I decided to give it a try.

I think we were less than half way there when I knew I was not going to make it. I tried to turn around to swim back, but the distance looked as great. I panicked, calling for my cousin to help me. I just couldn't keep my head above water, nor could I seem to get enough air in my lungs. My cousin did turn and try to help me but she was inexperienced in handling this type of rescue. I immediately grabbed on to her and tried to keep my head out of the water by standing on her shoulders, which pushed her under!

Only with the intervention of the lifeguard were we both saved.

Jesus is our Lifeguard in life. Usually it's when I get so deep in trouble that I can't keep my head up any longer that I panic. That's when I call out for Jesus to help me. Yet it's only when I let go of all my human devices that Jesus can act as my lifeguard and come to my rescue.

Romans 10:13 tells us

"For, 'everyone who calls on the name of the Lord will be saved.'"

Jesus saves. But sometimes it takes nearly drowning to realize it.

THE PIECES OF THE PUZZLE

John 12:41

Suppose a group of people were working on a jigsaw puzzle, each person bringing his/her own pieces to the table. As they work their pieces together a pattern begins to emerge. Finally the complete picture is revealed when the last piece is put in place.

No one coordinated this better than the prophet Isaiah and he did it over 700 years prior to the birth of Jesus. Isaiah is called the Messianic Prophet because he was thoroughly convinced that one day a great and wonderful blessing would come from God.

God gave Isaiah his pieces of the puzzle and he began adding them to the pieces others had already put compiled.

John the Apostle in the New Testament affirms that:

"Isaiah said this because he saw Jesus' glory and spoke about Him." John 12:38 & 41

Isaiah fit together the pieces of the puzzle concerning Jesus into a marvelous one-book account.

This pre-written story of Jesus, recorded centuries before He came, is so true in every detail that it could have been an eyewitness account.

Just One in all eternity could only have masterminded this. For as the pieces of the puzzle fit together they pointed to the glory of Jesus Christ, Incarnate.

Then as Jesus was born the final piece fell into place and the picture was complete.

SEPTEMBER 4

THE HISTORY OF WRITING

Genesis 4:15b

Anyone who is interested in the history of writing knows that archaeologists have now uncovered evidence that written languages date back into the pre-flood era.

In fact, when Ur, Abraham's birth city, was recently excavated, not only were advanced public libraries and complete schoolhouses uncovered, but also the evidence of written materials were found in common homes, proving beyond a shadow of doubt that the written language was widely practiced. Some of these materials, including informal letters and common cooking recipes, are on exhibit at the University Museum of Pennsylvania.

This has to mean that literary skills were common to all the people, not just the elite, throughout civilization prior to the year of 2400 BC (the timeline of the flood).

There is a tradition among the Jews and the Arabs alike that Enoch invented writing and left a number of books. Since Enoch was born around 3300 BC that would put the invention of writing at least 900 years before the flood.

Adam, who lived to be 930 years old, was only 622 years old at the birth of Enoch. That means that Enoch had at least 300 years to have either taught Adam to write or to record the exact account of history as Adam verbally relayed it to him. This proves Biblical history probably was not handed down orally as formerly thought. Most of it may have been recorded in written form as it occurred.

Then again, maybe all of history was recorded in written form as it occurred if what other scholars think is true. That is, the possibility that writing may have begun even earlier that this, dating back to the time when God put a "mark" or "sign" on Cain:

"So that no one who found him would kill him." Genesis 4:15b

KNOWING EMILY

Psalm 139:15

Technology is so wonderful. It's just so amazing how we've progressed.

In my day and age we had to wait until a child was born before we knew who that child would be.

Now, with ultra-sound and modern technology, we not only know who that child will be but we also are able to take pictures and videos of that child before he or she is born!

Just recently, while waiting for my granddaughter, Emily, to be born, I became aware of what a miracle that really is. It was incredible to me that I was knowing Emily before she was born. It was as if I was receiving a most special gift, one that in centuries past had been God's alone.

In my great joy Psalm 139 sprang to my lips and my excitement increased as I remembered the words of David:

"My frame was not hidden from You when I was made in the secret place. When I was woven together in the depths of the earth, Your eyes saw my unformed body." Psalm 139:15

I praised God and prayed for His grace to always be revealed in Emily.

Modern technology has provided us the means to know our children and grandchildren before they are born. Yet it was God who created us, the world and all that are in it. Thus He made modern technology possible.

That's how God allowed me to share with Him in knowing Emily before she was born.

GENTLE AND QUIET

I Peter 3:4

Our middle daughter calls Stephanee, her youngest, her quiet one. And she is. She is bright eyed and active; always into something, but she gets into it ever so quietly. She is so alert. Nothing gets passed her and once her mind is set on something she is not about to let it go.

Her quick mind and inquisitive nature fascinate me as I watch her gently allow those around her into her world – but on her terms only!

She is learning to walk, climb and explore her world. So there is also such sense of wonderment and joy in her spirit that is filled with true beauty.

I Peter 3:4 talks of:

"Your inner self, the unfading beauty of a gentle and quiet spirit which is of great worth in God's sight."

That describes our granddaughter, Stephanee. Stephanee has that type of gentle and quiet spirit.

Once again I find myself stepping into a child's mind in order to understand God. God does not delight in my busy-ness, nor does He consider my impatience beautiful. I need to approach God with the same sense of wonderment and joy in my spirit that Stephanee does.

My inner self must develop the unfading beauty of a gentle and quiet spirit in order to be of any worth in God's sight.

MY CRAVING

Matthew 5:6

One night not so long ago I found myself standing with the refrigerator door open, searching for something.

Only I had no idea what that was and nothing sounded good.

So I closed the refrigerator door and opened the pantry door instead. I was hoping I would find something there that might satisfy my vague, elusive craving.

Finally when nothing seemed to sound good I started to experiment. I bit into a cookie and nibbled at some cheese.

Anything to satisfy my craving that wouldn't go away.

But, no, neither the cookie nor the cheese satisfied my craving. No matter what I tried I couldn't find anything that could.

Man is a complex creature, designed by God to be multidimensional so it's really not surprising.

The craving physical food can't satisfy is probably really a craving for Spiritual food.

Jesus said it best in the Sermon on the Mount while He was trying to explain to His disciples and the people the different types of Blessedness.

We have come to know them as "the Beatitudes":

"Blessed are those who hunger and thirst for righteousness, for they shall be filled." Matthew 5:6

So the next time you get a craving that nothing else seems to satisfy, turn to Jesus and ask Him to fill you with the Spiritual food that completely satisfies the soul and never leave you craving for anything else.

LET'S MAKE A DEAL

Genesis 18:17

Abraham had a very special relationship with God. Not only did He love the Lord with his whole being, he believed in God for all things. Maybe that's why Abraham is known as the "father of all who believe". This special relationship was so intimate between Abraham and God that God actually confided in Abraham His plans.

The first time God confided in Abraham was in a dream as he slept. He told Abraham that his descendants would be enslaved for four hundred years in a country not their own.

Then a little less than fourteen years later God confided again in Abraham, this time appearing in angelic form. As the Lord prepared to leave He said to the angels accompanying Him,

"Shall I hide from Abraham what I am about to do?" Genesis 18:17

And so God told Abraham His plan to destroy the cities of Sodom and Gomorra. However, this time Abraham challenged God, "Hey, hold up there, God. Let's make a deal!"

That's how Abraham and God came to the agreement that if ten righteous people were found in the city of Sodom, God would not destroy it.

I always wondered why Abraham hadn't tried to make a deal with God the first time God confided in him. If he had I think God may have cut down the number of years his descendants would be enslaved. So why Abraham didn't try to make a deal with God the first time?

The answer, of course, is so simple I completely missed it.

The first time Abraham was asleep and unable to make a deal. Even if Abraham had wanted to make a deal with God, he couldn't. All he could do was listen.

That is why God's decision remained firm.

PERSISTENCE

Luke 18:2-5 & 7

Just as I sat down to record a terrific thought I had, our cat jumped up on my lap. Meow! She wanted to be petted. I pushed her aside and picked up my pen.

Meow! She was persistent. She jumped back up impeding my progress by rubbing her head against my pen. I firmly set her back on the floor and picked up my pen again.

As I tried to regain the thought I had, she jumped back up on my lap. Meow!

(O.K., O.K! I'll pet you!)

After a few minutes she settled down, purring, allowing me at last the opportunity to record the insight I had.

"You have the persistence of the widow in the parable Jesus told His disciples!" I told the cat.

Jesus said

"In a certain town there was a judge who neither feared God nor cared about men. And there was a widow in that town, who kept coming to him with the plea, 'Grant me justice against my adversary.' For some time he refused. But finally he said to himself, 'Even though I don't fear God or care about men, yet because this widow keeps bothering me, I will see that she gets justice, so that she won't eventually wear me out with her coming.'" Luke 18:2-5

Like the widow in this parable my cat persisted until I gave her what she wanted. Likewise, we are to be persistent in bringing our needs and wants to God, because

"... will not God bring about justice for His chosen ones who cry out to Him day and night? Luke 18:7

SEPTEMBER 10

THE FACE OF JESUS
Ephesians 6:13

John DeVito, in his story of September 11th published in the December 2001 edition of Guidepost, said that on his descent from the 87th floor in Tower One, he saw the face of Jesus in everyone around him. Jesus was in the face of a young Asian woman helping an older woman down. Jesus was in the face of a fireman determinedly pressing his way up to save others. He was also there in the faces of all those John passed who were holding on to each other for support, as well as in the many others who called out constant hope and encouragement.

John recounted that it wasn't too long after he emerged that Tower Two came thundering down in a hot black cloud. John described that cloud as an organic breathing malevolent blackness trying to devour them all.

As I read his story I realized John was presenting the classic struggle between good and evil.

Both Jesus and Satan were present in the tower with John that day. Jesus was in the faces of the people as they helped each other down. Satan was in the acts of the terrorists and in the black acrid smoke trying to envelop the people within its hideous thick blanket. It was almost like Satan was attempting to blind the eyes of the people so they wouldn't be able to see Jesus in each other's faces. Maybe Satan thought if he could keep the people from seeing the face of Jesus, they would lose hope.

However, Satan once again underestimated the power of God. As John DeVito and his companions made their way down, God strengthened them so they stood fast in the darkness. They were obeying Ephesians 6:13

"Therefore put on the full armor of God, so that when the day of evil come, you may be able to stand your ground, and after you have done everything, to stand."

Darkness will never hide the face of Jesus. For darkness must always flee from the Light.

COWARDS

John 3:19

I think my pastor said it best. In our church newsletter he was challenging Osama bin Laden's chilling message: America is "full of fear from its north to its south, from its west to its east."

Rev. Jim Roberts said, "Aside from the fact that his words are not true – our country is not "full of fear," I couldn't help but note the irony of the situation. A man hiding in a cave, accusing others of being afraid. Isn't there something wrong with this picture?"

President Bush called bin Laden and the terrorists, "Cowards" and their acts, "Cowardly acts of terror." The Bible says

"This is the verdict: Light has come into the world, but men loved darkness instead of light because their deeds were evil." John 3:10

Only cowards do their deeds in darkness so no one sees. Only cowards sneak in and strike down the innocent, then run and hide in caves. Only cowards turn their faces from the light and worship death and destruction.

Then dance in the streets with the Prince of Darkness.

What they didn't count on was our fierce unity in the face of their attack. Seldom has there been an act in all of history that could have produced this complete oneness that all of America instantly felt.

Those cowards awoke a sleeping Giant!

America is good. America is strong. And America has the Light.

Be warned terrorists: Darkness and cowards can not hide from the Light!

THE SAME VARIATION

Hebrews 13:8

At a church-planning meeting I attended not so long ago the Minister of Music was outlining the selection of music being considered for the Christmas pageant. As he did he made a very intriguing comment.

He stated that there are really only about three variations of music and that all our music – past, present and future – all fall within one of these three. For instance: The music from Starwars, Beethoven and Bach are all of different composition but of the same variation.

I was fascinated.

You know, that could also be applied to the composition of man also. I'm not thinking about the different mixture of ethnic backgrounds we enjoy today. America was designed to be a melting pot and although we are all of only one human variation, we are composed within our backgrounds slightly different. No, I'm thinking of the different ways we worship.

There are many ways to worship and our souls – past, present and future – all fall within one of them. For instance: We usually have a mixture of music, prayer, Scripture and a study on God's word all within one hour of worship. Some souls are lifted by music. Some are transported to the feet of Christ through prayer. Others feed their souls through Scripture and study. Yet this mixture is united in purpose: It is all designed to glorify God.

Hebrews 13:8 tells us

"Jesus Christ is the same yesterday and today and forever."

We all have different ways to worship but no matter the way we worship who we worship falls within the same variation – Jesus Christ.

OPEN AND HONEST

Proverbs 27:6

The other day an incident occurred that provided me with a good example of what Proverbs 27:6 really means.

"Wounds from a friend can be trusted, but an enemy multiplies kisses."

Not so long ago I invited someone very close to us over to our house for dinner. Although she accepted, she called the day of the dinner and canceled. She was not feeling well. Besides, she also shared, she was the only one of her family that even liked what I had intended to serve!

I hung up feeling a bit hurt and slighted. I had so looked forward to having her and her family over to our house. Was the menu more important to her than our relationship?

Later that same day she called me back to invite us over to her house for desert, explaining that she was feeling better now.

Privately I fumed. My first impulse was to tell her no. If she couldn't come to my house, why should I drop everything and go to hers? However I told her I'd check with my husband and give her a call to let her know. As I waited for my husband to come in I started obsessing about the situation.

Suddenly it occurred to me that maybe I was looking at it wrong. Perhaps this person loved me so much she felt comfortable being open and honest with me. If that were so then it would be my choice whether to feel hurt and in the process hurt her or to simply accept her open and honest nature, matching her love with my own.

WITHOUT QUESTION

Luke 18:16-17

The weekend I helped with the deaf "Walk with Jesus" retreat our son-in-law came over to help my husband finish building the shed we had started the weekend before. He brought along our five-year-old grandson with him to "help."

As David surveyed the half-finished building he inquired, "Pop, what's that?" His grandfather teased him by saying, "That's my house." Then as they were finishing up, David turned to his grandfather and asked, "Are you going to put your bed in there now?"

Suddenly Pop realized that David had literally taken him at his word. He had accepted his grandfather's answer to his query without question.

It never occurred to him that he was being teased.

You know that has to be the way God wants us to be with Him.

I believe He expects us to accept His answers to our prayers without question, especially when it doesn't make sense.

We need to come to Him as trusting as a little child.

Jesus emphasized this when He

"...called the little children to Him and said, 'Let the little children come to me and do not hinder them, for the Kingdom of God belongs to such as these. I tell you the truth, anyone who will not receive the Kingdom of God like a little child will never enter it.'" Luke 18:16-17

I NEVER KNEW THAT BEFORE

Luke 9:43-44

As I was driving my grandchildren home from school David suddenly asked, "MiMi, what are all those things sticking up on the roofs of those houses?"

I looked up at all the vents, pipes and chimneys on the housetops and quickly tried to form a truthful but understandable answer on his level. I focused on the vents. "That's where the hot air can go out of the attic so the houses stay cool."

David wasn't sure of that answer so he asked, "Why?" I tried to explain, "When it's too hot to play outside we play inside where it's cool. And, in order to make the inside stay cool we need to let the hot air go outside. That's what some of those things sticking up on the houses are for—so the hot air inside has a place to go outside."

David understood. His face lit up and he exclaimed, "I never knew that before!"

When Jesus was on earth walking with His disciples and performing many miracles they were amazed at His greatness.

"While everyone was marveling at all Jesus did, He said to His disciples, 'Listen carefully to what I am about to tell you: The Son of Man is going to be betrayed into the hands of men.' But they did not understand what that meant." Luke 9:43-44

Like David, at first they weren't sure of what Jesus was telling them. And like David, they probably wanted to ask, "Why?" After Jesus came back and walked among them, their unspoken "why" question was answered.

Then, their faces must have lit up as they exclaimed to each other, "I never knew that before!"

That precious moment of understanding comes as truth clicks in place and wisdom grows.

SEPTEMBER 16

BIG TREE, LITTLE TREE

Philippians 1:6

Our youngest daughter must have been eight or nine years old when she and her dad joined a Father-Daughter club known as Indian Princess. The fathers and daughters in the club formed a tribe and chose Indian names for the tribe and themselves.

Our daughter and her dad chose: "Big Tree" for him and "Little Twig" for her.

As they told me their names my memory flashed back to when I was around my daughter's age.

I had just gotten my first pair of glasses and was standing at the front door of our house looking out toward the road. I was focusing on one of the trees across the street. I put on my glasses, which magnified my vision. Then, out of curiosity, I lifted them up so my vision was not enhanced. I stood there lifting my glasses up and putting them back on, until my mother came up behind me to ask what I was doing. She had been in the other room and heard me chanting: "Big tree…little tree…big tree…little tree…"

Now looking at my husband and daughter standing before me, I couldn't help but think, "Wow! It's my big tree and my little tree come to life!"

Philippians 1:6 says

"Being confident of this, that He who began a good work in you will carry it on to completion until the day of Christ Jesus."

I, as a child in play, visualized a big tree and a little tree, both from the same source.

A generation later, my Big Tree and my Little Twig stood before me, both also from the same source.

OLD LETTERS

II Corinthians 3:2-3

Paul, in one of his letters to the Corinthians (II Corinthians 3:2-3), wrote:

"You yourselves are our letter written on our hearts, known and read by everybody. You show that you are a letter from Christ, the result of our ministry, written not with ink but with the Spirit of the living God, not on tablets of stone but on tablets of human hearts."

As I looked through the family records I have for the documented account of how my great, great grandfather escaped from Ft. Pickens during the Civil War by using his supper spoon to dig out, I came across some old letters written by my dad during World War II.

Since he had been killed in that war, I found myself, once again, re-reading those letters and reflecting on the person he must have been. He was killed when I was a little over two years old so I never knew him. His letters and the stories my mother and grandparents used to tell are a few of the only things I had to help me get to know the person he was.

Although Jesus never, to our knowledge, wrote a letter to anyone, we have a wonderful collection of letters others wrote about Him. Those old letters are compiled in the book called the New Testament.

Since Jesus died for my sins, I find myself also re-reading those old letters and reflecting on the person He must have been. Like the letters my father wrote, the letters about Jesus help me to not only get to know the person He was, but also His standards and His virtue.

They help me know how to live my life to become the person He would like for me to become.

THE TEST

Genesis 22:1-2

"Sometime later God tested Abraham: He said to him, 'Abraham!' 'Here I am!' he replied. Then God said, 'Take your son, your only son, Isaac, whom you love and go to the region of Moriah. Sacrifice him there as a burnt offering on one of the mountains I will tell you about.'" Genesis 22:1-2

If God had said that to you, concerning your child, what would you do?

Probably not what Abraham did. He got up, saddled his donkey and took his son and set out for the place God had told him about.

Why did Abraham obey God?

Better yet: Why did God test Abraham in that way? That certainly was putting Abraham's faith and loyalty to the supreme test.

All we really know for sure is that Abraham's trusting response was prompt and complete.

One significant meaning God's testing of Abraham had was to give us a foreshadowing of the sacrifice another of Abraham's offsprings, generations later, would undergo.

The immediate fulfillment of Abraham's unquestioning obedience was in the ram God provided as a substitute for Isaac.

But the ultimate fulfillment was in Jesus, the Lamb of God, He provided as a substitute for us.

As the ram died in Isaac's place so did Jesus die in our place as a ransom for us all.

IT BEGINS

Matthew 20:8-10

The other Sunday, a member of our Sunday school class rushed in a few seconds after class had started. As she took her seat she breathlessly exclaimed, "I'm sorry I'm late!"

As the class reassured her that we had just begun and she hadn't missed a thing, I told her, "Anyway, it never begins for you until you get here."

In a sense, that's one point Jesus trying to make in His parable of the workers in the vineyard. You remember the story.

The landowner went out early in the morning and hired men to work in his vineyard for a denarius a day. Later he went back and hired more men to work also. Still later, one hour before quitting time, he hired still others to work. Then,

"When evening came the owner of the vineyard said to his foreman, 'Call the workers and pay them their wages, beginning with the last ones hired and going on to the first.' The workers who were hired about the eleventh hour came and each received a denarius. So when those came who were hired first, they expected to receive more. But each one of them also received a denarius. When they received it, they began to grumble against the landowner. 'These men who were hired last worked only one hour,' they said, 'and you have made them equal to us who have borne the burden of the work and the heat of the day.' But he answered them, 'Friends, I am not being unfair to you. Didn't you agree to work for a denarius? Take your pay and go. I want to give the man who was hired last the same as I gave you.'" Matthew 20:8-14

You see it began for those who were hired last when they got there the same as it began for those who were hired first when they got there.

THE ONE TEACHER

John 3:2

Shortly after my mother moved from Michigan to Texas to live closer to us, I went with her to the grocery store. As we paid for our groceries and headed toward the car, one of the carryout boys came up to ask if he could help us. In fact he was almost leaping over people to get to us!

Then he turned to my mother and asked, "Aren't you Mrs. Luther?"

My mother was surprised. She hadn't been in Texas long enough to know anyone except a few neighbors and us. "I knew it was you!" the young man continued. "I couldn't forget you. You were my teacher when I first started school."

My mother, before her retirement, had been a special elementary education teacher in the Michigan School System. Her students were the ones who had "special needs" mentally. She had worked with her special students, some for many years, until she could promote them to the next grade. Now, here years later was one of her former special students, carrying her groceries and giving her a very priceless gift in the process.

He had never forgotten the one teacher who had cared enough to teach him how to overcome his disadvantages and to become all he could be!

We all have a Teacher who cares enough to teach us ways to overcome our disadvantages and to become all we can be. That Teacher is Jesus. It was Nicodemus, we learn from John 3:2, who came running up to Jesus, much like mother's former student did with her.

"He came to Jesus at night and said, "Rabbi, we know You are a Teacher who has come from God for no one could perform the miraculous signs You are doing if God were not with him."

Never forget the one Teacher who has come from God, for He is God!

THE WILLINGNESS

II Corinthians 8:12

In our Bible Study class one Sunday we had a lively discussion about our need to give to those less fortunate than ourselves. Inevitably our attention was turned toward the people we so often see on our city streets holding signs and begging for help.

The questions were asked: "How do we know if it's right to give those people help or not? We often see the same ones over and over again. How can we tell if it's just a guise to get money for another drink or for drugs? Are we really being good stewards when what we give unwittingly contributes to their addictions and sins? How can we tell if their needs are real or not?"

Suddenly I remembered where in Corinthians Paul says,

"For if the willingness is there, the gift is acceptable according to what one has, not according to what he does not have." II Corinthians 7:14

What we don't have are the answers to these questions. Particularly the one of, how do we know if their needs are real or not? Only God knows the heart and soul of another and can truly say if he or she is being honest about needing help. We don't have that insight. We can make judgment calls based on previous experiences but we can't look into a person's heart and soul like God can.

Perhaps Paul was reminding us that it really doesn't matter if the person asking for help is being honest with us.

All that matters is our willingness to help as we can, when we can, and where we can.

Judging if another person's circumstance is genuine is not our responsibility.

SEPTEMBER 22

WHEN GOD SPEAKS

John 10:26-27

Last night during our Experiencing God class we were exploring how we can tell when God speaks and how we can be sure it's really Him. There's so many mixed messages filtering in to us daily.

However, one member of our class brought it all into perspective for us. He likened it to listening to a ball game on the radio.

He said we can't even begin to hear the ball game unless we first turn on the radio. We must make the connection. Then, because there is so many different radio waves in the air, we must adjust the radio dial so it singles out the one signal we want to hear. If we don't adjust it correctly we end up with garbled sound or static. So, not until we have turned on the radio and the connection is made and we have adjusted the dial to the correct wavelength will we be able to hear the game.

That same principle applies to hearing God speak. We can't begin to hear God speak until we first turn to Him. We do that through Prayer. Prayer makes the connection. Then, because there are so many mixed messages in the world we must adjust ourselves to single out the ones from God. If we fail to filter out the world's messages we won't recognize God when He speaks.

Jesus tells us,

"My sheep listen to my voice; I know them, and they follow Me. I give them eternal life and they shall never perish; no one can snatch them out of My hand!" John 26-27

In other words, we must turn to God in Prayer, listen for His direction and then adjust ourselves to make the connection by singling out His voice.

Only then we will be able to know when God speaks.

UNDERSTANDING WHY

I Thessalonians 5:16-18

Little Hannah, an eighteen-month-old, was scheduled for some tests at the Children's Hospital. Since Hannah and her mom had no relatives living close I met them at the hospital that day to be their support.

During one test in which Hannah needed to remain completely still, we all participated. I helped hold Hannah's precious little legs while her mom held her arms and spoke to her in soothing tones.

But Hannah was too young to understand. At one point, Hannah, not happy with being restrained, looked up at her mother with that pleading look that clearly said, "Help me!"

It just about broke her mother's heart.

Sometimes we are all like Hannah when we are not happy with what is happening to us. We tend to struggle against our circumstances while looking up at God, crying, "Help me!"

Can't you just imagine how that must just about break God's heart?

God knows we can't understand why that particular circumstance (whatever it may be) has to happen in our life. Remember what Paul told the Thessalonians in I Thessalonians 5:16-18?

"Be joyful always; pray continually; give thanks in all circumstances for this is God's will for you in Christ Jesus."

Like a loving Father, God never wants us to suffer. But He, like every mother, knows that sometimes some things, no matter how hard they are for us, are for our own good.

Sometimes our greatest blessings come from our worst circumstances.

FIVE SMOOTH STONES

I Samuel 17:40

Last Sunday we visited a local church whose pastor blessed us by using the story of David and Goliath as a teaching tool.

It was the Spirit of the Lord who empowered David while it was David's faith that strengthened him for the fight. David's power was in God. He knew that God would deliver Israel from the hands of the Philistines. Therefore, little David had no fear in fighting the big giant, Goliath.

Total reliance on the Lord was essential in David's life.

So David prepared for the battle. Yet, in preparation David refused the protective armor and helmet offered him, for he was not use to wearing them. He simply went down to the stream and chose five smooth stones for his sling, which was his weapon of choice.

"Then he took his staff in his hand, chose five smooth stones from the stream, put them in the pouch of his shepherd's bag and, with his sling in his hand, approached the Philistine." I Samuel 17:40

Suddenly I was struck with two thoughts:

First, I think God was showing us through this incident that we can't fight His battles using anything but our own weapons. Like David did, God expects us to use the tools we know how to use.

Secondly, I noticed that 1 Samuel 17:40 says David went down to the stream and *"chose five smooth stones."* David trusted God to see that he won. Yet David didn't step back, veg out and wait for a miracle. David took action. He went down and picked up the stones.

Through this I believe God is showing us that He will bless us, but like David we need to work for the blessings we receive.

INGREDIENTS

Colossians 2:8

My husband is diabetic so I am somewhat careful when preparing food for him – especially deserts. So, when I heard of a banana bread recipe that used extra bananas for sweetness instead of sugar, I was excited. Banana bread is one of my husband's favorites.

So as soon as I got the recipe I set out to make it. I measured the ingredients, mixed them, then poured the mixture into a loaf pan and baked it. However, when I served it that night we found it entirely unedible. I couldn't figure out what had happened so I went back over the recipe trying to pinpoint the problem.

Then as I was studying the ingredients it suddenly occurred to me. I store all my dry ingredients in Tupperware containers to keep them fresh and protected. Perhaps I had grabbed the wrong container while measuring the ingredients…

That's exactly what happened. Although I had carefully measured the ingredients it hadn't helped because my ingredients were wrong.

It's no different in our own lives. You see it doesn't matter how accurate we are in our life's measure of worth if the proper ingredients have not been used. Our lives, like my banana bread, can end up no good if the proper ingredients have not been used.

Even Paul warns us about that in Colossians 2:8

"See to it that no one takes you captive through hollow and deceptive philosophy, which depends on human tradition and the basic principles [ingredients] of this world rather than on Christ."

In other words, if your life's ingredients come from Jesus the end results of your life will always be good.

BE YOKED

II Corinthians 6:14 & 7:1

I was listening to Chuck Swindoll speaking on the verse from II Corinthians 6:14:

"Do not be yoked together with unbelievers. For what do righteousness and wickedness have in common? For what fellowship can light have with darkness?"

Now, I always had considered this passage meant do not associate with non-believers. But Chuck Swindoll tweaked my interest when he suggested that that might not be the case.

He explained that when Paul said, *"Do not be yoked with unbelievers"* he might not have been speaking of the separation of believers from non-believers. We are supposed to go into the world seeking out and proclaiming to those who do not know Christ the Good News.

Perhaps we get the idea Paul was indicating "non-believers" because that's where we usually stop reading. But Paul goes on.

In chapter 7:1 Paul continues by urging us to:

"Purify ourselves from everything that contaminates body and Spirit."

Could it be that Paul meant separation must come from within our own selves? In other words, maybe if we allow unpure, unchristian thoughts to remain in ourselves, we will become yoked with them. Then it would be those thoughts that shape and direct our actions, leading us away from God.

A mind filled with darkness always turns away from the light.

Jesus sends us out into a world of unbelievers and doubters. But in order for us to be a light to them we must first be yoked with a right mind and Spirit.

We must be yoked with Jesus.

FOR A LIFETIME

Acts 3:6

One day Peter and John went up to the Temple to pray and saw a crippled beggar at the Temple gate. When the crippled beggar saw Peter and John, he asked them for money.

"Then Peter said, 'Silver or gold I do not have, but what I have I give you. In the name of Jesus Christ of Nazareth, walk.'" Acts 3:6

Now, I am sure that between Peter and John they may have been able to scrape up a few cents to give him, but Peter chose not to.

You can almost see Peter's thought pattern: The crippled beggar asked for money because begging was his only means of support.

I am reminded of the saying,

"Give a man a fish and you feed him for a day, but teach him how to fish and you feed him for a lifetime."

This is what Peter was doing. Instead of giving the crippled beggar a few coins that would feed him only for one meal, Peter sought to have Jesus heal him so he could earn all the coins he needed to feed himself for a lifetime.

In so many ways we are that crippled beggar. We ask God for our needs of the moment to be met. Yet, usually what God gives us are the tools, revelations or lessons we need to master in order to meet our needs for a lifetime.

So, the next time God answers your prayer with something other than what you expect, look at it closely.

Chances are God is feeding you for a lifetime.

BACK PORCH

Luke 6:38

The back porch of my grandfather's house was reminiscent of the poem, "A House by the Side of the Road." For whenever anyone needed a helping hand all they needed to do was to find their way to his back porch.

My grandfather always shared what he had with those in need, and in such a way that each of them retained their honor and dignity.

He did this because he had learned that people couldn't survive without help from neighbors. He himself had a meager beginning, going to work at the age of thirteen picking and chopping cotton for four and a half dollars plus board a month. If someone hadn't shared with him back when he needed it, he would not have been able to reach the point where he, in turn, could help others.

He never forgot that.

For me he was my example of how I should live my life. He taught me that our true wealth is in giving.

Recently Jesus led me to read His Word in Luke 6:38. I think it fairly accurately sums up my grandfather's philosophy:

"Give and it will be given to you, a good measure, pressed down, shaken together and running over, will be poured in your lap."

My grandfather never turned anyone away.

So many a good measure, pressed down, shaken together and running over, were given and received on that back porch of my grandfather's house.

CIRCUMVENT THE LAWS

Luke 11:46

Years ago my husband cut out a "Gem of the Day" he saw in the newspaper and put it on our refrigerator. It has since turned yellow but it's still has its place on the door.

It asks the question: "Doesn't it seem strange that we have 50,000 laws trying to enforce the Ten Commandments?"

That seems like going to extremes, yet we know it is probably not far from the truth. After all, don't we need laws to keep order?

However, given our nature, we seem to spend more time and energy trying to circumvent the laws to our own advantage than we do in following them.

Jesus accused the Pharisees of this very thing. He said to them in Luke 11:46:

"Woe to you experts of the law because you load people down with burdens they can hardly carry while you, yourself will not lift one finger to help them."

The Pharisees circumvented the laws to their own advantage by oppressing the people. Jesus knew this and was quick to let them know He knew. Jesus also knew that it was not the laws themselves that did this: It was in the ways that the Pharisees applied the laws.

We see that even today. At times we watch the guilty circumvent the laws to their advantage and get off scott free, while the innocent remain oppressed. We are fully aware that bad men can take good laws and use them for bad. On the other hand, given the same drive and determination, good men can take bad laws and use them for good.

The point Jesus was trying to make was that it is not the laws that are good or bad; it's the people who use them.

MADE NEW

Ephesians 4:22-24

I remember the year my mother decided to re-paper our downstairs bathroom. She spent a great deal of time choosing a design, a color scheme and gathering the tools.

Then as she surveyed the room she noticed several tears and bumps in the old paper. If she pasted the new wallpaper over the old, the tears and bumps would weaken the new paper and cause it to crack and tear. She decided she would have to strip the old paper down to the bare wall before she could begin.

No sooner had she begun stripping off the old paper than she discovered that there were layers upon layers of old wallpaper! Not only wallpaper, she discovered, but also the last few layers were actually old newsprint.

What she though would be an afternoon transformation of the downstairs bathroom suddenly turned into weeks of hard labor.

You know I'm like those downstairs bathroom walls myself. I look O.K. on the outside until I am inspected closely. Then all my human defects and sins begin to show. Usually I am hasty to cover up these defects and sins with another layer that "looks good" but I know and God knows that it is weakened by the defects I left in myself.

Ephesians 4:22-24 tells us what to do:

"...With regard to your former way of life, put off your old self, which is being corrupted by its deceitful desires, [and]...be made new in the attitude of your minds; and...put on the new self, created to be like God in true righteousness and holiness."

I must be willing to let myself be stripped by God so that the layers upon layers of self-righteousness, pride, guilt, and other sins can be removed. Then I can be made new and put on my new self that will be free from my former defects.

TIME TO TEACH

Matthew 4:23

One of our youngest daughter's artistic release and passion has always been dance. While in high school she pushed herself to become more limber and fluid in motion. She constantly worked on exercises designed to stretch her back to develop the range she needed for ballet. I remember one night her coming in from dance class and collapsing on the floor in tears because her back hurt so much.

It was time to find out what was wrong.

X-rays showed a minor defect of her spinal column. The bottom vertebra had fused to her tailbone, which prevented her from developing the natural curvature she worked so hard to obtain. Our daughter was crushed. Without this graceful bend to her back she was afraid she would never attain the dance goals she had set for herself.

However, her dance instructor took the time to teach her ways to compensate. What she learned were techniques designed to create the illusion of a natural curvature of her spine in spite of her lack of normal extension. In fact, she learned to compensate so well that she went on to take first place, not only statewide but also nationwide, in dance competition!

Jesus takes time to teach us to do the same thing in life. Matthew 4:23 tells us:

"Jesus went throughout Galilee, teaching in their synagogues, preaching the good news of the kingdom..."

Jesus knew that without a graceful giving in our lives we would never attain the promise of life everlasting. We are a stiff-backed people and our human limitations and the defects caused by sins and temptations mar our lives. Jesus knew in order for us to compensate we would need to learn ways of maintaining a sanctified life in Grace, in spite of our lack of perfection. He came to teach us those ways. In fact, if we follow His instructions we too can go on to take first place, not only in the guarantee of life everlasting, but also in the heart of our Lord.

PARABLE OF THE LOST COIN

Luke 15:8-9

One of my duties as the accountant for a Christian school was to take the deposits to the bank. One particular day, one of the deposits was found to be twelve dollars short, so I brought that deposit back to the office so we could determine the difference.

We knew that certain deposit had been created from several sources, so there had been different vouchers for each fund. One voucher had contained exactly twelve dollars. It made us wonder if the money had failed to be removed from the envelope attached to the voucher before being discarded. However, the custodians had already picked up the trash.

Yet on the outside chance the money could be recovered, we paged the head of our maintenance department to help us search for it. But the envelope was nowhere to be found.

Then a miracle happened.

As the head custodian stopped his search, he noticed a bag in the back of the school van that had been missed. Even though he was almost sure it couldn't be a bag from the central office he went ahead and opened it. There, in the neck of the bag, right on top, was the envelope containing the twelve dollars! He grabbed the envelope and ran back to our office to tell us the good news.

We praised God and rejoiced with him. The lost had been found.

It reminded me so much of the parable Jesus told us of The Lost Coin found in Luke 15:8-9:

"Or suppose a woman has 10 silver coins and loses one. Does she not light a lamp, sweep the house and search carefully until she finds it? And when she finds it, she calls her friends and neighbors together and says, "Rejoice with me; I have found my lost coin!"

OCTOBER 3

THE WAY GOD WATCHES

Psalm 121:8

Some years back my husband was downsized from his job, which was the beginning of some delightful blessings in our lives.

Of course, we couldn't see the blessings until we could look back on them.

It was during this time that my husband accepted a position out of town and we sold our home, preparing to move. Just as we closed on our old home and put a bid in for a new home in the other area, my husband, with good cause, decided against accepting that position.

This, of course, left us virtually homeless. Our Realtor invited us to stay at one of the townhomes she owned until we could get situated.

As we moved in I noticed a barn swallow nest with freshly hatched fledglings under the eaves of the attached covered patio. I then discovered that if I stood inside the house on the third step of the staircase leading upstairs I could lean over and peek out the top of the sliding glass door located next to the staircase directly into the barn swallow nest.

So, until the babies grew and flew off I kept watch, checking in daily on them. They never knew I was there, but I watched and prayed, delighting in their growth and accomplishments, much like I would have done had they been my own babies.

It crossed my mind that this must be similar to the way God watches me. Sometimes I don't know He's there, but I can now imagine Him smiling with delight at my accomplishments and growth, drawing close to me in my prayers because I am His own.

Psalm 121:8 says

"The Lord will watch over your coming and going both now and forever more."

OCTOBER 4

I CAN SEE!

John 16:16

It was my first trip back home after leaving for college. Although I had been gone just a short time, it felt strange to walk back into a familiar setting seeing familiar faces.

The next afternoon I enjoyed spending time with my brother and sister in front of the TV. We were watching "The Three Stooges." All of a sudden, my brother, seated between my sister and myself on the couch, clutched his eyes and yelled, "I can't see! I can't see!"

Extremely concerned, I immediately responded, although I had no idea of what to do. "What happened? What's wrong?" I glanced over at my sister, silently imploring her for help.

She just gave me one of those "Heaven help us" looks, then said to him, "Why don't you try opening your eyes!" To my astonishment, my brother blinked a few times and then said, "Oh, hey thanks! Now I can see."

I must have looked bewildered because they both burst out laughing. Then my sister told me, "He does that all the time. He loves The Three Stooges."

I realized, then, in the short time I had been away, a change had occurred. Because I no longer had that daily contact with them our relationship had entered into a new stage.

I wonder if that was how the Apostles felt when Jesus appeared to them in His glorified state. In the short time He had been away from them, He had changed. They knew they would no longer have that daily contact with Him. They must have recalled His words:

"In a little while you will see Me no more, and then after a little while you will see Me." John 16:16

Their relationship with Christ had entered into a new stage.

RACHEL

Genesis 29:16

We hear a lot about Joseph and his coat of many colors, his brothers, and Jacob, his father. But we seldom hear much about Joseph's mother, Rachel. Just who was she?

She must have been a very highly intelligent and quick-witted person. She was raise by a father who was a master of deceit, skilled in tricks and very quick-witted himself.

Rachel's older sister, Leah, however, was probably somewhat slower for that is how the scriptures describe her:

"Laben had two daughters, Leah and Rachel. Leah had 'weak eyes' but Rachel was lovely in form." Genesis 29:16

Rachel was more than likely the buffer between Leah and their father. Given Laben's quick-wit and deceitful nature I can just imagine he might have been continually irritated with Leah's slower wit.

Just think how remarkable Rachel must have been to be able to balance so well between these two opposites on a daily basis and to successfully mediate between them. And because both Leah and Rachel became the wives of Jacob, who was the match of Laben in deceit and wit, Rachel must have carried these mediator skills into her marriage as well.

Jesus Christ came to earth as our Mediator. He, like Rachel, came to balance Himself between us who have 'weak eyes' and are slow in coming to the Lord and a God who is, by definition, total Perfection!

How Jesus must love us to continually protect us as tenderly as Rachel protected her sister.

Jesus said, *"I am the Way, and the Truth and the Life. No one comes to the Father except through Me."* Jesus offers us His mediation, for love and life everlasting.

MIRACLES

Psalm 57:9-10

Yesterday afternoon was one of those days for me! My car had stalled on a main street at a busy intersection during rush hour traffic. I was blocking traffic, but no matter how hard I tried I couldn't get it to start again.

The only help I received from my fellow commuters was limited to very irritated looks and the melodious melody of their car horns as they maneuvered around me and sped away. Yet, there was nothing I could do. I kept wishing I could just sink down in my seat and disappear!

If I ever needed a miracle, it was now.

Isn't that typical of how bad things need to get before I ask God for help? It must amaze Him the lengths to which I have to sink before He can get my attention.

Yet God always comes through.

Finally a Good Samaritan stopped to help me by pushing my car out of the line of traffic. Then after allowing my car time to cool down I was able to restart it and make it to a repair shop nearby. The problem turned out to be dirty fuel line, which, while complicated, was not as major as I had feared.

All the bad melted away – like a miracle.

In thanksgiving I raised my voice in praise to God for His goodness and bounty, especially in the time of my need.

"I will praise you, O Lord, among the nations; I will sing of You among the peoples. For great is Your love, reaching to the heavens; Your faithfulness reaches to the skies." Psalm 57:9-10

TEAM PLAYERS

Acts 1:8

When I was a child we had two pets that I fondly remember. A Calico named "Mother Cat" and a Cocker Spaniel named "Skipper". The two got along famously. Mother Cat earned her name by having kittens with regular dependability so it wasn't unusual to see her dozing in the sun next to Skipper who always had kittens chasing his tail or ears or cuddled up in his fur asleep.

We always made a bed for the kittens in the shed, but Mother Cat preferred to bring them inside the house whenever she could. She would pick up a kitten, take it to the back screen door, hook her claws into the screen and pull it open enough to get her head and the kitten inside. Then she would slip in the rest of the way, deposit the kitten in a closet or our toy box and then push out the screen door to go get the next one.

After watching Mother Cat a few times, Skipper figured out how to help her. As Mother Cat took one kitten inside, Skipper would run to the shed and pick up another kitten – by gently placing the whole kitten's head in his mouth. Then he'd take the kitten to the back door and wait. When Mother Cat came out Skipper would drop the kitten on the steps. As Mother Cat picked up the unharmed (but wet) kitten to carry inside, Skipper would run back to the shed to get the next kitten!

Teaming together, Mother Cat and Skipper could get those kittens into the house before we realized what was happening.

I got to thinking… The help Skipper gave Mother Cat is the same type of help we need to give Jesus. Jesus needs us to team with Him. All we need to do is to bring others to the door. Jesus will be there to open that door for them and take them on inside. That's what He's asking us to do in Acts 1:8:

"You will be My witnesses in Jerusalem and in all Judea and Samaria, and to the ends of the earth."

FRIENDS

II Timothy 2:13

Some years ago I wrote a poem about friends, which goes like this:

"Friends are like flowers:

Some are staunch perennials and are always there;

Some must be nursed and handled with delicate care.

Friends are like flowers:

So let me be this type of friend –

A perennial upon whom hearts can depend.

jkh

Most of us have experienced the hurt that comes from friends who are undependable. I know I have.

How reassuring it is to know that there is One who is dependable and forever faithful in everything. That One is, of course, God. Because of His very nature God could not be God and be unfaithful.

We read in II Timothy 2:13:

"If we are faithless He will remain faithful...for He cannot disown Himself."

God never changes. He is the perennial that is always there. He can never go back on even one of His promises. God, being Who He is cannot cease to be What He is. Because He is dependable He will always be faithful in His actions.

We may have to nurse our friends and at times be careful not to hurt their feelings. None of us are perfect so sometimes we do hurt our friends and they hurt us. All of us are delicate and must be handled with care. However our God, who is our Perfect Friend, will always be the perennial upon whom our hearts can depend.

FISHING FOR MEN

Luke 5:4-6

Do you enjoy fishing?

My Grandmother did. I learned from her that those of us who do fish usually have our favorite spots and our own special techniques. I doubt that even my Grandmother would have listened if someone (let's say a carpenter who had never held a fishing pole) came up to her and proceeded to tell her how to fish!

Yet, this is exactly what happened to Simon Peter in Luke 5:4-6 when Jesus came to him and told him to go out and let his nets down after a full night of not catching anything.

"When [Jesus] had finished speaking, He said to Simon, 'Put out into deep water, and let down the nets for a catch.' Simon answered, 'Master, we've worked hard all night and haven't caught anything. But because you say so, I will let down the nets.' When they had done so, they caught such a large number of fish that their nets began to break."

Now Peter could have said, "Lord, you are a carpenter. What do you know about fish? We do this for a living and we know what we're doing. Just leave the fishing to us."

But instead Peter said, *"But because you say so, I will let down the nets."*

Folks, that's the secret of faith.

Because Simon Peter did what Jesus asked, his reward was great. Fish filled his nets to the point of breaking and the other fishermen had to come out to help him bring in his catch. And because Peter acted on faith Jesus went a step further. He took Peter from the water into the world to fish for men.

His example is what we are to do today. Jesus is still asking us to go out and let our 'nets' down and fish for mankind.

OCTOBER 10

TRUST

Jeremiah 17:7

Susan Lenzkes, author of "When the Writing on the Wall is in Brown Crayon," tells of a wonderful little event she witnessed about trust.

She had just stepped into her kitchen with an armload of wash when she caught sight of her two boys on the back porch. As she watched, the little one wrapped his arm around his brother's knees and tilted his head back, gazing up. He barely reached his brother's belt loops. In a tiny voice he said, "Bend your ear down here a minute. I want to tell you a secret." Then, very quietly he whispered something that delighted them both.

Then Susan wrote:

"You know, Jesus, I can't help thinking...After all these years of walking with You I still don't stretch up to Your knees. Bend Your ear down here a minute. I want to tell You a secret. I think You are wonderful. And I really do trust You. When I grow up I want to be just like You."

Jeremiah 17:7 says:

"But blessed is the man who trusts in the Lord – whose confidence is in Him."

When was the last time you gazed up at the Lord and trustingly said, "Jesus, bend Your ear down here a minute. I want to tell You a secret."

Remember, Jesus, who knows our every need and hears our every thought, is always ready to "bend His ear down here a minute" just for you.

LOVE ONE ANOTHER

Romans 13:8

He drew a circle that shut me out: Heretic, rebel,
A thing to flout. But Love and I had the wit to win:
We drew a circle that took him in!

No matter who we are or where we are, we are always within the circle of God's love. We have all been created in love, for God, our Creator is pure perfect love. He made us to come into this world ready to love and be loved. Ready to see and accept the best in others and ourselves.

Love lifts us up when we feel down. Love is forgiving and encourages us to forgive. Love builds and repairs our relationships when they break – especially our relationship with God. Love heals us. Love gives to us generously with no thought of return. We live and function within the circle of God's love that is always radiating out. We can never move beyond the blessing of it touch – no matter how far we go.

Jesus said, "Love one another as I have loved you." Romans 13:8 says,

"Owe no one anything, except to love one another."

So, when God draws a circle that takes us in no matter where we go or what we do we will always function within that circle.

See how clear it becomes when we revise this anonymous little poem?

We drew a circle that shut God out: Heretic, rebel,
A thing to flout. But Love and God had the wit to win:
He drew a circle that took us in!

Revision by jhh

RAIN LINE

Acts 2:17

As a child part of my youth was spent in a cozy little home nestled in the center of a cornfield in Robertsdale, Alabama. My step dad ran a chicken business and my mother taught private kindergarten.

One day as my brother, sister and I played on the playground equipment in our backyard we heard our mother's voice calling for us to 'quick, come in out of the rain!' The urgency in her voice was clear.

My siblings and I looked at each other, puzzled, then up at the clear sunny sky. Had our mother lost her mind? We responded back to her 'It's not raining.' All we got back was a more firm command for us to get into the house and out of the rain!

I guess because we were not running toward the door as my mother had anticipated she dashed out around the house to get us. Then she stopped short.

It wasn't raining on our side of the house although it was a downpour on the other side! As we watched we were able to visibly see the 'line' of rain slowly move over our house and across the roofline until we were standing in the downpour.

Then it was my step dad yelling out the door for us 'crazy' folks to get out of the rain into the house! Acts 2:17 tells us that

"In the last days, God says, 'I will pour out My Spirit upon all people. Your sons and daughters will prophesy, your young men will see visions, your old men will dream dreams. Even on My servants, both men and women, I will pour out My Spirit..."

I think it may be like that day when we witnessed the 'rain line' moving across our house. But in the last days it will be the 'Spirit line' moving across the souls of all mankind.

OCTOBER 13

CENTERING

II Peter 3:9

To center myself in prayer, I must first find a quiet place. I need to visualize myself lying face up with my heart's door open revealing my treasures (memories, experiences, and thoughts – everything that makes up Jeanne).

Then I can invite God to look into my heart and choose something from it. I do this by allowing God to bring what He chooses to the surface of my mind. At this point I try not to judge what that will be. God could choose a "rose" to bring forth, or He could choose to strip that "rose" and only bring forth its "thorns".

However, more often than not my human condition unconsciously leads God to bring forth a "thorn".

Why?

I visualize myself looking through God's eyes. "Child, you are looking at that "thorn" from way over there, and you are only looking at the outside. Come closer and examine this one with Me so I can show you its inner beauty and its worth."

Together we examine the one He chose inside out, upside down, and backwards. He leads and I follow. Then He moves it and myself into the brightness of His light so I can begin to see the wonderful design of it and the perfect pattern it gives to my life. Together God and I move that "thorn" in my life from the dark corner of my heart to a place of honor and show. Together we rejoice and I praise my God sincerely and in boundless joy, not only for Him showing me the beauty He sees in my life, but for the relief I feel in the lifting of another burden that never was a burden at all, except in my own mind.

II Peter 3:9 says,

"[God] is patient with you, not wanting anyone to perish, but everyone to come to repentance."

OCTOBER 14

KEEPING PERFECT BALANCE

Matthew 14:23

The daughter of a former co-worker, who had taken ballet for a number of years, was in training to go on Pointe. Knowing that our youngest daughter was a dance instructor with a dance degree, she decided to consult her. Going on Pointe was her heart desire and she was pursuing it with a passion.

So she wrote my daughter a letter and asked me to deliver it, which I did. As a result, my daughter and I began talking about the exercises needed to strengthen the ankles and feet in preparation for Pointe.

I finally admitted that I had always been amazed at the way a dancer could balance on one toe. It seemed impossible to me how one could stay so steady and so effortlessly poised. Then my daughter shared with me a simple truth I have never forgotten. She said, "In Pointe, you first must find your center and once you find it you will always keep your balance, no matter how you move."

That made a profound impact on me, for I realized that also applies to life. We need to find our center and once we find it we will always keep our balance, no matter how we move.

For me, that Center is Jesus. His life is my example. I read that Jesus taught the multitudes, fed the 5,000, and washed the disciples' feet. He was very actively involved with life. Yet, just as often He also withdrew to be renewed and to pray.

"After He had dismissed them (the crowd), He went up on a mountainside by Himself to pray. When evening came, He was there alone." Matthew 14:23

We need to keep Jesus somewhere between our involvement and our withdrawal. He is that Center our daughter talked about. Only with Jesus can we keep perfect balance.

OCTOBER 15

A PLACE TO CALL HOME

John 14:2-4

There's a scene in the movie, The Horse Whisperer, where Annie and her daughter, Grace, are guests at a Booker family reunion and barbecue. Tom Booker's mother asked Annie where she was from. Annie revealed that she had been born in London, England and had lived in many places since. Her family had constantly moved: Never putting down roots in any one place like the Bookers had.

In fact, Annie told the elder Mrs. Booker that there was never any one place she could consider home.

Mrs. Booker reflected on that a moment and then made the wise observation that many folks carry their place with them in their hearts wherever they go.

It made me think immediately of Jesus who so often told us that the Son of Man has no place to lay His head. He never had any one place He could consider home either – at least, not here on earth.

Jesus told His disciples,

"I am going ... to prepare a place for you. And if I go and prepare a place for you, I will come back and take you to be with me that you also may be where I am. You know the way to the place I am going." John 14:2-4

When Jesus went to prepare us a place, His Holy Spirit came to reside with us in our hearts.

Therefore, we have been born of the Spirit and are children of God. So no matter if we have put down roots in one place or not, we carry our place with us in our hearts wherever we go.

THE SON'S LIGHT

II Corinthians 3:18

Usually when we go to a movie there is at least one scene I can relate to Jesus. That was the case with the movie "Primary Colors."

There was one scene near the end of the movie where Libby sat in her truck looking out the window at the moon.

"See that there?" She asked. "That moon is me. It doesn't have any light of it's own; it just reflects the sun's light."

That was Libby's way of telling her companion that she felt she had no life, because everything she did reflected the life of another.

I thought how much like Libby we should all be.

We live because God breathed life into us. That means we don't have any light of our own. We were not self-created.

We can only reflect the light God gave us.

That light is, of course, God's only Son, Jesus. We should live our lives so that even when we are unaware of it we reflect Jesus by example. Our lives should always be a reflection of His.

Paul, in his second letter to the Corinthians, wrote,

"We, who with unveiled faces all reflect the Lord's Glory, are being transformed into His likeness with ever-increasing Glory, which comes from the Lord who is the Spirit." II Corinthians 3:18

Like Libby pointed at the moon, we need to point to Jesus and say, "I don't have any light of my own. I just reflect the Son's light."

WALKING BACKWARD

Proverbs 16:9

While attending High School in Michigan, my friends and I walked over a mile to and from school each day. We could have ridden with my step dad, who was a teacher, but we girls treasured the time we had together, even if that meant walking.

However, in mid-winter that walk was hard. Some days the wind would send ice and snow swirling around our heads from snow banks that were piled high on the sides of the road.

On the worse days it seemed that the raw cold wind always hit us square in the face, blinding us so we couldn't see where we were going. On those days we would turn our backs to the wind and walk backward, checking over our shoulders occasionally to stay on course.

Sometimes life is that way for us. Trials and tribulations can hit us square in the face, blinding us so we can't see past them. When this happens, we usually are tempted to turn our backs to our troubles and continue on.

However, when we do, we end up spending most of our lives moving backwards, looking over our shoulders at the past. This puts all our focus on our trials and tribulations, allowing them to set our course of action.

Proverbs 16:9 tells us,

"In his heart a man plans his course but the Lord determines his steps."

Now, that's good news! That means if we turn our backs on our trials and tribulations we can move forward without looking back! Only then will we find ourselves face to face with God, who was behind us all the time!

God is the One who will keep watch over our shoulders for us and keep us on course.

BRIDGES

John 14:6

After my husband and I married and the girls were small, we use to travel to El Paso, TX at least once a month to visit his mother. We considered the long round-trip (usually on a Sunday) a small price to pay to allow our children the benefit of growing up knowing their grandmother. As my mother lived in Michigan during this time, our visits with her were almost as frequent but by phone.

We knew that if our children were going to get to know our parents it would be up to us to make that happen.

We made it our priority.

Therefore we became the bridge that allowed our children to cross over into their grandparents' lives.

You know Jesus did that same thing for us.

He knew that we had no way on our own to get to know our Father God. So, He chose to be our Bridge that would allow us to cross over into God's presence.

In John 14:6 Jesus revealed to Thomas:

"I am the Way and the Truth and the Life. No one comes to the Father except through Me."

Jesus knew that if we were going to get to know and love God it would be up to Him to make that happen.

He made it His priority.

THE TRAIN CONDUCTOR

John 3:17

There's an old story about a train conductor that I've heard many times:

There was a time when a large passenger train pulled out of the station gathering speed toward its designation. Passengers, large and small, from all walks of life occupied every seat. There was an air of festivity and excitement, especially for one of the passengers toward the back of the car.

He had looked forward to this trip for as long as he could remember, and now he was finally on his way.

As the train settled down to its rhythmic movement, our passenger noticed the conductor begin to move through the car checking and punching tickets. He panicked. He couldn't remember purchasing a ticket, though he was sure that he must have. Anxiously he searched through his pockets while the conductor moved closer and closer.

"Oh well," he thought. "I'll just buy another from the conductor." Nothing was going to ruin this trip for him. Somehow it felt like the most important trip of his life. So he felt in the breast pocket of his coat for his wallet. It wasn't there!

Suddenly the conductor stopped in front of him. Our passenger checked his pockets briefly one more time before looking up at the conductor. He looked into the most loving and understanding eyes he had ever seen. "I – I don't have a ticket" he whispered, fearing he would be told to get off at the next stop.

But the conductor smiled. "You don't need a ticket, my child. I've already paid the price for you." Then the conductor held out a ticket.

As our passenger reached out and took his ticket from hands that were pierced, he knew.

"For God did not send His Son into the world to condemn the world but to save the world through Him." John 3:17

A VISION

Hebrews 11:1

Once in my quiet time with God I had a vision of standing at the edge of angry waters with no way to cross. Then Jesus came and stretched out across the waters forming a bridge for me.

He lay face down with His hands touching one bank and His feet the other.

Without hesitation I joyfully stepped out and walked toward the middle of His back. There I paused to look around.

When I looked down Jesus had disappeared! I was standing on nothing. I looked at the angry waters beneath me and froze. Oh, I dare not move or I would fall!

"Jesus," I cried. "Where did You go? Come save me or I will fall."

Jesus replied, "I did not leave. I'm still here. When you could see Me you didn't hesitate to step out because you knew I was here. But now that you can't see Me you are afraid to continue.

Just remember --

'Faith is being sure of what we hope for and certain of what we do not see.'
Hebrews 11:1

Never forget that, especially when you do not see Me, I am always there.

Now, in the confidence that goes with faith, take another step and continue the journey I lay down before you."

HEALING

James 5:14-16

I have been present at a healing.

A young son of a good friend of ours was scheduled for surgery after a x-ray revealed a large mass forming in the site of a recently reconstructed hip joint. The young man had been thrown from a horse, which had shattered the ball in his hip socket.

The hip was healing nicely, but the discovery of this large mass was disheartening. We were told that the prognosis was not favorable, given the fast growth and size of the mass.

The cry went out.

Prayer warriors were called together and a healing ceremony was scheduled. My husband and I were among those called.

This was in accordance with the instructions found in James 5:14-16:

"Is any one of you sick? He should call the elders of the church to pray over him and anoint him with oil in the name of the Lord. And the prayer offered in faith will make the sick person well; the Lord will raise him up...The prayer of a righteous man is powerful and effective."

Later during surgery, the doctors were amazed. They did not find anything abnormal. The mass they had identified previously simply ceased to exist!

They couldn't explain it, but we knew. We had called on the name of our Lord and claimed His healing for this young man.

Jesus had healed him instantly and completely.

Our God is great.

GOD'S GRACE ROPE

John 6:44

My husband was telling me the other day about a talk he recently heard in which the speaker compared the old fashioned rope ski rope lift that manually pulled the skiers up the hill to a life in Grace.

This type of ski lift works fine, but only if you physically grab on to it. That's also true for a life in Grace. It also takes action on our part. We must reach out and grab on to God's Grace rope.

The practice slopes where I trained for ski team competition while in high school were equipped with rope ski lifts, so I was very familiar with them.

However, I had never heard them compared to a life in Grace. It was intriguing.

Then I began thinking of the dangers we have to watch for when using a rope ski rope because it runs continuously.

One danger is in not being prepared to catch the rope properly. Another is to make sure no loose clothing or equipment can get twisted into the rope.

That actually happened to me once. Somehow my jacket sleeve got twisted around the rope so that when I reached the top I couldn't break free. The rope continued to drag me until my weight tripped the safety and stopped the lift!

There are similar dangers to look for when using God's Grace rope.

We must be prepared to catch God's Grace rope properly. We do this by reading the Word and practicing its truths. Also, we need to be sure our faith is solid with no loose ends. Otherwise our faith may unravel, get twisted up into lies and drag us away from Jesus! Jesus tells us to remember,

"No one can come to Me unless the Father who sent Me draws him..." John 6:44

God uses His Grace Rope to draw us to Jesus.

FEAR NOT

Luke 2:10

I remember the time a few years ago when my boss called my whole department into her office just at closing time and gave us the news that due to the company being sold, we were no longer employed. I didn't know what I would do. Close to tears, I walked out to my car, got in, and slowly let my breath out as I turned the key to start the engine.

Just then, a message came on the Christian station I always listen to. It was an advertisement for employment within my chosen profession! Suddenly I knew that this was God's way of reaching down with encouragement.

It was like He was saying, "See? Fear not, for there are jobs out there for you!"

I felt the comfort of His Presence. My spirit began to lift and my distress turned to joy. For me it was like the time in Luke 2:10 when the angels appeared to the shepherds in the fields saying,

"Fear not, for behold I bring you good tidings of Great Joy!"

God's good tiding to me in this incidence was not in a guarantee of being hired for this particular position. Rather, it was His good tiding in bringing me the hope and assurance that I would find another position.

Like the angels to the shepherds, God said to me, "Fear not." Which for me meant, "I will provide."

And He did.

I applied for that position and was the one chosen to fill it!

Praise God.

THE MIND'S EYE

Philippians 1:3

When we moved from New Mexico to Texas we moved not only to a different state but also into a different climate. We traded dry air and mountain tops for humid air and flat green plains.

It took us a long time to adjust and although that was over thirty years ago, at times I still miss my mountains.

It seemed no matter what happened I could look up and my solid, unmovable range of mountains would always be there. Now that I can't do that, I have to look into my mind's eye to see my mountains.

It isn't quite the same, but I've found that those mountains do stay in my memory and that they are there ready for me anytime I decide to recall them.

When Paul wrote the Philippians to thank them for the gift they had sent him while he was imprisoned in Rome, I think he was experiencing this same type of thing. He missed his friends and family and longed to see them, so he had to look into his mind's eye to see them.

That's why Paul wrote in Philippians 1:3:

"I thank God every time I remember you."

Although Paul was in prison and not free to come and go, he, like me, could recall the stable "mountains" he left behind. He learned to recall his friends and, while it wasn't quite the same, those Paul longed to see stayed close in his memory.

Paul had learned to look into his mind's eye, which allowed him to recall precious friendships whenever he needed.

HIDING

Jeremiah 23:23-24

"I want you to meet a clown named Sparky." Our church administrator told the children as he motioned for my husband (clown name, Sparky) to come forward.

"Now, Sparky may look like a clown," he continued, "but I bet there's someone else hiding under there. What do you think, boys and girls?"

The occasion was our Sunday school Fall Rally. Every class from toddler to senior had gathered for our fall kick off.

As trained Christian clowns my husband and I were part of the program. Our church administrator was using Sparky to bring home an important point he wanted to make.

That point was, even though at times we present ourselves to be someone we're not, we still remain ourselves underneath. No matter how we try to hide, God can always find us.

In fact, God made this same point to Jeremiah:

"'Am I only a God nearby,' declares the Lord, 'and not a God far away? Can anyone hide in secret places so that I cannot see him?' declares the Lord." Jeremiah 23:23-24

To illustrate this point at the Sunday school Fall Rally, our church administrator began wiping off Sparky's face paint until …

"What do you know! Just as I thought! It is our good friend who's been hiding under there all along!"

THE RELATIONSHIP

Hebrews 4:16

Last Halloween was the first Halloween in quite some time that we actually went out "trick or treating" in our neighborhood. I hadn't done that in ages! Yet, there I was, on the street, dressed like a pumpkin – walking the neighborhood with my family and close friends – following our grandchildren, just like we had followed their mother on halloween nights when she was around their ages.

Some houses in the neighborhood went all out with all types of Halloween decorations – from pumpkins and lights to cute goblins and ghosts – all designed to awe and impress every age child.

Some house just had the porch lights on while their occupants simply stood in the doorway handing out treats to the children.

Some houses remained dark and closed – choosing not to participate at all.

Yet the extent of participation never in any way altered the relationship of any house to the neighborhood.

As a human race we tend to worship God in a similar manner.

Some of us go all out – loudly praising and raising our hands to Jesus, praying in tongues and being filled with the Holy Spirit.

Some of us enjoy a more sedate manner of worship with traditional hymns and prayers – being quietly filled by the Holy Spirit.

Some of us tend to limit our worship to a personal experience, praying silently to ourselves – choosing to experience the Holy Spirit privately.

Yet the manner in which we choose to worship does not in any way alter the relationship of ourselves to God. All of us may

"... Then approach the throne of grace with confidence, so that we may receive mercy and find grace to help us in our time of need." Hebrews 4:16

OCTOBER 27

BASEMENTS

Psalm 56:3-4

When I was a child it wasn't until we moved from Alabama to Michigan that I discovered houses could have basements.

The first house in which we lived in Michigan had an old coal-burning furnace that had been converted to gas. This furnace was huge and black with "arms" (heat ducts) snaking out everywhere. It was pretty scary. My mother often referred to it as the "monster." This "monster" lived in a partially enclosed area of the basement located to the left of a steep staircase. The nearest light, a single low wattage bulb, hung overhead on exposed wiring in an open area located right of the staircase base.

How my imagination would run wild every time I had to go down into that basement for any reason! In fact, having to travel down those basement stairs anytime in its constant dark atmosphere to reach the light terrorized me. That was because I always had to step out of the light at the top of the stairs and walk directly down into the unknown darkness where the "monster" lived.

Sometimes I'd sing or talk real loud to make myself brave enough to make the trip. At other times I'd hold my breath, thinking that my not breathing would force fear to freeze in time…(at least for enough time for me to reach the light!) I knew that if I could just reach the light nothing would get me.

There are times all of us let our imaginations run wild. When I do, I usually find that Psalm 56:3-4 helps me bolster my courage and ease my fears:

"When I am afraid I will trust in You. In God whose Word I praise, In God I trust; I will not be afraid."

God promises to be with us and guarantees that His light will break through our deepest and darkest basement fears.

DECEPTION

Mark 13:5

I remember a Halloween party in which my husband went as three different characters: A robot, a devil and an old man. It took planning and split timing, but he pulled his deception off perfectly. We first arrived at the party with him dressed as a robot. Then, after most people had guessed who he was, he slipped out, coming back in dressed as a devil. This time he fooled everyone because no one could guess correctly who he was.

(It couldn't be my husband because he had already arrived and, besides, he was the robot, right?)

After a while he slipped out again and returned dressed as an old man.

It wasn't until someone missed my husband and others became aware that the robot and the devil had both disappeared that the scheme was uncovered.

When Jesus said,

"Watch out that no one deceives you." Mark 13:5

His main purpose was to alert His disciples to the dangers of this type of deception.

My husband's identity switches at the Halloween party may have been all in fun, but it illustrates an important point. It shows us just how easily we can be fooled when we are not paying attention.

Jesus knew Satan would come to us in many forms, sometimes fooling us into believing he is not who he is. Jesus also knew how easily we can be fooled if we are not on guard.

We must watch out that we are not deceived, for the deception Satan brings us leads to death.

NOT REAL

Colossians 2:17

I have never seen any, but I've heard of fireplaces that are constructed with custom-made openings. Instead of fire grates to hold burning logs, TVs with built-in players are installed inside. Then, special videos of a roaring fire, complete with sound effects, are played to simulate the effect of a real fire.

I have been told it's sometimes hard to distinguish the video fire from a real one. Yet, I am sure that if you walked up to it and spread your hands out, you would not feel any warmth.

Its fire is not real.

On Halloween we sometimes like to dress up in costumes and pretend to be something we are not. We think it's fun to try to fool others, yet we know that they know that we are not real.

Paul wrote us a warning about that in his letter to the Colossians. Paul said,

"These are a shadow of the things that were to come; (our) reality, however is found in Christ." Colossians 2:17

Some Christians are like that.

They look so good and sound so wonderful that they often fool many into thinking that they are real. But when you get close to them, long enough, you will discover that they have no warmth.

Their inner fire is not real.

True reality is only found in Christ.

HALLOWEEN

Isaiah 55:8

Some years ago my husband and I decided we would throw a Halloween Party for our co-workers and friends. We really went all out decorating the house, turning it and the garage into a "hall of horrors".

Our oldest child, who was only five years old at the time, delighted in watching the transformation. She even helped us as we turned the family room into a haven for paper spiders and string webs with sheet ghost in the corners and our garage into a spooky "tunnel" fashioned out of sheets, with all sorts of twists and turns, pop-up surprises and recordings of strange sounds.

Finally we were done and as we stepped back to survey the finished product, she tugged at my hand to get my attention. She looked up at me and asked, "Can we leave it up until Christmas?" "Oh, no." I replied. "We can't. Besides it might scare Santa away."

As I turned to walk away, feeling pleased that I had satisfied a five-year-old's inquisitive mind, I almost missed her response.

"No, it'll scare Santa Clause so he'll drop <u>all</u> the toys and leave them for me and Cheri!"

You know, when God asks us a simple question we usually try to come up with an answer we think will satisfy Him.

Too often we are so pleased with our own inspiration we almost miss His response. Then His response to our answer – like our oldest daughter's was to mine – surprises us.

However it really shouldn't.

"'For My thoughts are not your thoughts, neither are your ways My ways,'
declares the Lord." Isaiah 55:8

OCTOBER 31

DO SOMETHING

Obadiah 13:5

Every day, if you just look, you can find something to do for someone who needs you. Now, there is always those for whom you are responsible; from your child needing a kiss to make it better after scraping his/her knee to your boss counting on you to meet that project deadline.

I'm not talking about that type of need.

There's a bumper sticker that says, "Practice random acts of kindness." That's the type of need I mean.

It's just another way of saying,

"...As you have done, it will be done to you. Your deeds will return upon your head." Obadiah 13:5

So, find someone and find something to do for him or her, no matter how small and for which there is no pay. What's so wonderful about that is that as we do for them they, in turn, will do for us.

Remember that none of us live in this world on our own. Just think of the countless people in the background waiting to do something for you - from the young man who stocked the grocery shelves last night with the very item for which you are reaching to the person who thought of you today while recalling a cherished moment.

When we do something for another we are, in essence, letting them know what we want from them.

Do something that helps them glorify God so that they will, in turn, do something that helps us glorify God.

THERE GOES THE NEIGHBORHOOD

Matthew 12:43-45

As my husband and I rounded the corner to our new neighborhood the marquee in front of a nearby church caught my eye. We had just recently purchased our present home and were busy moving in. We were so excited and were looking forward to getting settled.

Our new neighborhood was just blocks away from one of the larger churches in our area. The marquee that weekend was advertising the subject of the upcoming Sunday message. There, big and bold as life, was the message: "There goes the Neighborhood"

I suspect that's similar to what Jesus was saying to the teachers of the law and the Pharisees in Matthew 12:43-45:

"When an evil spirit comes out of a man, it goes through arid places seeking rest and does not find it. Then it says, 'I will return to the house I left.' When it arrives it finds the house unoccupied, swept clean and put in order. Then it goes and takes with it seven other spirits more wicked than itself, and they go in and live there. And the final condition of that man is worse than the first."

In other words, "There goes the Neighborhood!"

Jesus was referring to our bodies as homes to our souls. He urgently warns us not only to keep our soul's homes clean but also to keep our souls filled with His Word and surround ourselves with others who do also. When we do that, there will be no room for anything ungodly to stay in our lives. Together our souls and our neighbor's souls create good neighborhoods.

It's amusing that the message "There goes the Neighborhood" concurred precisely with our move into the neighborhood. My husband and I looked at each other and, because we are such good friends with that church's pastor, we couldn't wait to tease him about that particular message that particular weekend.

OCTOBER 2

YO-YO

Proverbs 16:9

My husband is a yo-yo master.

He can really make a yo-yo sing, sleep, walk or anything you have ever heard of a yo-yo doing. So it was natural for him to use it in one of his sermons to illustrate the ups and downs of life.

As he worked the yo-yo, he applied his skills and let the yo-yo point out what happens. He visually showed us what happens when our lives run smoothly; when our lives get "stuck" and seem to be on hold; when we run our lives on a fast track and even what happens when our lives get all tangled up or spin out of control.

Then he turned our attention to the string itself. He pointed out that he was the one manipulating the string and perhaps that wasn't such a good thing. The best thing to do is to transfer our lives' string controls to God because:

"In his heart a man plans his course, but the Lord determines his steps."
Proverbs 16:9

God is the One who ultimately decides when our lives need to go up or down, sleep or even when we need to carry His message around the world.

Of course, He will never take control of our lives' strings unless we ask Him to, because He won't cross the line of our free will. But if we transfer our lives' string controls to Him, He will accept control and help us to align our will with His.

That's so comforting to me because it lets me know that when my life's strings become tangled I can let go and trust God to untangle them.

God is The Master Yo-Yo Master.

FILTERS

John 14:6

Thomas Kinkade, the painter of light, has explored extensively the purpose of filters in our lives. He said:

"Properly maintained filters will actually bring you closer in touch with the deepest form of reality."

As I read that I remembered what Chuck Swindoll recently said about the perfection of God. He said that God, being Perfect, cannot look on anything less than perfection.

Because of our sin we are therefore permanently separated from Him.

However, God couldn't bear that to happen, so He sent us His Son to be a filter for Him. Now Jesus stands between God and us.

Jesus is the properly maintained filter that screens out our imperfections and sins so that God, through His Son, Jesus, can look upon us and have fellowship with us.

No one can come to the Father except through Jesus, the Son.

Jesus Himself told Thomas this in John 14:6:

"I am the way and the truth and the life. No one comes to the Father except through Me."

Jesus is our filter sent to us by God, not to force us into perfection, but to screen out our imperfections.

So, it is only when we come through Jesus that God can truly see us.

Jesus is the truly the Filter that saves.

THIRST MECHANISMS

John 4:13-14

An article I recently read contained several interesting facts concerning thirst. It stated that it is likely that about ½ of the world's population are chronically dehydrated without knowing it. Dehydration is so common that at least half of those chronically dehydrated will often mistake their thirst for hunger.

That's because overtime their thirst mechanisms become that weak.

Those statistics could just as well apply to our spirituality.

Nearly ½ of the Christian population are likely to be spiritually dehydrated without knowing it. And about ½ of those will mistake their spiritual thirst for self or secular unfulfillment. They may try to satisfy their thirst by accumulating material things.

That's because overtime their spiritual thirst mechanisms become that weak.

Jesus may have had something like this in mind when He stopped at Jacob's Well in Sychar. You remember...

When a Samaritan woman came to draw water Jesus told her

"Everyone who drinks this water will be thirsty again, but whoever drinks the water I give him will never thirst. Indeed the water I give him will become in him a spring of water welling up to eternal life." John 4:13-14

In other words, only the water Jesus gives us can satisfy our thirst mechanisms.

GOD'S CHOICE

Romans 10:13

God is never changing. He chose us and His choice has not changed. In fact the ark Noah built emphasizes that. Some people believe that because of Adam's sin God wanted a fresh start so He decided to "start over" by using the flood. But God did not use the flood to "start over".

If that had been the case there would have been no need for an ark!

Noah was a descendent of Adam so mankind, through the creation of Adam, is still God's choice. So, although we sin and fall short God spared all of us – first through the ark, then through another:

"For everyone who calls on the Name of the Lord will be saved." Romans 10:13

Sometimes looking at a diagram helps us to understand how it all fits:

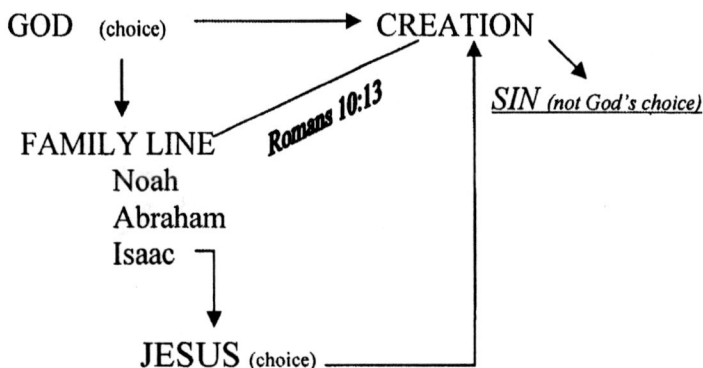

GOD (choice) ⟶ CREATION

FAMILY LINE ⟍ *Romans 10:13* ⟍ SIN (not God's choice)

Noah
Abraham
Isaac

JESUS (choice)

God's choice is for His crowning creation – mankind. But mankind chose sin. God then bypassed that sin through His Son, using the family line of His creation to do so. Now mankind can choose either to sin or to call on the Name of the Lord.

But God's choice remains the same and will never change.

OCTOBER 6

A TOUCH

John 14:30

When I saw my grandson, David, being placed in the arms of my daughter for the first time my heart exploded. There was just something about witnessing the first time she touched him.

It was a touch I knew well:

It drew me back to the first time she had been placed in my arms and I touched her. Now the part of me that lives in her will also live in him and, no matter where the future takes us, we are connected. The bond of mother and child is magnified and enhanced with the addition of each new generation.

I wonder if that's how God must have felt when He saw His own precious Son being placed in the arms of Mary for the first time. Jesus, being 100% God, was no stranger to God. How could God not know Himself?

However, this was the first time that God the Father witnessed God the Son in infant form cradled in His mother's arms.

There must have been something miraculous and breath taking about the first time Mary touched Jesus. Mary was not only cradling her son she was the one chosen to touch God while God watched.

It was a touch God knew well.

It was no accident that God came to us, taking the form of an infant. The bond of God to man was now complete, and through Jesus, God would magnify and enhance this bond daily with the addition of each new generation.

Later Jesus was to remind us of that when He said,

"...I am in my Father and you are in Me and I am in you." John 14:30.

ANALOGIES

II Samuel 12:4

The use of analogies to make a point has existed since the beginning of time. We all use them, sometimes in fun and sometimes to make a more serious point.

I remember one afternoon as my husband and I was traveling to some destination, I spotted a battered old tennis shoe on the side of the road. Drawing his attention to it, I made the remark, "It's all by itself, poor thing. Bless it's little 'sole'!"

Entering into the spirit of the game, my husband observed, "I think it's a 'heel'! It probably ran away from its 'mate'."

(You know I just had to come to its rescue!) "It had to." I countered "Can't you see the 'lacing' it took? See? Its little 'tongue' is hanging out." Back and forth we bantered until we had exhausted all analogous terms between a human and a shoe that came to mind. That analogy was in fun.

Now when the Lord sent Nathan to rebuke King David, Nathan used a little ewe lamb as an analogous term for Bathsheba. Nathan told David a story about this little ewe lamb as being the only and beloved' possession of a poor man.

"Now a traveler came to the rich man, but the rich man refrained from taking one of his own sheep or cattle to prepare a meal for the traveler who had come to him. Instead, he took the ewe lamb that belonged to the poor man and prepared it for the one who had come to him." II Samuel 12:4

When David expressed horror at the rich man's actions Nathan turned to him and said, "You are the man!" Realizing this, David then acknowledged, "I have sinned against the Lord." That analogy made a more serious point.

FINISH THE RACE

II Timothy 4:7-8

I remember the day our youngest daughter came running in the house waving a red ribbon and bursting with pride. She had won third place in one of her elementary school field day races! We were so proud of her. We naturally wanted her to share every last detail of her accomplishment so we could rejoice with her. As we did, her dad asked her, "How many were in the race?"

With great enthusiasm she replied, "There were three of us. We all got a ribbon!"

Now there were several ways we could have responded here.

Yet, at the time her attitude conveyed pure excellence. Her self-confidence confirmed that in spite of the head count she had run her best and in the process had won her place with honor and dignity! Whether we come in first or third God always expects us to finish the race. He wants us to do our best and, like our daughter, run our race with honor and dignity. Then we can, like Paul, say,

"I have finished the race. I have kept the faith. Now there is in store for me the crown of righteousness which the Lord, the Righteous Judge, will award to me on that day – and not only to me but also to all who have longed for His appearing." II Timothy 4:7 – 8

Our daughter finished her race that day and, along with those in it, was rewarded. She kept the faith and did her best. For her efforts she was awarded a ribbon of excellence.

Jesus never expects us to always come in first. He just expects us to finish our races to the best of our abilities.

Everyone who finishes his or her race and keeps the faith will be rewarded.

AN INTIMATE RELATIONSHIP

John 10:14

Our dinner conversation centered on basketball. We became quite animated as we discussed the attributes of several well-known players.

I became amused as it dawned on me that we were seriously analyzing the accomplishments of these famous players like we had an intimate relationship with them. We were acting as if they were such close personal friends that we knew them better than they knew themselves!

Wouldn't it be wonderful if we centered on God with the same enthusiasm as we do famous sports figures? Or if we studied the Bible with the same concentration as we do the player stats and the finer points of the games?

Think how refreshing it would be for us to seriously spend hours analyzing the attributes of Jesus and His accomplishments like we have an intimate relationship with Him.

Chances are if we do, we will.

The biggest difference in discussing famous sports figures and God is that those players do not and probably never will know us personally. However, God knows each one of us personally and better than we know ourselves.

Never has any famous sports figure claimed, "I am the good player; I know my fans and my fans know me."

But Jesus says,

"I am the good Shepherd; I know my sheep and my sheep know me." John 10:14

ILLUSION OF PEACE AND BEAUTY

Psalm 56:3-4

The other day I was watching a sci-fi movie in which four people were traveling through some glorious garden in order to reach their ultimate center of inner-peace and beauty. However, as they traveled one of the four became aware of unrest and ugliness behind the beauty and kept telling the others that something did not seem quite right. Yet the others pleaded with him to only look at the beauty and ignore his feeling.

But they failed to convince him. As the feeling of unrest became stronger, the vines at the edge of the path began wrapping themselves around his legs and began pulling him toward a horrible monster that suddenly broke through a hole in the serene sky. As all this was happening the others kept screaming for him to focus on the beauty and not to look at the monster. The scene implied that was the only way to make the monster go away and save himself.

How like Satan that monster is for all of us!

Satan wants us to close our eyes to the ugliness of his true self and to only focus on the illusion of peace and beauty he feeds us. That way he can keep us content and serene in his death grip. We can't see his vines wrapped around our arms, feet and neck pulling us toward eternal damnation as long as we choose to focus on the illusion and ignore the realities.

What does God say?

"Don't be deceived, my dear brothers. Every good and perfect gift is from above, coming down from the Father of the heavenly lights, who does not change like the shifting shadows."

We, as Christians in the world, are the ones who sense the unrest and ugliness behind Satan's lies and illusions. We must stand firm and help others become aware of Satan's deceits and guide them to Jesus. Only Jesus can break us free from Satan's illusion of peace and beauty.

THE POOR FEEDING THE POOR
I Kings 17:9-12

The Lord was speaking to Elijah, the Tishbite, during the drought:

"'Go at once to Zarephath of Sidon and stay there. I have commanded a widow in that place to supply you with food.' So he went to Zarephath. When he came to the town gate, a widow was there gathering sticks. He called to her and asked, 'Would you bring a little water in a jar so I may have a drink?' As she was going to get it, he called, 'And bring me, please, a piece of bread.' 'As surely as the Lord your God lives,' she replied, 'I don't have any bread - only a handful of flour in a jar and a little oil in a jug. I am gathering a few sticks to take home and make a meal for myself and my son, that we may eat it - and die.'" I Kings 17:9-12

It is interesting to note that the widow God sent Elijah to was extremely poor. In fact, she was gathering wood to cook the last of her food for herself and her son, knowing that after that there was no more. They would starve.

Then here comes Elijah wanting her to split that last meal three ways!

God was using the poor to feed the poor. And because this poor widow was obedient and shared her meager fare with Elijah, God blessed her so that her food supply never depleted.

Think about it.

Had God sent Elijah to a well-to-do household that could have easily spared Elijah all the food he could have eaten, this blessing would have been lost. Those with an overabundance already would never have noticed more added. But to give a starving widow who had nothing an endless food supply…

Only a poor widow without means to feed herself or her son would realize this great blessing of a food supply that could never be depleted.

THE WORD OF GOD

Luke 8:11

Jesus often used the planting of a seed in His parable. And to make sure we grasped the significance of this He told us why. Jesus said,

"This is the meaning of the parable. The seed is the Word of God." Luke 8:11

The seed symbolizes the Word of God. Jesus told us that we are suppose to go out and sow the Word of God so that others can hear, believe and grow in the Truth.

There's one important item to be noted here: Jesus made us responsible for sowing the Word of God among our fellowmen. We are to see to it that others hear.

However, He never made us responsible for their believing or growing in the Truth. That responsibility belongs to Jesus.

Trouble is, we tend to forget that. We have this mind-set that what we have planted we must water, tend and cause to grow. In other words, we tend to self-appoint ourselves responsible for the entire harvest. When we do, we become obsessed with the complications of reaping results instead of simply sowing seeds.

There's a quote I once heard that fits perfectly here:

"We plant a seed and then kill it by continually digging it back up to see if it has grown."

We need to concentrate on sowing the Word of God and leave the growth and harvest to Jesus. We need to plant, nurture and cultivate The Seed into our fellowmen's hearts.

Then we need to step out of the way and let Jesus bring home the harvest.

PLAIN AND SIMPLE

John 16:5-7

Once I went to pick up David and Emily from school, David came running up to me shouting, "Hey, MiMi, I got this for you!"

He had found a stone on the playground shaped like a heart and he couldn't wait to give it to me.

Since that day I always carry it with me. That plain and simple little stone shaped like a heart reminds me of the plain and simple treasure I have in my grandchild's heart.

The way God extended His love to us is that He sent His Son, His only Son Jesus, to us. God personally placed His Son on the earth to live among us. You see, in His heart God loved us so much He wanted to give us the plain and simple Truth found in His Son.

Then, when Jesus knew the time was short for Him to stay with us, He couldn't wait to give us, His disciples, another gift from His heart, the Holy Spirit.

Can't you just see Him?

Jesus, running up to His disciples shouting, "Hey, Disciples, I got this for you!"

Jesus knew He had to go, but He did not want to leave His followers comfortless. So He said,

"But I tell you the truth: It is for your own good that I am going away. Unless I go away the Counselor [Holy Spirit] will not come to you; but if I go, I will send Him to you." John 16:5-7

The plain and simple words of Jesus remind us of the plain and simple treasure we are in His heart.

OCTOBER 14

THE ONE WHO IS IN YOU
I John 4:4

"You, dear children, are from God and have overcome [the spirit of the antichrist] because the One who is in you is greater than the one who is in the world." 1 John 4:4

The One who is in you.

Paul is talking about the Holy Spirit. Jesus sent the Holy Spirit to us, upon His ascension, to live in our hearts. Jesus promised not to leave us alone and He didn't. He sent the third member of the Holy Trinity to remain here on earth with us.

The main thing we need to remember is that Jesus will only go where He is invited.

First we must believe in the One True God. Then we must open our hearts to His Son, Jesus Christ.

There's one other thing I might add: We will always have a choice. I mean, we will never find Jesus standing outside our hearts' doors, trying to pick the locks to get in!

No, Jesus is a gentleman. He won't force His way into our hearts. He may stand there and knock, or He may simply wait. But He will never enter until we open the doors.

However, once we have opened the doors, Jesus will send the Holy Spirit to come live within us. That's because, once we have invited Jesus in, He will help us live our life through the Holy Spirit.

It's the Holy Spirit who will guide us in all circumstances.

Yet, once again, although the Holy Spirit is willing to do this for us, we still have a choice. We will always have the option of accepting His help at any point or to continue doing things in our own ways.

Regardless of our decision, the Holy Spirit will quietly stand by us, waiting to be the One who is in you.

NO SENSE

Acts 7:8-10

The sermon this past Sunday focused on Stephen, one of the seven, full of the Spirit and wisdom, chosen to look after the needs of the people by the Apostles.

"Now Stephen, a man full of God's Grace and power, did great wonders and miraculous signs among the people. Opposition arose, however, from members of the Synagogue of the Freedman (as it was called) – Jews of Cyrene and Alexandria as well as the Provinces of Cilicia and Asia. These men began to argue with Stephen." Acts 7:8-10

Our pastor then described Stephen as one of 'those who believed in Jesus and didn't have the sense to keep it to himself'!

He pointed out that there have also been many before and since Stephen who didn't have the sense to keep Jesus to themselves.

Instantly I thought of someone close to my husband and I who does not share our beliefs and constantly argues with us trying to discredit our God. Not only have our e-mail messages, which are designed to encourage and uplift fellow believers, been rejected, but any light, whimsical or humorous joke that has any moral message to it, that we pass on, has been taken as a personal attack by this individual.

Yet, we keep praying for this individual, resisting the urge to do as we have been instructed. That is: To keep Jesus out of our relationship.

I guess it's because, like Stephen (and so many who came before and after him), we have no sense either.

It's because we believe in Jesus and don't have the sense to keep it to ourselves!

OCTOBER 16

WHO TRAPPED WHO?

Matthew 22:15, 17-21

"Then the Pharisees went out and laid plans to trap [Jesus] in His words... 'Tell us, then, what is your opinion? Is it right to pay taxes to Caesar or not?' But Jesus, knowing their evil intent, said, 'You hypocrites, why are you trying to trap me? Show me the coin used for paying the tax.' They brought Him a denarius and He asked them, 'Whose portrait is this?' 'Caesar's,' they replied. Then He said, 'Give to Caesar what is Caesar's and to God what is God's.'" Matthew 22:15, 17-21

What exactly was Jesus saying here?

That money only belonged to Caesar and not to God? I don't think so.

Jesus asked to see *"the coin used for paying the tax"* not all coins. As a result the Pharisees' well thought out plan backfired because Jesus' answer actually satisfied both sides of the question: It is right to give to Caesar what belongs to Caesar and it is right to give to God what belongs to God.

On the surface Jesus' answer seemed innocent enough. However there was deeper truth hidden within His answer.

Jesus clearly stated that it is right to give to Caesar what belongs to Caesar and it is right to give what belongs to God to God. Therefore, by distinguishing between them, what Jesus was actually doing was pointing out the fact that Caesar was not God as he claimed to be!

The Pharisees completely missed this important historic distinction until it was too late to object.

So, now you tell me.

Who trapped who?

TAKE, EAT

Genesis 3:6 & Mark 14:22

There are so many interesting parallels in the Bible and recently I learned of one more that was pertinent to the fall and salvation of man.

The fall of man took place in the Garden of Eden at the beginning of time, as we know it.

God had told Adam and Eve not to eat the fruit of the tree in the middle of the garden or they would surely die. However, the serpent, a crafty one, caused Eve to doubt God's word.

So

"When the woman saw that the fruit of the tree was good for food and pleasing to the eye, and also desirable for gaining wisdom, she took some and ate it. She also gave some to her husband who was with her, and he ate it." Genesis 3:6

The salvation of man took place in the Upper Room while Jesus and His Disciples were celebrating Passover.

"While they were still eating, Jesus took bread, gave thanks and broke it, and gave it to his disciples, saying, 'Take it, this is My body.'" Mark 14:22

Eve said, "Take, eat."

Thus sin entered the world creating a division between God and man.

Jesus said "Take, eat."

Thus salvation entered the world erasing the division between God and man.

OVER THE RAINBOW

John 4:13-14

The movie, Wizard of OZ, begins with Dorothy standing in a field singing "Over the Rainbow". She pours her heart out to Toto, her dog. She knows she should be satisfied with what she has. She has everything she could need – a warm home, friends and family, people who love her.

But she can't help but feel there's something missing. It's right there – just out of sight – somewhere… "Over the Rainbow"!

Recently our pastor used Dorothy to make a point.

We are all seeking for something we feel is missing. It's our human nature to constantly seek and to continually accumulate more and more – whether it is possessions or knowledge. Yet the more we get the less satisfied we are.

Like Dorothy, we can't help but feel there's something missing.

That's because what's missing can't be filled with worldly things. "Stuff" can never satisfy us.

Jesus knew this. He made this point at a well with a Samaritan woman. He told her:

"Everyone who drinks this water will be thirsty again, but whoever drinks the water I give him will never thirst. Indeed, the water I give him will become in him a spring of water welling up to eternal life." John 4:13-14

When we allow that which is missing in our lives to be filled by Jesus, we will never have to look "Over the Rainbow" again.

JESUS LOVES YOU

Ephesians 2:8-9

"Jesus will not love you for what you can or can not do
Jesus will love you just because you are you.
So just when you might question your worth,
Remember, Jesus loves you more than anything else on earth!"

jhh 1995

There's absolutely nothing in this world that you can do to make Jesus stop loving you.

Have you really thought of what that means?

It means, no matter what you do, Jesus will still love you. That doesn't mean He will approve of or even like what you do. He may not approve at all of your actions or your lack of action. But He will still love you. He knows that it is only in loving Him back, that we become willing to act and behave in a way pleasing to Him.

Love, as every parent learns, has very little to do with how our children behave. We don't just love our children when they are living up to our personal or self-conceived standards nor should we threaten to take away any type of support from them when they misbehave. If children were led to think our love was only reserved for good behavior, they would never learn how to give or receive unconditional love. It is in allowing our children the grace to be loved and to love us back, regardless of their behavior, which motivates them to willingly act and behave in a way pleasing to their parents.

Love can't be forced or earned. In just the same way, salvation can't be forced or earned.

It's a gift of Grace from God to all who believes in and loves Him.

"For it is by faith – and this not from yourselves, it is the gift of God – not by works so that no one can boast." Ephesians 2:8-9

WRITE

Revelation 3:12

"Write injuries in dust, benefits in marble." I came across that saying the other day while I was thumbing through a collection of bits and pieces of wisdom and sayings I have accumulated over the years. It caught my attention so I pulled it out to study.

- Write injuries in dust. When I get hurt by others I, more often than not, nurse those injuries, as if seeking some sort of restitution. As I do, I focus on perceived injuries, which etch bitterness deep in my heart. When that happens, my injuries might as well be written in marble and stay with me forever!

- Write benefits in marble. When things don't go just right I, more often than not, forget to look for the blessings in them. As I do, I fail to focus on how those situations could benefit my neighbor or myself. When that happens, my benefits might as well be written in dust and be blown away!

Jesus is recorded in Scripture only twice to have written anything. The first time was in the temple courts when the teachers of the Law brought in a woman caught in adultery. They were trying to trap Jesus, so they asked Him what they should do. Before He answered, however, Jesus bent down and wrote in the dust with His finger... Jesus wrote her injuries in dust. Then, in the Book of Revelation Jesus promises:

"Him who overcomes, I will make a pillar in the temple of My God. Never again will he leave it. I will write on him the Name of My God, the New Jerusalem, which is coming down out of heaven from My God; and I will also write on him My new Name." Revelations 3:12

Jesus will write our benefits in marble.

FEVER DREAM

Matthew 1:20

Ever since I can remember I've had the same dream whenever I have a high fever. It only takes a moment, but it is always exactly the same and can occur multiple times as long as I am feverish.

Although my fever dream always means I'm sick, most dreams we have do not have meanings. Usually I can't remember what I was dreaming shortly after I wake and move around some. It might be that most dreams are from the imaginative part of our brain trying to entertain us while we sleep. I recall from my psychology class in college that while our bodies need periods of rest our brains never sleep.

So it is possible that God could still use our dreams today as a way to communicate with us. After all, the Holy Bible is full of instances of God working in the lives of His people through their dreams.

One of the most memorial times God used a dream to work in the life of another was when He spoke to Joseph concerning Mary, his betrothed, who was found to be with child before they came together.

Joseph, being a just man had decided to quietly divorce Mary and send her away.

"But after he had considered this, an angel of the Lord appeared to him in a dream and said, 'Joseph, son of David, do not be afraid to take Mary home as your wife, because what is conceived in her is from the Holy Spirit.'" Matthew 1:20

Although the coming of Jesus was first announced to Joseph in a dream, the reality of our salvation and life everlasting is definitely not a dream.

ALIGNMENT

Luke 11:1-4

When our vehicles are driven over deep ruts in the road or perhaps hit one of those potholes so prominent on many streets our tires suffer. Eventually this abuse throws the tires out of alignment, which means that the vehicle wheels are no longer traveling in the exact same direction. Even a slight deviation in direction can cause the entire vehicle to shudder and shake.

In order to regain a smooth ride the tires need to be brought back into alignment.

When our souls slip into the deep ruts in our lives that sin creates or perhaps encounter one of those temptations designed to throw us off course our souls suffer. Eventually this continual moral eroding throws our souls out of alignment, which means that our souls have moved away from the presence of God. Even a slight deviation from God's presence can cause our souls to lose hope.

In order to regain a smooth connection our souls need to be brought back into alignment.

"One day Jesus was praying in a certain place. When He finished one of His disciples said to Him, 'Lord teach us to pray just as John taught his disciples." Luke 11:1

Jesus knew that prayer brings our souls back into alignment with God.

"He said to them, 'When you pray, say: "Father, hallowed be Your name, Your kingdom come. Give us each day our daily bread. Forgive us our sins, for we also forgive everyone who sins against us. And lead us not into temptation.'" Luke 11:2-4

IT'S A GOOD DAY

Psalm 118:24

David stopped a moment, then twirled around with the look of pure joy on his face. He smiled at me and with breathless delight announced,

"It's a good day!"

It was David's birthday weekend. We were watching him play and enjoy his gifts while visiting with each other. I was sitting on the floor while David was running and jumping in my arms.

It was one of those perfect moments everyone experiences occasionally.

David was right. It was a good day.

There's another David long ago, who experienced this same breathtaking delight in a similar perfect moment and announced,

"This is the day that the Lord has made. Let us rejoice and be glad in it!"
Psalm 118:24

Psalm 118 is a hymn of thanksgiving. In it the Psalmist is giving thanks to God for His awesome gift of deliverance. The hymn continues to praise God and bless His name while declaring with delight the marvels God is doing among His people.

I can almost see David of long ago, like my grandson, David, stop a moment, then twirl around with the look of pure joy on his face.

As he tells us to rejoice and be glad, I can just imagine him smiling up at God and announcing,

"It's a good day!"

"CHY-MI-TEA"

Mark 6:12-13

One Thanksgiving Chyann and I created a special type of tea we call "Chy-Mi-Tea". Actually, the only difference between regular iced tea and "Chy-Mi-Tea" is Chyann. She helped her MiMi make it.

Hence the name, "Chy-Mi-Tea".

However, everyone agreed it was Chyann's four year old touch that made our "Chy-Mi-Tea" the highlight of the meal.

Once, long ago, a Jewish carpenter named Jesus along with his disciples created a special type of worship that many called "The Way". Actually, the only difference between regular Jewish worship and "The Way" is Jesus. For even Jesus admitted He came to fulfill the Jewish law, not to change it. Jesus is the Christ, the one and only begotten Son of the true God.

Therefore He is the only way to the Father. Hence the name, "The Way" or, as we refer to it today, Christianity.

It was Jesus who appointed the twelve who would carry His message out into the world. He commissioned them to preach, anoint and heal anyone who would come to them in His name.

Therefore, as the twelve spread the Good News,

"They went out and preached that people should repent. They drove out many demons and anointed many sick people with oil and healed them."
Mark 6:12-13

Everyone the twelve touched came to know Jesus as the Highlight of their lives.

SUNSHINE

Hebrews 13:5

Several years ago, my husband and I were flying to North Carolina to spend Thanksgiving with my sister and her husband. The weather was on the verge of storms all the way, especially around Atlanta, Georgia. In fact, our flight was delayed due to heavy rains.

Once we were allowed to take off, our ascent was very jerky and bumpy. The winds and the sheets of rain really pounded at our plane. I'm not real fond of flying and this didn't help my confidence much. My husband and I didn't say anything but we looked at each other and held hands.

All the passengers were as silent.

All of a sudden we broke through the layer of clouds surrounding our plane. The sun was shining. The sky was joyously blue and so peacefully calm. A perfect day.

Then I looked down toward earth and, in a break in the clouds, I could see the dark linings, the flashes of lightning, and the haze of distant and heavy rains. I looked back up at the sun shining so bright.

Suddenly I knew!

The sun is shining whether it is raining or not. It never stops. It never disappears. It's still there. Just like Jesus is always there even when it is raining in our lives.

In Hebrews 13:5

"...God has said, 'Never will I leave you; never will I forsake you."

Like the sun, God is constant in His light. But sometimes until we break through the dark clouds of our pain and troubles we can fail to see His light or feel His calming presence.

WATCHING

Matthew 26:38

This week we start celebrating the first week of Advent. It is during this week we begin the "watch", looking for signs that Jesus Christ is coming.

In doing so, we need to be aware that this type of watching is not passive but action.

This type of watching does not suggest that we sit back and wait, but that we need to actively seek the Christ Child. This type of watching suggests that we need to take some type of action to begin to prepare our hearts, minds and souls to be ready for His coming. It signals the beginning of all the flurry of Christmas and its activities, songs, and excitement. The excitement Jesus always brings us.

Then we notice it.

We are not alone. Jesus is not just waiting for us to seek Him.

He loves us so much that He is right here beside us, watching with us!

As Jesus said in Matthew 26:38 to His disciples, He still says to us who are His disciples today:

"Keep watch with me."

Like the wise men of old, we today need to keep actively seeking Him.

Let us remember that as we light this first candle – the candle of Watching – it is as if its light is our Star of Bethlehem, guiding us to actively seek the One born to give us eternal life.

So actively seek Jesus to discover where the candle of Watching is leading you.

GO AHEAD, MAKE MY DAY!

Isaiah 53:2-3

If Jesus were to appear today would we recognize Him?

Would He look as we picture Him, or would we have to admit He might not be exactly what we had in mind? Could it be that we would prefer to find the spectacular in our God, not mildness?

Maybe what we really want is a "Dirty Harry" type of Messiah – One who will rescue us – One who will stand between us and evil – One who will look our temptations square in the eye and declare,

"Go ahead, make my day!"

But is that really who Jesus is?

"He [Jesus] grew up before us like a tender shoot and like a root out of dry ground. He had no beauty or majesty to attract us to Him, nothing in His appearance that we should desire Him. He was despised and rejected by men, a Man of sorrows, and familiar with suffering. Like one from whom men hide their faces He was despised, and we esteemed Him not." Isaiah 53:2-3

This week as we light the Candle of Watching, the first candle of Advent, remember for whom we are watching.

Memorize His nature so that when He comes we will recognize Him.

Then when we see Him we will run to Him and entreat Him to please

"Go ahead, make my day!"

OCTOBER 28

ON WATCH

Matthew 24:42

A few weeks before Christmas a dear friend of ours told us he thought he had seen a mutual friend of ours in church that Sunday. He was referring to a friend who lives out of town but comes back occasionally unannounced. So, we were not surprised. What surprised us was that my husband and I were the Prayer Partners that Sunday, so we were very visible to everyone at the close of that service.

Since we hadn't seen him, our friend would have had to leave knowing we were there. We were really puzzled.

Had our dear friend seen someone who resembled our mutual friend or had he really been there?

I thought that maybe we had missed him somehow.

"Therefore keep watch because you do not know on what day your Lord will come"

from Matthew 24:42 popped into my mind. We had not looked for our friend, so maybe that's why we hadn't seen him.

We do that to Jesus. We go through our daily routines wondering where Jesus is, yet we forget to look for Him! When that happens Jesus could walk right pass us without us even noticing.

This first week of advent we light the Candle of Watching. We begin our watch for the birth of the Savior who came to save all mankind. When we light this candle let us do so in remembrance to be constantly on watch for our Lord.

It's only when we keep watch that we will see our Lord when He comes.

START WATCHING

Luke 2:19

When I brought our youngest daughter home from the hospital, I could hardly believe she was real. I marveled over how perfect she was, and I never grew weary of watching her.

Sometimes while she slept I'd slip in to reassure myself that she was still real. As I'd stand by her bassinet watching her tiny chest rise and fall, I'd constantly study her lips, her eyes, and her tiny fingers as they curled around mine. She was so perfect.

I just couldn't keep my eyes off her!

It occurred to me that if I was so consumed with my newborn, how much more Mary would have been with hers. Because not only was she watching her newborn son she was actually watching God.

Also, Mary had the unique experience of being able to watch those who came to watch Jesus with her.

Luke 2:19 tells us:

"...Mary treasured up all these things and pondered them in her heart."

As we light the candle of watching this first week of Advent, we join those who came to watch with Mary.

Thus, we begin anew our watch for the One who came to save us.

Get ready.

Start watching.

Mary's newborn Son, Jesus, is coming.

READY OR NOT, HERE I COME!

Luke 12:40

Do you remember playing hide and seek when you were a child?

The one who is "it" hides his or her eyes and counts. When the predetermined count is complete he or she loudly announces,

"Ready or not, here I come!"

Jesus spent much time with His disciples telling them of events that would take place. He told them He had to go but would come back again when God's predetermined count was complete.

Jesus wanted to be sure all His followers everywhere would be ready for the time the count would be complete.

As we light the first candle of Advent, the candle of watching, remember that no one, not even Jesus, knew when God's predetermined count would be complete, but Jesus gave us signs to watch for so we'd be ready.

Jesus emphasized over and over the need for His disciples to watch for Him and to be ready.

"You also must be ready, because the Son of Man will come at an hour when you do not expect Him." Luke 12:40

In other words, Jesus is "it" and He is counting from His Holy Place. When the predetermined count is complete Jesus will loudly announce,

"Ready or not, here I come!"

KEEPING WATCH

I John 5:8

While I was keeping watch for my granddaughter, Emily Frances, to be born, I began praying for her birth to be easy. While doing so, I marveled over God creating her and bringing her forth through the water and blood of her mother, our daughter.

The miracle of birth is awesome.

I kept watch and prayed for God to hold both mother and child safe.

This week we begin keeping watch for another.

It is a very special One, God's own Son, whom God brought forth through the water and blood of His mother, Mary.

In fact, John testifies to this in I John 4:8:

"This is the One who came by water and blood – Jesus Christ. He did not come by water only, but by water and blood."

But it didn't end there.

Jesus went one step further. He came to us through the water and blood of His mother, Mary. Then He turned around and saved us all through His own water and blood on the Cross!

As we light the candle of watching to begin this Advent Season, we do so to symbolize our keeping watch for the birth of our Lord and Savior, Jesus Christ.

Let us also realize that this candle also represents the birth of our own new life and salvation through Him for whom we are waiting.

ANGELS

Luke 1:26-27

There are many people who collect angels and I have accumulated a fair collection of them myself. Except I have to giggle every time I think of our pastor's definition of angels at Christmas time.

Christmas seems to be the most popular time of the year for angels. He said,

"Christmas, of course, is a time when you can't swing a cat without hitting an angel. They are everywhere!"

We usually portray all angels as female, but it's interesting to note that all the angels mentioned in the Bible are male.

It was the angel "Gabriel" that appeared to Mary and his message to her changed her life, not to mention the whole course of history.

"In the sixth month, God sent the angel Gabriel to Nazareth, a town in Galilee, to a virgin pledge to be married to a man names Joseph, a descendant of David. The virgin's name was Mary." Luke 1:26-27

An angel appeared to Mary.

Then another appeared to Joseph.

Then a whole host of angels appeared to the shepherds.

Our pastor was right. You can't swing a cat without hitting an angel at Christmas time. They are everywhere!

As we light the Candle of Watching this week stay alert. For no matter how many angels appeared or to whom they appeared, their message was always the same:

"Jesus, the Christ, is coming!"

TRANSITION

Matthew 11:28

I picked up the phone and the voice at the other end said, "I can't go on. I've tried but it's not working. I can't even find God." A young lady, suffering depression, was contemplating suicide.

Even though I was a commissioned Stephen Minister I wasn't prepared for this.

It was Christmas week. Our family had just gathered together for the first time in over a year. As I transferred the call to the bedroom and excused myself from the festivities, I prayed, "God, I know You are there for her. I ask You to be here for me also. Help me put on the mind of Christ and help her find the hope she needs to hold on."

I recalled a time when I myself had cried out for help. I too had longed for that "rest." Quietly I became one in spirit with her as I listened and calmed her, allowing Jesus to work through me to guide her to a more stable place.

After contacting my pastor to ensure her safety I rejoined my family.

I was amazed at the calmness Jesus had given me.

This young lady had reached out to me, weary and carrying heavy burdens, and Jesus had put His yoke upon me and walked her to safety in His Name. Matthew 11:28 promises us,

"Come to me, all you that are weary and carrying heavy burdens, and I will give you rest."

Suddenly, the transition from deep fear to celebration seemed very natural.

This week we light the Bethlehem candle of transition reminding us of the dark night when Joseph and Mary found "rest" in the stable after being turned away. They also experienced that transition from deep fear to celebration, found only in the Lord Jesus Christ.

DECEMBER 4

COMPASSION

Philippians 2:9

One Christmas my family spent the holidays with our Grandpa and Grandma in the trailer park where they lived. After we had opened our gifts, my sister, brother and I took our new toys outside to play. My brother played with his new truck while my sister and I took our baby dolls for a stroll through the "park."

We soon noticed two girls close to our own ages watching us. We proudly showed them our new dolls that Santa had just brought us then asked them what Santa had brought them. The younger girl said, "Shoes."

Thinking she misunderstood us, we asked again. Then the oldest simply stated, "Just shoes. Shoes is what we needed so shoes is what we got."

When we got back to our grandparent's trailer we shared our unbelievable shock that all they got for Christmas was shoes. Then we asked our mother if we could give the girls the old dolls we had brought with us since we now had new ones. My sister and I had never before witnessed the plight of the less fortunate. But something happened in our young hearts as we poured out the details of their circumstance.

Our transition from shock to compassion became the most lasting gift we received that Christmas. Paul summed it up perfectly in Philippians 2:9.

"Each of you should look not only to your own interest but to the interests of others."

This week as we light the second candle, the Bethlehem Candle of transition, let us also remember the innkeeper who out of his compassion gave Mary & Joseph shelter. The plight of this young couple caused something to happen in his heart. And it became his gift to the Christ Child.

DECEMBER 5

HOLOGRAMS

Luke 12:3

I've always been fascinated by those hologram pictures. You know the ones that are a composite seemingly of patterns and objects and lines. Yet, if you focus on a point and shift your eyes -- just so -- a completely different picture within the composite appears. Not only is this new picture 3-D, it leaves you to wonder if you just somehow stepped into the picture itself.

That's because its depth seems so real you are taken within it instantly. It is a transition created from what first meets the eye into the very soul of the picture.

Reading the Bible can be that type of experience for us also.

We read the Scripture over and over, seeing the words and hearing their messages. Yet, when we focus on the Scripture, it's meaning and our understanding shift. We become aware of a deeper and greater meaning.

Unlike the hologram, its depth is real and instantly known. It is the true transition from what first meets the eye into the very soul of the Scripture -- Jesus!

In fact, Jesus hinted at this Himself. He said,

"There is nothing concealed that will not be disclosed, or hidden that will not be made known." Luke 12:3

This week as we light the Candle of Transition, let us remember that greatest transition of all. The transition Christ made for us. He who was with God and was God came to earth as a helpless baby to save us. Our Lord became human so that all humanity might live.

Our understanding shifts, and Lo!

Instantly Jesus is there.

SEASON CHANGE
Luke 2:9-11

Miss Catherine Utz.

I'll never forget her. She was my senior class literature and English teacher. She was not only a great teacher; she was a champion of students. Everyone knew what a profound difference she had made in many young lives over the years. Many students went on to college because Miss Utz recognized a potential.

She personally extended scholarships to those whom would not have had a chance to go otherwise.

But the most remarkable thing I remember about Miss Utz was that even the seasons in my hometown followed her lead.

You see Miss Utz had two pair of shoes; a pair of black ones and a pair of white ones. The whole town would wait for her to announce the transition of the seasons by changing her shoes. Only then would the change of seasons for our town be official.

As we light the second candle of Advent, the candle of transition, lets think back around 2000 years ago to some shepherds keeping watch over their flocks by night.

The transition they experienced was to change all seasons forever.

"An angel of the Lord appeared to them, and the glory of the Lord shone around them and they were terrified. But the angel said to them, 'Do not be afraid. I bring you good news of great joy that will be for all the people. Today in the town of David a Savior has been born to you; He is Christ the Lord." Luke 2:9-11

Suddenly the season changed for the world forever as the angel of the Lord announced the Birth of our Lord Jesus.

GETTING TO KNOW YOU

Psalm 138:1

The other day I was humming the melody "Getting to Know You" from Anna and The King. I immediately thought of my youngest son-in-law and his thoughtful caring nature.

Shortly after I met him, before he and our youngest daughter began to date, he and a friend stopped over one evening to visit. It really surprised me because our daughter wasn't home. She and her Dad had gone deer hunting that weekend.

Now, I know the boys had better things to do with their time. Youth is so fleeting. Yet, they chose to spend some of that evening with me.

Just so we could get to know each other.

> "Getting to know you.
> Getting to know all about you…"

Then another thought struck me.

"Jesus, you do that same thing, don't you? You come by to visit me during prayer time, just so we can get to know each other!"

I exclaim with the Psalmist,

"O, Lord, You have searched me and You know me." Psalm 138:1

As we light the second candle of Advent, the candle of transition, remember the transition the Son of God, Jesus, made for us.

God came to earth, taking human form, just so He could get to know us.

DECEMBER 8

NEW BEGINNINGS

Genesis 12:1

Facing new beginnings is hard.

There's no activity that proves that more than the process of moving. That is, uprooting oneself from the area in which you have vested your life, leaving behind those you've grown to love, and traveling to a strange area to call it home.

It's hard. My husband and I have done it.

There was another long ago that had to face new beginnings too: Abram.

"The Lord had said to Abram, 'Leave your country, your people and your father's household and go to the land I will show you.'" Genesis 12:1

Abram, acting solely on God's word, uprooted himself and his household from the area in which he had vested his entire life. He not only left behind those he loved, he was traveling to an area which had not been revealed to him yet!

In other words, Abram had no idea where he was going.

It's something to know where you're going, like my husband and I did. Abram didn't have a clue, yet he went anyway!

As we light the second candle of Advent, the candle of transition, let's reflect on Abram and his courage in facing new beginnings. As we do, think about another one who faced new beginnings for us. God uprooted Himself from His heavenly domain, leaving behind paradise to come to earth in the form of a defenseless newborn babe.

His new beginnings saved us all.

NEVER PUT JESUS AWAY

Matthew 15:8-9

During the time I worked for a Baptist church I displayed a beautiful hand carved nativity set on the top shelf of my bookcase. This rare set had been a gift years ago from my sister-in-law. It had been given to her by a Chaplain in the Army on base in Frankfort, Germany during the time my brother had been stationed there.

My sister-in-law chose to pass it on to me so I have always treasured it.

Around June last year someone walked into my office to confer with me on another matter and noticed the nativity set. After admiring the workmanship of the pieces, the person asked me if I had forgotten to put it away after Christmas.

"No" I answered. "I didn't. I never put Jesus away."

Always after Christmas we take down the entire tree trimmings and decorations and put them away until next year. And although I don't think we mean to but often we also take Jesus down at the same time and put Him away too.

Jesus spoke out against people who treat Him like a Christmas tree ornament and only worship Him when it suits them.

He cautions us from doing that.

"These people honor Me with their lips, but their hearts are far from Me. They worship Me in vain." Matthew 15:8-9

As we light the second candle of Advent, the Candle of Transition remember that Jesus is more than glint and glitter.

If Jesus is to be Lord of our lives we can never put Him away.

TO GOD BE THE GLORY

Psalm 113:1

A few years ago I had a recurring dream. It was the same theme over and over. Every night, usually, right at 3:00 a.m., I would awaken and the dream would slip just out of reach. I would be left with the haunting refrain of a song.

During the day I would find myself humming parts of that refrain with the only words that I could remember: *"Praise the Lord. Praise the Lord…"*

Then it would dissolve. I search though our hymnals at church every chance I got and had everyone I knew trying to help me identify the song I kept dreaming over and over each night. Then one Sunday, during the service at church, I opened my hymnal as directed, to the hymn, "To God Be the Glory."

As the congregation began to sing, I recognized it as the song of my dreams.

"Praise the Lord, Praise the Lord. Let the earth hear His voice. Praise the Lord, Praise the Lord. Let the people rejoice. Come to the Father through Jesus the Son and give Him the Glory. Great things He hath done!"

I have no doubt that song was a message to me from God reminding me that in all things I must give Him alone the Glory.

My recurring dream stopped but my joy and praise of God never has.

As we light the third candle of Advent, the Candle of Praise, let us remember and be thankful that God has done great things for us. Psalm 113:1 tells us to

"Praise the Lord. Praise, O servants of the Lord, praise the Name of the Lord."

THE SONG

Psalm 149:1

Recently I ran across a little quip that a friend of mine had copied down for me a few years ago:

"A bird does not sing because it has an answer

It sings because it has a song."

That caught my attention because it's so simple, yet thought provoking.

Just imagine all those simple and pure melodies floating in the air!

Every time I catch the harmony of those songs filling my universe I never cease to be amazed. The birds share their audible beauty with all that would listen. Not because we would learn anything from them but simply because they have a song to sing.

We have a song too. His name is Jesus. And like the birds we are simply supposed to sing because we have a Song.

We don't have to worry about the answer either. Jesus is the only One who has the answer and He came to earth to share that answer with us.

Psalm 149:1 tells us

"Praise the Lord. Sing to the Lord a new song, His praise in the assembly of the saints."

So, as we light the third candle of Advent, the candle of Praise, let us remember that our Song is Jesus and He alone is worthy of our praise.

Never stop singing the Song we have been given to sing.

Sing to Him a new song, a song filled with praise.

THE PSALMS

Psalm 146:1&2, 10

The Psalms are full of praise. In fact the traditional Hebrew title of the Psalms is "tehillim," which means "praises."

The Psalms speak of God in praise, faith and trust. For example, Psalm 146 begins with

"Praise the Lord. Praise the Lord, O my soul. I will praise the Lord all my life; I will sing praise to my God as long as I live."

And ends with

"...Praise the Lord." Psalm 146:1&2, 10

Look also at Psalm 148, 149 and 150. Almost every sentence begins with *"Praise the Lord."*

You know it is impossible to harbor unpleasant thoughts in our hearts when we are consumed in praise. Praising God softens our hearts and heals our hurts.

It's the balm that allows us to cleanse ourselves and be filled with the joy that comes from a loving God.

The Psalms remind us over and over that while we worship God we need to praise Him and keep praising Him. Only He is worthy of our praise.

This week as we light the third candle of Advent, the Candle of Praise, let us remember that God Himself gave us the ability to praise Him and that He works in us through that praise.

So, this Christmas season let us praise God with psalms of praise.

IN THE GARDEN
Ezekiel 28:13

One Sunday in church while we were singing "In the Garden", which was my Grandmother's favorite hymn, I visualized her reaching down to take my hand.

As I raised my hand for her to take, I felt we were spiritually holding hands, joining the past and the future with the present through this classic hymn.

That's when I remembered the classic film, "Places in the Heart".

"In the Garden" was the background music of its wonderful but unique ending. The finale was a church service in which the Lord's Supper was being shared as the elements were passed from person to person. The hired hand passed the tray to the blind boarder who passed it to the two children. The children passed it to their mother who gently handed it to her murdered husband now seated beside her. He took it and lovingly handed it to the person next to him – the slain young man who had killed him!

The young man accepted the tray, smiled back at him in pure love, affectionately murmuring, "Peace of God".

Just as I joined spiritual hands with my Grandmother, so did the characters in this film. Past, present and future were joined together in both incidences through the act of communion and within the ageless music of "In the Garden."

As we light the third candle of Advent, the candle of praise, let us remember that we are all joined together as one in the Lord.

Lift your voice and praise God that because He lives we can all belong in the garden with Him. God Himself told us this in Ezekiel 28:13 when He proclaimed:

"You were in Eden, the Garden of God."

NEWSWORTHY

Luke 2:17-18

Not so long ago I read in the paper about a frail but mischievous elderly woman who was celebrating her 104th birthday in a local nursing home. All her friends and relatives had gathered for the occasion as well as a few members of the local press.

After all, attaining the age of 104 was certainly newsworthy.

As one reporter interviewed her during the celebration, he asked her "What is the best thing about turning 104?" Eyes twinkling she responded, "There's no peer pressure."

Over two thousand years ago a young woman celebrated a birthday by giving birth to the only begotten Son of God, Jesus. Angels went out and proclaimed the news so that even shepherds from the field came and gathered for the occasion.

After all, God becoming man was newsworthy.

"When they had seen Him [Jesus] they spread the word concerning what had been told them about this Child, and all who heard it was amazed at what the shepherds said to them." Luke 2:17-18

This week we light the third candle of Advent, the candle of praise. As we gather with the shepherds awaiting the arrival of our Lord and Master let's join them in proclaiming Jesus as our Lord and King.

Let us praise God! Raise your hands and praise His name!

For He is the only One truly newsworthy!

ON OUR SPIRITUAL TOES

John 14:25-26

The Spanish Professor I had for my first year Spanish in college was really tough. Not only did she give exams weekly; she expected Spanish to be the only language to be used in class.

One of my roommates had a more lenient professor for her first year Spanish so I found myself searching for ways I could switch to that class. But my schedule would not allow it.

I just had to tough it out.

At the end of the semester, when grades came out, I discovered I had scored above my roommate. All those exams and classroom practice had kept me on my toes.

The same holds true in our Spiritual growth. Just as a student needs exams and classroom practice to keep him/her on academic toes, a growing Christian needs Biblical study and Christian fellowship to keep him/her on Spiritual toes. The Holy Spirit is our Spiritual professor, appointed by God to test and guide us in our growth.

Jesus confirmed this for us:

"But the Counselor, the Holy Spirit, whom the Father will send in My name, will teach you all things and will remind you of everything I have said to you." John 14:25-26

This week as we light the third candle of Advent, the candle of praise, give God thanks and praise for His loving gift of our Spiritual professor, the Holy Spirit.

It's God's way of keeping us on our Spiritual toes!

NINE LIVES

I Peter 1:3-4

When I was in grade school we lived in a very rural area so when a classmate of mine invited me to spend the weekend at her house I was very excited. She lived on a working farm.

That mid-winter Saturday morning she woke me early before the sun rose. We bundled up and ran out to the barn to begin her morning chores and to watch the milking. But as we reached the barn we discovered that sometime during the night one of the cows had rolled over on top of the barn cat. When the cow rose that morning the barn cat was flat – stiff as a board and exhibited no signs of life. My classmate's father threw the cat outside the barn to "see to later" after the chores were done.

Then after we finished the morning chores we headed back up to the house for breakfast.

As we reached the house, imagine how amazed we were to find the barn cat yowling at the back door for his breakfast like nothing had ever happened!

Either the sun rising that morning after being thrown outside the barn warmed and revived the cat, or it's really true that cats do have nine lives!

As we light the third candle of Advent, the candle of Praise, let's remember what Peter had to say:

"Praise be to God and Father of our Lord Jesus Christ! In His great mercy He has given us new birth into a living hope through the resurrection of Jesus Christ from the dead, and into an inheritance that can never perish, spoil or fade – kept in heaven for you." I Peter 1:3-4

That's even better than nine lives!

WHICH PERSON ARE YOU?

Matthew 28:20

Bruce Willis, in the movie "Signs", said there were two types of persons, and I paraphrase: There are those that feel that no matter what happens they are on their own. Then, there are those that feel that no matter what happens there will always be someone there for them.

Then he asked, "Which person are you?"

We have all been in that place where someone has promised to be there for us but when we needed them they were not there. If that happens enough times we do begin to feel like we are on our own – that no one cares. It's hard to hold on to the promise of hope when there is no hope in sight.

Jesus knew that. That is why He tells us in Matthew 28:20 to always remember that

"Surely I am with you always, to the very end of the age."

We might not be able to trust our fellowman all the time to always keep every promise he/she makes but we can trust Jesus 100% of the time to keep every promise He ever has or ever will make.

That's why I am one of those persons that feel that no matter what happens there will always be someone there for me.

That someone, of course, is the King of Kings, our One and Only Lord of all Lords – Jesus Christ.

As we light the fourth candle of Advent, the candle of promise, remember this promise Jesus gives – He promises us all that He will be with us now and forever, even to the very end of the age.

GOD SAID IT

Isaiah 45:19

The other day someone repeated that old saying:

> "God said it, I believe it and that settles it."

But one of my friends took it one step further. He said the saying really should be:

> "God said it and that settles it whether I believe it or not!"

That made sense to me. God's Word is the truth, the whole truth and nothing but the truth. It doesn't matter if we believe it or not.

God never consulted any one of us (that I'm aware of) to find out what we considered true before He spoke! So regardless of whether we believe or not, God's Word shall always remains true.

What does God, Himself, say about it?

"I have not spoken in secret from somewhere in a land of darkness; I have not said to Jacob's descendants, 'Seek Me in vain.' I, the Lord, speak the truth; I declare what is right." Isaiah 45:19

This week we light the fourth candle of Advent, the Candle of Promise. As we do, let's reflect on what God's Word promises us.

God spoke His Word into being. His Word is Jesus Christ, who is the Way, the Truth and the Light. And Jesus promises us everlasting life.

It's the truth.

God said it.

A COUCH?

Isaiah 7:14

Around ten years ago our whole family gathered together to watch the converted VHS version of our family reel to reel movies we had taken over the years. The time span covered my husband's high school days as well as our wedding and the precious growing years of our daughters.

We were taking special delight in showing our two young grandsons, Kevin and Travis, their mother as a tiny baby. At one point we told the boys to get ready because they were going to see what their mother had gotten for Christmas when she was just two months old.

However, our timing was off slightly. The next scene was not the one we expected, even though it was still of their mother. Instead of their mother lying in the arms of an over-stuffed bear twice her size, she had been asleep on a couch!

Travis studied the scene, paused a moment, then inquired, "She got a couch?"

Travis had taken us at our word. We had told him he would see what his mother had gotten for Christmas. He tried to figure it out and came up with the only thing that was in the scene with his mother. The couch. We all became so tickled we laughed until tears streamed down our faces.

As we light the candle of promise this fourth week of Advent think about when Isaiah told the Israelites to get ready because the Deliverer God promised was coming.

"Therefore the Lord Himself will give you a sign: The virgin will be with child and will give birth to a son, and will call him Immauel." Isaiah 7:14

Isaiah made this statement at least 740 years before Jesus was born. Like our grandson Travis, the Israelites had to wait until the next "scene" before they were to see the prophecy come true.

NEVER WILL GOD LEAVE YOU

Hebrews 13:5

Open your Bible and look up these passages:

Deuteronomy 31:6

Deuteronomy 31:8

Joshua 1:5

1 Chronicles 28:20

They all say the same as Hebrews 13:5:

"Never will I leave you; never will I forsake you."

Each of these passages contains that same promise. Five times God tells us that He will never leave us. His promise spans from the beginning of creation to our present day.

God is consistent in His promise, but to make sure we never forget, He tells us over and over again.

We may leave God but God can never and will never leave us.

As we light the fourth candle of Advent, the Candle of Promise, whisper this message in your heart.

"Never will God leave me; never will He forsake me."

Soon we will celebrate the birth of Christ. Let God's promise remind us that He sent His only Son to tell us again in yet one more way:

"Never will I leave you; never will I forsake you."

YOU PROMISED

Haggai 2:5

Her words echoed in my ears.

"But you promised, Mom."

I still remember how she looked. Her hurt was written on her face. Her hurt hurt me because I had no excuse.

My only honest reply was simply: "I forgot."

Another broken promise.

We all break promises at times and each broken promise hurts either others or ourselves. Usually both. Then we work hard to receive forgiveness and vow to do better at keeping our promises. And we do.

Until something happens and we again break a promise.

God, however, always keeps His promises. In Haggai 2:5 God said,

"This is what I covenanted with you when you came out of Egypt. And My Spirit remains among you. Do not fear."

That is a promise God has kept for thousands of years!

Why? There is no one alive today who can personally remember that promise after all these years to say, "But you promised, God!"

The answer is, God remembers and just as He promises, He will remain faithful to His promise throughout all generations.

This week we light the Candle of Promise. As we do, we are reminded that our God is still in the business of keeping promises. His greatest promise to us was in the form of His Son, our Savior.

As we look forward to celebrating His birth, let's celebrate God's faithfulness to us in all His promises.

THE PERFECT GIFT

James 1:17

The other night my husband reminded me of a time years ago when I was preparing a Christmas box to send overseas to my brother stationed in Korea. I had wanted to send him a little something that would remind him of Texas.

What I had found was a very nice-sized stuffed armadillo. Instantly I knew it was the perfect gift.

Later I carefully examined the armadillo before I wrapped it to be sure the price tag had been removed. As I turned it over I noticed the little manufacturing sticker on its underside.

It read, "Made in Korea."

What I had thought I had done was to buy the perfect Texan-made gift for my brother in Korea.

What I had actually done was to purchase a Korean-made gift to send back to Korea!

When God wanted to send us something that would be the perfect gift, He knew that gift would be Jesus, His only Son. Because

"Every good and perfect gift is from above, coming down from the Father of Heavenly Lights, who does not change like shifting shadows." James 1:17

This week as we light the fourth candle of Advent, the candle of promise, let's remember the perfect gift we have been given in Jesus.

Like those shifting shadows, the perfect gift I had found for my brother changed in value and meaning as I learned its origin.

But the perfect gift we find in Jesus increases in value and meaning as we learn His origin.

CHRISTMAS EVE

CHRISTMAS EXCITEMENT

Isaiah 7:14

I remember as kids choosing to sleep together on Christmas Eve, mainly because we were too excited to sleep. We'd whisper and giggle and try to figure out what we would find in the stockings we had hung.

We had this family rule.

No one was allowed downstairs on Christmas morning until our parents were ready. So we made a deal with each other. Whoever was the first to wake would wake the others so we could get our parents up quickly.

I think it added to our excitement as we held hands, waiting for our parents to join us at the top of the stairs.

I realize now that our family rule was so that our parents would not miss a moment of our Christmas surprise and blessings. Actually, without knowing it, that was our greatest Christmas gift to them.

Isaiah, years before the birth of Christ, told us that Jesus was coming:

"Therefore, the Lord Himself will give you a sign: The virgin will be with Child and will give birth to a Son and we will call Him Emanuel." Isaiah 7:14

So the people began waiting, like we did at the top of the stairs.

Only they had to wait 740 years for the Lord to join them at the birth of His only Son, our Savior.

Each Christmas we experience anew the miracle and excitement only Jesus can bring. Our excitement builds as we hold hands and wait to re-experience the moment of His birth.

And I think, without knowing it, that is our greatest Christmas gift to Him.

CHRISTMAS DAY

THE KING

Luke 2:7

It was an ordinary night, much like others.

She was young and accompanied by her husband. She was with child, much like hundreds of women. So there was nothing that set them apart, unless it was that they were far from home and she was about to give birth.

Even that drew little attention, what with all kinds of people pouring in due to the census. In fact, they hardly found a place to stay.

"Then she gave birth to her firstborn, a Son. She wrapped Him in cloths and placed Him in a manger." Luke 2:7

No hoopla. No party. Just another birth…or was it?

Strange things begin to happen. Shepherds actually left their sheep and came into the city seeking the child about which the Angels told them. Kings from other countries came bearing expensive gifts, talking of a Star they had followed.

Both the shepherd and the kings came to worship a New King. And they all came to the Baby who had been placed in a manager.

Just imagine.

This is Christmas Day. As we light the Christ Candle we are aware that it is now time for us to come seeking the Baby in the manager. We come recognizing Him as our Lord and King. We have followed His Star through the lit candles of Advent and have spent weeks preparing our hearts and minds to receive Him.

We are ready. The time has come.

It's Christmas.

IT'S ABOUT A BIRTHDAY!

Luke 2:7-8

It was Christmas Morning. We had set our alarm so we'd be up before our granddaughter, Chyann, awoke. We didn't want to miss a minute of her Christmas excitement!

Later that morning, at breakfast, I felt very blessed by my family. I remarked on what a joy it was to once again experience Christmas through the eyes of a child.

In fact, my heart was full as I summed it all up by saying, "You know, that's what Christmas is all about."

Very softly and quietly, Chyann said, "It's about a birthday."

I almost missed it.

I asked, "Chyann, what did you say?"

She repeated, "It's about a birthday – Jesus' birthday!"

Wow.

We celebrate Christmas because Jesus had a birthday.

"While they were there the time came for the Baby (Jesus) *to be born, and she gave birth to her firstborn, a Son. She wrapped Him in cloths and place Him in a manger, because there was no room for them in the inn."* Luke 2:7-8

Sometimes the tinsel, glitter and, yes, even the special times we spend with family divert us from the real reason of Christmas.

Then it takes a little child to lead us back to the true meaning:

It's about a birthday – Jesus' birthday!

A MIRACLE

Genesis 21:6

If you were to ask me to define a miracle, I'd only have one word to say:

Chyann.

I'm sure God always knew His gift of her to our middle daughter was to be, but years and years were to pass before she came.

Yet, God's perfect timing left no doubt in our minds that His gift of Chyann was nothing than less a miracle.

Actually the story of our middle daughter and her husband is similar to the story of Sarah and Abraham.

God also promised them a child of their own, but it was also years and years before he was born.

Yet, God's perfect timing leaves no doubt in our minds that His gift of Isaac was nothing less than a miracle.

Like the story of Abraham, Sarah and Isaac, the story of our daughter, her husband and Chyann reminds us once again of God's great love and overwhelming compassion.

I know our daughter must have felt exactly as Sarah did when she looked at her child and exclaimed,

"God has brought me laughter and everyone who hears about this will laugh with me!" Genesis 21:6

Because, you see, Chyann is our child of laughter.

We will never cease to praise God for His gift of this beloved miracle, our Chyann.

THE THOUGHT THAT COUNTS

John 3:16

I smile as I remember the story my grandmother use to tell me about two of her sisters.

Over the years of living together, they had developed their own Christmas morning ritual. They would exchange gifts with each other before they opened anything else.

Now, the elder of the sisters always planned her sister's gift, making sure it would be special – something perhaps that she wanted but would never buy for herself. Unfortunately, the only thing her younger sister disliked more than shopping was spending money. She never gave her choice of a gift much thought. So she would wait to the last minute to dash out and purchase whatever was on sale and available.

This would drive the elder sister crazy, especially the explanation that always accompanied the gift:

"It's not much, but remember, it's the thought that counts."

So one Christmas the elder sister decided it was time to do something about it. As usual she carefully thought out and planned her gift for her sister, placed it in a small box, wrapped it and put it under the tree. That Christmas morning when her sister unwrapped the box she found that it was empty except for a note, which simply stated,

"Just a thought!"

Actually, both the sisters had good points, for without the thought or the planning the gift is meaningless.

As we light the Christ candle let's remember that God over 2,000 years ago made those same points. He had a Thought that counted and then planned His gift to us, wrapping it in the body of a young virgin.

"For God so loved the world that He gave His one and Only Son, that whoever believes in Him shall not perish but have eternal life." John 3:16

DECEMBER 28

THE FIRST CHRISTMAS

Luke 2:7

What was that first Christmas like? We sing songs of awe, wonderment, love, new life and joy. We sprinkle them liberally with snow, bright lights, angels, trees, gifts and beauty on earth.

Is that how it was like?

We know Mary must have been a very scared teenager trying hard to understand what was happening to her. As was Joseph. I mean, they both had been visited by angels and had accepted what the angels said.

But now what?

The angels were gone and they were left to fend for themselves. They had struggled through all the whispers, the side-glances and gossip. Now it was time for Jesus to be born.

On top of that, Joseph and Mary had to travel back to Bethlehem to register for the census, since both of them were from the house of David. Joseph must have at the very least questioned the wisdom of Mary traveling during this time.

Yet they had no choice.

Once they reached Bethlehem, the only shelter they could find was a lean-to that had been hastily erected to shelter the travelers' animals.

"And she [Mary] *gave birth to her firstborn, a son. She wrapped him in cloths and placed him in a manger, because there was no room for them in the inn."* Luke 2:7

This makeshift nursery was probably dirty and smelled of dust, chaff and wet animal fur among other foul odors. All types of insects, including fleas and mites, probably called it home.

Yet, God looked down and smiled, and the heavens opened. The angels sang as our Salvation and Mercy entered the world.

DREAM TRIP

Luke 1:35

One of my husband's and my dreams has always been to visit the Holy Land so that we could walk where Jesus walked. So, the year we were extended an invitation to visit the Holy Land with our Bishop on a special group tour package we were ecstatic!

However, finances and other circumstances prevented us from participating. We would have to put our dream trip on hold for another time.

And I had so looked forward to standing in birthplace of our Savior.

But, just as I started feeling sorry for myself I remembered something a pastor friend of ours once said in a talk on Justifying Grace.

"You don't have to cross the sea to see the Cross."

Most of us will never be able to visit the physical birthplace of Jesus or to visit the area in which He practiced His ministry on earth. But all of us can expect to be where Jesus lives.

He lives within us all. When we accept Jesus as our Savior, it becomes for us as the Angel Gabriel said to Mary,

"...The Holy Spirit will come upon you, and the power of the Most High will overshadow you. So the Holy One (which is within you) will be called the Son of God." Luke 1:35

My husband and I don't have to travel overseas to visit the birthplace of Jesus.

He was born within us the moment we accepted Him as Lord and Master of our lives.

His true birthplace is within each one of us.

DECEMBER 30

EVERYTHING FROM JESUS

Luke 2:19

Recently I heard an intriguing story about a little girl who unknowingly became one of Jesus' greatest witnesses.

It was Christmas time and the little girl was standing in a department store check out lane with her mother. An elderly gentleman, standing in line behind them, struck up a conversation with them to pass time while they waited.

After a few minutes the gentleman turned to the little girl and asked, "And you, young lady. What is Santa Claus bringing you for Christmas?"

She looked straight into his eyes and answered, "Nothing."

Then she added. "Cause Jesus gives me everything."

That wasn't what the elderly gentleman expected to hear, which left him momentarily at a loss for words. As he watched the little girl leave the store with her mother, he found himself wondering over her simple message.

I think he did as Mary did so long ago in Luke 2:19.

"Mary treasured up all these things and pondered them in her heart."

Today is New Year's Eve.

As we take time to ponder where the past year has taken us, let's use this little girl's testimony so innocently given to be our measure of our hope and future for the New Year:

"Jesus gives me everything!"

Scripture Guide

OLD TESTAMENT:

GENESIS

1:1 – January 4 The Word

1:1 – January 26 God's Heart

1:1-2 – June 1 Water

1:3 – January 4 The Word

2:18 – February 20 The Rib

2:18 – June 28 One Perfect Being

2:19 – March 2 The Chicken or The Egg?

2:21-24 – February 20 The Rib

2:22 – June 28 One Perfect Being

3:1 – January 22 Overstatement

3:1 – July 31 The Lie of Omission

3:4 – January 3 Temptation's Strategy

3:6 – November 18 Take, Eat

4:15b – September 5 The History Of Writing

6:22 – June 7 Trust Me

9:20 – April 7 My Prayer Stool

12:1 – December 9 New Beginnings

18:17 – September 9 Let's Make A Deal

21:6 – December 27 A Miracle

22:1-2 – September 19 The Test

24:3-4 – May 18 Rebecca

29:16 – October 6 Rachel

45:5 – January 2 God's Purpose

EXODUS

1:15-18 – January 5 Standing In The Gap

3:19-20 – January 15 The One and Only True God

32:7 – January 17 Your People

32:11 – January 17 Your People

DEUTERONOMY

33:12 – February 4 Shielded

JOSHUA

24:15 – February 24 Choose Jesus

24:15 – March 8 Whom Will You Serve?

RUTH

1:16 – February 13 As Ruth Loved

3:18 – March 11 Be Still

I SAMUEL

17:40 – September 25 Five Smooth Stones

II SAMUEL

12:4 – November 8 Analogies

I KINGS

17:9-12 – November 12 The Poor Feeding the Poor

19:11-12 – January 27 Where Are You?

II CHRONICLES

7:14 – June 14 Forever Love Our Country

JOB

1:21 – February 21 Angel Checks

PSALMS

8:4 – January 23 God Cares

10:14 – August 23 Bee Sting

16:11 – May 22 Nudges

16:11 – July 2 Fireworks

20 – April 11

Praying Psalm 20

20:7 – January 12 Trust

23 – July 13 God's Word

31:16 – August 10 Mercy

48:14 – August 19 My Pilot

51:10 – August 9 Harmony

56:3-4 – October 28 Basements

56:3-4 – November 11 Illusion of Peace & Beauty

57:1 – August 10 Mercy

57:9-10 – October 7 Miracles

91:14-16 – January 13 Turning Point

100:3 – April 9 Manipulating the Strings

113:1 – December 11 To God Be The Glory

118:24 – November 24 It's a Good Day

119:27 – July 17 The Heart Of The Author

119:35-38 – August 11 Discovering the Banquet

121:7-8 – July 25 Keeping Us From All Harm

121:8 – October 4 The Way God Watches

122:1 – January 30 Toys

122:2-3 – February 18 Our Church Home

124:7-8 – August 28 Safe Spot

138:1 – December 8 Getting To Know You

139:15 – September 6 Knowing Emily

139:16 – March 22 Jellybeans

143:9-10 – August 24 Who's In Your Driver's Seat?

145:8-9 – August 4 Encouragement

146:1-2 –December 13 The Psalms

146:10 – December 13 The Psalms

149:1 – December 12 The Song

PROVERBS

3:5 – May 11 "I Shot Cheri"

3:5-6 – April 2 Instincts

8:33 – July 4 Peaches

12:17 – February 25 Witness

14:10 – March 21 Bitter or Better

15:5 – April 10 God's Beauty of The Pattern

16:9 – October 18 Walking Backward

16:9 – November 3 Yo-Yo

18:24 – March 12 The Kind That Sticks

19:2 – June 16 Missing The Point

27:6 – September 14 Open And Honest

ECCLESIASTES

3:6 – February 16 Trains and Stations

4:12 – May 29 A Cord of Three Strands

SONG OF SOLOMON (SONG OF SONGS)

4:9 – June 27 Snapshot In Time

ISAIAH

7:10 – July 15 A Sign

7:14 – December 20 A Couch?

7:14 – December

24 Christmas
Excitement
11:6 – March 23
Let's Go Play
11:6 – May 7 Baby
Birds
11:6 – July 10 Love
Or Likes?
29:13 – March 9
Making It
Special
40:28-31 – May 8
The Game
42:9 – July 23
Spring Into
Being
43:10 – March 15
Our Past and
Our Future
43:25 – April 4 For
My Own Sake
43:25 – July 21
Forgive and
Forget
45:19 – December
19 God Said It
49:16 – March 16
An Old Irish
Blessing
53:2-3 – November
28 Go Ahead,
Make My Day!
55:2-3 – February 7
Feeding Wood –
And Souls!
55:8 – October 31
Halloween
64:8 – June 10
Oops!
65:24 – June 21
Chasing Rabbits

JEREMIAH
17:7 – October 11
Trust
23:23-24 – October
26 Hiding
29:11-14a – July 30
The Gift is
There

EZEKIEL
28:13 – December
14 In The
Garden
36:26 – January 31
ReSouling Our
Souls

HOSEA
11:8 – July 11
Change Of
Heart

OBADIAH
13:5 – November 1
Do Something

JONAH
1:1-2 – March 29
Meant To Be

HAGGAI
2:5 – December 22
You Promised

**NEW
TESTAMENT:**
MATTHEW
1:20 – November
22 Fever Dream

2:11 – January 6
Epiphany
4:23 – October 2
Time To Teach
5:6 – September 8
My Craving
5:8 – September 8
My Craving
5:16 – June 20 You
Do Your Father
Proud
7:7-8 – August 7
Pictures
7:28-29 – June 30
The Secret of a
Long Life
10:19-20 – May 30
Arrested
10:22 – June 6 A
Few Good Men
10:26 – April 5 No
Place To Hide
10:34 – July 27
Bumps In The
Road
11:2-3 – February
10 Are You the
One?
11:11 – May 6
Three Things
11:28 – February 9
The Purse
11:28 – March 28 It
Doesn't Matter
the Words
11:28 – December
4 Transition
12:43-45 –
November 2
There Goes The
Neighborhood
13:13 – May 28

Scripture Guide page 3

Some Dumb
13:44 – July 9
Hidden
Treasures
14:23 – October 15
Keeping Perfect
Balance
14:29 – July 19 In
A Row Boat
15:8-9 – December
10 Never Put
Jesus Away
16:26 – March 18
A Complete
Blessing
18:2-3 – April 1
Change
19:14 – April 15
The Man
20:8-10 –
September 20 It
Begins
21:18-19 – August
15 The Fig Tree
22:37 – May 16
With All Our
Hearts
22:15 – November
17 Who
Trapped Who?
22:17-21 –
November17
Who Trapped
Who?
24:30 – April 8 The
Master Will
Appear
24:35 – January 21
God's Word
24:42 – November
29 On Watch
26:13 – April 30 A

Simple Thing
26:36 – May 15
Gardens
26:38 – November
27 Watching
27:5 – April 14 A
Condition of the
Heart
27:19 – April 18
Pilate
27:21-23 – April 19
Barabbas or
Jesus
28:5-6 – April 24
He Has Risen
28:16-20 – August
3 God's
Fingerprints
28:20 – June 9 No
Matter What
28:20 – August 22
Lost Keys
28:20 – December
18 Which
Person Are
You?

MARK
6:12-13 –
November 25
"Chy-Mi-Tea"
10:25 – August 13
Eye of A Needle
10:31 – June 5 Last
Shall Be First
13:5 – October 29
Deception
13:37 – June 2
Watch For Me
14:22 – November
18 Take, Eat
14:22-24 –

February 2 The
Most Precious
Gift
14:60-61 – March
10 Doing As
Jesus Did
15:34 – May 12
Unforgettable
Fear
16:2-4 – March 25
Christian
Symbols

LUKE
1:26-27 –
December 2
Angels
1:35 – December
30 Dream Trip
1:37 – June 18 Do
It Again, Daddy
2:7 – December 25
The King
2:7 – December 29
The First
Christmas
2:7-8 – December
26 It's About A
Birthday!
2:9-11 – December
7 Season
Change
2:10 – October 24
Fear Not
2:17-18 –
December 15
Newsworthy
2:19 – November
30 Start
Watching
2:19 – December

Scripture Guide page 5

Scripture Guide page 6

PHILIPPIANS

1:3 – October 25 The Mind's Eye
1:6 – September 17 Big Tree, Little Tree
2:9 – December 5 Compassion
3:13-14 – March 19 Press On
4:6 – May 5 Rains

COLOSSIANS

2:8 – July 12 In The Light
2:8 – September 26 Ingredients
2:13 – August 31 The Right Tour Guide
2:17 – April 28 The Reality Of Christ
2:17 – October 30 Not Real
3:8-10 – June 22 Weeding Out

I THESSALON-IANS

5:11 – May 31 The Future
5:16-18 – September 24 Understanding Why

I TIMOTHY

4:9 – April 26 Easter Monday

II TIMOTHY

2:13 – October 9 Friends
2:15 – January 16 Life Stories
4:7-8 November 9 Finish the Race

TITUS

2:11-12 – March 26 Strung Together

HEBREWS

2:3-4 – January 20 Outside Your Expiration Date
2:18 – August 29 Dilemma
4:12 – April 6 The Wrong Territory
4:16 – October 27 The Relationship
9:14 – August 14 Spot Of Shame
10:7 – May 20 Photo Album
10:25 – February 11 Confident In Our Direction
11:1 – January 14 Faith
11:1 – October 21 A Vision
11:40 – February 19 God's Plan
13:5 – March 6 Never Will I Leave You
13:5 – November 26 Sunshine

13:5 – December 21 Never Will God Leave You
13:8 – February 3 Who Moved?
13:8 – July 7 Frozen In Time
13:8 – September 13 The Same Variation

JAMES

1:16-17 – August 8 Illusions
1:17 – December 23 The Perfect Gift
4:7-8 – July 26 The Right Connection
4:8 – June 12 Wanna Talk
5:14-16 – October 22 Healing

I PETER

1:3 – January 1 New Birth Into Living Hope
1:3-4 – December 17 Nine Lives
1:18-20 – January 18 Did He Know?
2:21 – May 21 Be A Model
2:24 – January 28 Healed
2:24 – August 17 Footprints
3:4 – September 7

Gentle and
Quiet
3:12 – April 13
    When God Calls
4:8 – August 20
    Stain

II PETER

3:9 – October 14
    Centering
3:13 – March 27
    Crisp And Sharp

I JOHN

1:9 – July 14 The
    Longest Walk
2:14 – June 19 The
    Point
3:9 – January 24
    Birth
4:4 – November 15
    The One Who is
    in You
4:4-6 – May 26 He
    Who Is In Us
4:7 – August 2
    Recognition
5:8 – December 2
    Keeping Watch

REVELATION

1:7 – January 10
    Sunbeam
3:12 – November
    21 Write

ALL SCRIPTURE QUOTED IN THE NEW INTERNATIONAL VERSION (NIV) unless otherwise noted

JANUARY

6. EPIPHANY. History from article in United Methodist Reporter, newspaper issued January 1997

7. HIGHER GROUND: CD – Columbia Records: Song "TELL HIM" sung by Barbra Striesand & Celine Dion

10. SUNBEAM SONG, Author unknown, Midi. Chorus of song as remembered from childhood

14. FAITH IS THE BIRD... Quote by Frank Dyer Heffern

IT IS ALWAYS DARKEST.... quote, Euripides (484-406 B.C.) Iphigenia in Tauris (tr. Sr. Gilbert Murray) line 115

15. THE PLAGUES, Disciple I Study Guide Session 5, Deliverance: God Hears the Cry pages 34-41 and the book of Exodus

16. EVERYLIFE HAS A STORY, quote and focus of the Ontario Black History Society: Understanding Black History web site featuring The Life Story of Jacklyn Blocker Scaife

17. DEREK PRINCE, Teacher, Author and Evangelist, daily radio program and founder of Derek Prince Ministries (DPM) reaching almost every country in the world

19. PALM VALLEY LUTHERAN CHURCH, Elroy Haverlah, Senior Pastor, Round Rock, TX

20. CHUCK SWINDOLL, Author, Evangelist and Bible Teacher for the daily radio program INSIGHT FOR LIVING. Also pastor of Stonebriar Community Church in Frisco, TX and Chancellor of Dallas Theological Seminary

21. CHUCK SWINDOLL, Author, Evangelist and Bible Teacher for the daily radio program INSIGHT FOR LIVING. Also pastor of Stonebriar Community Church in Frisco, TX and Chancellor of Dallas Theological Seminary

22. MARK TWAIN (Samuel Langhorn Clemens) 1835-1910 – A paraphrased excerpt from "Pudd'nhead Wilson" in the Mississippi Writings published by Library of America

25. PRAYER: MY SOUL'S ADVENTURE WITH GOD (A Spiritual Autobiography) © 1995 book by Robert H. Schuller, publisher Thomas Nelson, Inc.

27. MY UTMOST FOR HIS HIGHEST by Oswald Chambers' classic daily devotional, May 1st, page 122

28. WOMEN OF FAITH Conference, "Outrageous Joy" San Antonio, TX 1999

29. HALLEY'S BIBLE HANDBOOK, 24th edition copyright 1965, Zondervan Publishing House

FEBRUARY

2. CLOWN COMMUNION: THE GIFT Adapted by Chrysalis (Youth version of Walk to Emmaus© Upper Room, Nashville, TN) from "Lamb of God" written by Floyd Shaffer, non-copyrighted material

3. GUESS WHO MOVED? Quote – Author unknown Cited in God's List as anonymous (Familiar Quotes) web-site, quote #1

6. THE CHAIR by Frank Peretti, Assemblies of God Minister, writer, musician, actor and pilot, as presented on

FOCUS ON THE FAMILY: Dr. Dobson

7. JUST AS WOOD CRACKS … quote by Frank D. Heffern

9. "LAMB OF GOD" written by Floyd Shaffer, non-copyrighted material

18. THE GREATEST OF THESE IS LOVE: from the Disciple I Study Guide Session 27, Love: a Congregation in Ferment, pages 198-205 and I Corinthians 13:4-7

15. PORCUPINE PEOPLE book by Lee Ezell, Ezell Communications, Newport Beach, CA 92658

16. OUR THOUGHTS ARE LIKE TRAINS Contemplative Prayer Work shop – Open Mind, Open

Heart by Father Thomas Keating, a Cistercian "Trappist" priest, monk and abbot St. Benedict's Monastery. Founder of the Centering Prayer Movement

17. PULL YOURSELF TOGETHER, old Joke, first told in ethnic form – Source and Author unknown

19. THE STEPHEN SERIES® "Christ caring for people through people" a one-on-one caring program founded by Dr. Kenneth Haugk

20. THE WEDDING SONG, song copyright 1971 Public Domain Foundation

25. KINGSLEY PLACE: An Assisted Living Facility in San Antonio, TX

29. "MAN'S WEAKNESS IS SATAN'S STRENGTH" Anonymous quote as remembered – not found recorded or quoted – Author/Origin unknown

MARCH

1. WILL YOU DIE FOR ME? A poem by Jean Howell Kopp Heffern – 1996

2. WHAT CAME FIRST – THE CHICKEN OR THE EGG? Age-old question, often referred to in materials depicting the myth of evolution. Author, exact wording, and Source unknown

4. THE SINGER NOT THE SONG, (1961) a movie based on the novel of the same name by

Audrey Erkine Lindrop

6. ABSENT YET PRESENT – A poem by Edward Bulwer-Lytton, Lord Lytton

14. DID YOU PRAY FOR ME? A poem by Jean Howell Kopp – 1965

15. STEP MOM, (1998) a movie. Story & screenplay by Gigi Levangie, directed by Chris Columbus

16. OLD IRISH BLESSING, prayer, Author unknown – quoted as handed down throughout the ages

18. OLD IRISH MORNING BLESSING, prayer, Author unknown – quoted as handed down throughout the ages

20. LIFE LESSON, e-mail by Brother Robb Wood, Director

of Protestant Religious Education and Ecumenical Family Ministries, Ft. Sam Houston, San Antonio, TX

24. "LAMB OF GOD" written by Floyd Shaffer, non-copyrighted material

27. "ALL YOU NEED IS NEW GLASSES" paraphrased quote – based on quote by Kenich Ohmae, Internet Collection 20th Century Quotes

28. WALK WITH JESUS Retreat for the Deaf. Based on the 3 day weekend Walk to Emmaus and is sponsored by The Methodist Mission Home located in San Antonio, Texas, a facility for unwed mothers, open adoption and the training

of the deaf to function in a hearing society and the workplace.

30. HOW TO GET THERE, Familiar illustration – quoted in many articles and talks: Original origin/Author unknown

APRIL

3. The definition of a VIBRATION: Not the true definition from the dictionary, but an anonymous verbal contribution as cited by a friend. Actual Author and origin unknown

8. THE STUDENT IS ONLY AS GOOD ... Paraphrased from Luke 6:40 "A Student is not above his teacher..."

WHEN THE STUDENT IS READY ... A

famous old yogic saying, reprinted in many sources, quoted by many authors – actual Author/ origin unknown

10. THE BEAUTY OF THE PATTERN: From the book "EACH NEW DAY" by Corrie ten Boom. Copyright © 1977. Fleming H. Revell Company

11. Adaptation of PSALM 20 by Jean Howell Kopp Heffern 1999

15. FOCUS ON THE FAMILY: Dr. Dobson "MARGINS IN OUR LIVES", as relayed by a guest speaker, Speaker/ origin unknown

16. THE MAN, Mini-Story: Author – Jean H. Heffern 2001

18. ONE HAND WASHING ANOTHER...

Quote, Origin unknown

19. CHUCK SWINDOLL, in a Mini-series for Easter, as presented on the daily radio program INSIGHT FOR LIVING. Author, Evangelist and Bible Teacher. Also pastor of Stonebriar Community Church in Frisco, TX and Chancellor of Dallas Theological Seminary

21. SEDAR, the Jewish holiday falling on Thursday before Easter, which is also celebrated by Jesus: His last as the "Last Supper" which is now celebrated by all Christians during the Holy Week of Easter

23. IT WASN'T ANY ORDINARY NAILS… quote as adapted from Hebrews 12:2 "…who for the joy set before Him endured the cross, scorning its shame, and sat down at the right hand of the throne of God."

25. THE CONTEST, Author Jean H. Heffern 2000

MAY

3. RESENTMENT, as quoted by Jonathan Clarke, commentator, CONTACT Radio Program "Breaking the Bonds of Resentment" produced by Jim Hone and presented by Mike Powers. Actual definition sources are unknown, however the Big Book of AA was alluded to in the program.

INSANITY, definition by Benjamin Franklin (1706-1790)

4. THE GREEN MILE, a 1999 movie based on the book by Stephen King of the same name. Directed by Frank Darabont

6. CHUCK SWINDOLL, Author and Evangelist, and Bible Teacher; daily radio program INSIGHT FOR LIVING. Also pastor of Stonebriar Community Church in Frisco, TX and Chancellor of Dallas Theological Seminary

11. I SHOT THE SHERIFF, song – words and lyrics by Bob Marley sung by Eric Clapton

26. ROD SERLING, (1924-1975) Author, playwright, The Twilight Zone –

CBS 1959-64
The "Hocus-
Pocus &
Fresby" episode

28. SUMDUM
GLACIER –
Life in the
USA– Reader's
Digest (old
issue, date and
author unknown
to me) retold as
remembered

30. MIRANDA
WARNING:
The warning
required by law
to be given to
suspects before
taking any oral
or written
confession

"YOU DON'T
HAVE THE
RIGHT TO
REMAIN
SILENT..."
Michael
Stewart, Lay
Speaker @
Oxford UMC
Wednesday
Night Lenten
Service, San
Antonio, TX

JUNE

6. A FEW GOOD
MEN, a 1992
movie by
Columbia
Pictures,

directed by Rob
Reiner

11. GIRL SCOUT
PIONEER
CAMP:
Primitive site
with emphasis
on pioneer/
primitive
camping and
outdoor
adventure

13. SOUTHWEST
STORYTELLERS
of the Cochiti,
Pueblo, Hopi
tribes featuring
work of Helen
Cordero,
Dorothy
Herrera, Ethel
Shields as well
as Tafoya,
Toya, and
Quitana, among
others.

16. FALLING IN
THE WELL
Illustration as
remembered,
Origin/Author
search
unsuccessful:
Unknown to
me. Cited as
remembered
from a mini-
sermon at a
worship service

18. MAX
LUCADO,

Well-known
Christian
Author and
Pastor, Church
of Christ, San
Antonio, TX

JUICE
COMMERCIAL:
An old Orange
Juice TV
commercial
about a father
"sipping" the
sun up with
orange juice.
Exact showing
dates and the
sponsoring
Juice Company
unknown to me

19. MISSING THE
POINT retold as
remembered
from an
illustration
heard in a
sermon some
time ago
Origin/Author
unknown to me

25. THE
PHYSICAL
AC-COUNT
OF CRUCI-
FIXION: © The
Review of the
News, April 14,
1976 from "A
Physician
Testifies About
The

Acknowledgment Guide page 6

Crucifixion" by Dr. C. Truman Davis, Ophthalmologist and Vice President of the American Association of Ophthalmology, President and Founder of the Trinity Christian School in Mesa, AZ

30. AN AMERICAN GREETINGS® A Birthday Card, message, an anonymous contribution. As remembered from a card purchased to sent to a friend

JULY

6. CLOWN COMMUNION: Adapted by Chrysalis (Youth version of Walk to Emmaus© Upper Room, Nashville, TN) from "Lamb of God" written by Floyd Shaffer, non-copyrighted material

9. HIDDEN TREASURE STORY, based on Matthew 13:44, origin unknown

11. THE WALK TO EMMAUS ©The Upper Room, Nashville, TN

16. FOOLS FOR CHRIST training by Terry Morgan, Austin, TX at The King's Klowns Workshop 1995 Mt. Wesley Kerrville TX

"DYING TO SELF" – Wiping out personal ego or agenda. The process of whiting the face symbolizing "putting on the essence of Christ" – I Corinthians 9:22 "I am made all things to all…"

17. LUDINGTON HIGH SCHOOL 1959, Ludington MI, Mr. Harry

Nuckolls, Journalism Instructor

18. FINISHING TOUCH, retold as remembered from a familiar story, Source, Author & origin unknown

19. TIM HANSEL notes from a personal appearance First United Methodist Church of Boerne, TX – well known author and evangelist

21. BEEHIVE from The Upper Room® Devotional – July/August 2000 issue

23. THE PILLSBURY® (General Mills) DOUGHBOY™, Trademark of Pillsbury®

27. "WHY MUST THERE BE BUMPS IN THE ROAD?" Larry Van Deventer, Author of "Bumps in the

Road: Things I have Run Across"

30. LUCI SWINDOLL – Excerpt from "Joy in the Journey", a collection from Women Of Faith

AUGUST

4. THE FAMOUS WRITERS' COURSE, a correspondent one-on-one writing course by mail

ROD SERLING, (1924-1975) Author, playwright, The Twilight Zone – CBS 1959-64; and an affiliated instructor with the Famous Writers' course

9. MAKE ME AN INSTRUMENT, song, words from Songs & Creations, the Yohann Anderson collection

14. LADY MCBETH, a Shakespearean Play, famous quote

17. I FOUND HIS FOOTPRINTS a song by Jean Howell Kopp Heffern

24. WHO'S IN YOUR DRIVER SEAT? Marquee University United Methodist Church, San Antonio, TX – sermon title

29. THE KING'S KLOWNS Christian Clown Ministry (see July 16)

SEPTEMBER

2. SAN ANTONIO MISSIONS – A Texas League Baseball Team, San Antonio, TX

5. HALLEY'S BIBLE HANDBOOK, 24th edition copyright 1965, Zondervan Publishing House

11. THE FACES OF HOPE by John DeVito, Guidepost, December 2001 Issue

12. THE OXFORD UMC GRAPEVINE, Rev. Jim Roberts, newsletter issue October 11, 2001

15. WALK WITH JESUS, a two-day retreat for the deaf community, modeled after The Walk to Emmaus®The Upper Room, Nashville, TN

17. INDIAN PRINCESS, a club formed exclusively for Fathers and their grade school aged Daughters

23. EXPERIENCING GOD – Knowing and Doing the Will of God by Henry T. Blackaby, a class study on how to discover God's will in your life

28. GIVE A MAN A FISH..., anonymous quote. Author unknown

29. A HOUSE BY THE SIDE OF THE ROAD, poem by Sam Walter Foss

30. GEM OF THE DAY of unknown origin from the San Antonio Express Newspaper 1994

OCTOBER

5. THE THREE STOOGES™ C3 Entertainment, A comedy trio popular in the 1960's – Mo, Larry & Curly.

9. FRIENDS ARE LIKE FLOWERS – A poem by Jean Howell Kopp Heffern

11. WHEN THE WRITING ON THE WALL IS IN BROWN CRAYON: Devotions for the Harried Homemakers by

Susan Lenzkes Copyright 1981 Zondervan Publishing House

12. OUTWITTED, poem, by Edwin Markham. Source: The Best Loved Poems of the American People. Doubleday, 1936. p.67

14. Inspired by the book THE GUARDIAN by Jane Hamilton Copyright 1994 Thomas Nelson, Nashville, TN USA

16. THE HORSE WHISPERER, a 1998 movie directed by Robert Redford, staring Robert Redford

17. PRIMARY COLORS, a 1998 movie Universal Pictures staring John Travolta, directed by Mike Nichols

20. THE CONDUCTOR, old story

(revised) One of several variations – Author unknown

30. Fireplace Videos: Phil Gary Enterprise USA, Deluxe Ultimate

NOVEMBER

1. PRACTICE RANDOM ACTS OF KINDNESS, a bumper sticker – origin unknown

2. THERE GOES THE NEIGHBOR HOOD – Marquee United Methodist Church, San Antonio, TX Sermon Topic

4. REFLECTIONS FROM THE HEART OF GOD: DEVOTIONAL BIBLE FOR WOMEN by Thomas and Nanette Kinkade, Publisher: Nelson Bibles

5. DEHYDRATION OR HUNGER –

a e-mail fun-
fact received
from a multiple
forward (origin
unknown) by a
friend over the
Internet
February 2003

11. AN OLD SCI-
FI MOVIE, as
remembered –
exact title
forgotten

19. WIZARD OF
OZ a 1939
movie – based
on the novel by
L. Frank Baum,
directed by
Victor Fleming,
starring July
Garland. Song:
"Somewhere
Over the
Rainbow"
Music by
Harold Arlen,
Lyrics by E.Y.
Harburg, sung
by Judy Garland

20. BECAUSE
YOU ARE
YOU, Author –
Jeanne H.
Heffern – 1995

"WRITE
INJURIES IN
DUST,
BENEFITS IN
MARBLE"
written by

Benjamin
Franklin (1706-
1790)

28. QUOTE from
DIRTY
HARRY of the
Dirty Harry
Collection,
property of
Warner Bros. –
Starring Clint
Eastwood as
Inspector
Callahan

DECEMBER

3. THE OXFORD
UMC
GRAPEVINE,
Rev. Jim
Roberts,
newsletter issue
December 16,
2001

4. LUDINGTON
HIGH
SCHOOL,
Ludington, MI.
Miss Catherine
Utz, English &
Literature
Teacher 1960

8. GETTING TO
KNOW YOU
song by Richard
Rodgers and
Oscar
Hammerstein II
on Pocket
Songs label,
from the
original THE

KING AND I,
staring Yul
Brynner,
screenplay

11. TO GOD BE
THE GLORY
hymn, from The
Methodist
Hymnal

12. A BIRD quote,
by Author &
Poet Maja
Angelou

14. PLACES IN
THE HEART
Classic film
starring Sally
Fields, John
Malkovich and
Danny Glover,
directed by
Robert Benton

IN THE
GARDEN,
Classic hymn
written in 1912
by C. Austin
Miles

16. WESTERN
MICHIGAN
UNIVERSITY
Kalamazoo, MI
1960-1962

18. SIGNS a
Touchstone
movie/video
starring Bruce
Willis, directed
by M. Night
Shyamalan,

Frank Marshall,
Producer

19. "GOD SAID
IT, I BELIEVE
IT, THAT
SETTLES IT"
Anonymous
quote, Author
unknown

30. "YOU DON'T
HAVE TO
CROSS THE
SEA TO SEE
THE CROSS"
Origin unknown

31. "JESUS GIVES
ME
EVERYTHING"
quote and story,
Author
unknown

About The Author

Jean Howell Kopp Heffern began her writing career early in life, exchanging original poetry with her grandfather, a noted journalist in his time. Due her grandfather's influence Jean went on to enroll in a creative writing course after college where she studied briefly under Rod Serling.

Jean has authored seven weekly devotional books and a variety of poems. In "Finding God's Fingerprints in Our Daily Lives" she opens a window in her life and allows us to peek inside at how God works through the smallest and most mundane events. She portrays a living relationship with God in her daily living that encourages and challenges the reader to find that same relationship within his or her own life.

Printed in the United States
27536LVS00001B/142